Education for Children of the Poor

Education
For Children of the Poor

A Study of the Origins and
Implementation of the Elementary and
Secondary Education Act of 1965

Julie Roy Jeffrey

Ohio State University Press : Columbus

Library of Congress Cataloguing in Publication Data

Jeffrey, Julie Roy.
  Education for children of the poor.

  Bibliography: p.
  Includes index.
  1. Socially handicapped children—Education—
United States. 2. Poor-United States. 3. Educational
law and legislation—United States. I. Title.
LC4091.J4   371.9'67'0973   77-14272
ISBN 0-8142-0277-2

FOR CHRIS, MICHAEL, AND SOPHIA

CONTENTS

Acknowledgments

I have accumulated many debts of gratitude to those who so generously helped me during the years that I worked on this study. My thanks go first to my professors at Rice University who aided me with my dissertation on the ESEA. Especially generous with his time was my adviser and friend Allen Matusow. He gave me good criticism and advice. Ira Gruber, Chandler Davidson, and Martin Wiener also helped me during graduate school as did my friend and fellow historian Carol Wiener. I appreciate both their patience and unfailing support. I would also like to thank Rice University and the Southwest Center for Urban Research. Each provided me with a fellowship that allowed me to work on the manuscript. Goucher College also supported me financially while I revised the dissertation one summer. John Walton of Johns Hopkins University was unfailingly helpful during its revision and my colleague Jean Baker, unfailingly supportive. I thank them both. Joy Pankoff, Catherine Grover, and Katherine Buckley all typed the manuscript at one stage or another; without their help, my work would have been much slower than it was. Finally, of course, I formally thank my husband, Chris, and my children, Sophia and Michael, for their years of patience and good humor.

Preface

When Lyndon Johnson so unexpectedly became president in November 1963, he discovered plans under way for an attack on poverty. The new president enthusiastically supported the planners' efforts and made the War on Poverty a major part of his 1964 legislative program. From the seeds of the antipoverty program grew the vision of the Great Society, "a challenge constantly renewed, beckoning us toward a destiny where the meaning of our lives matches the marvelous products of our labor."[1]

For Johnson, who often stressed his own humble origins, the idea of an attack on poverty, with its implications for a better world, was most congenial. Congenial, too, for the former schoolteacher, was the poverty program's major emphasis on educational solutions. The conventional picture of education as "the only valid passport from poverty" corresponded to Johnson's view of his own past.[2] And, as a traditionally acceptable means of achieving social goals peacefully, educational programs also fit in with Johnson's belief in consensus politics.

Johnson, therefore, worked hard to ensure that the educational aspects of the antipoverty effort became realities. The

Economic Opportunity Act passed in 1964 encouraged community action groups to establish educational programs and subsidized work-study arrangements. But the Elementary and Secondary Education Act (ESEA) of 1965 was the administration's major educational assault on deprivation. One billion dollars flowed to almost every school in the country to pay for special programs for poor children. In the confident rhetoric of the mid-60s, Johnson described the bill as "the giant stride toward full educational opportunity for all of our school children. . . . It will help five million children of poor families overcome their greatest barrier to progress—poverty."[3]

The support of federal aid to education as a crucial element in the attack on poverty rested on the belief that schools were effective agents of upward mobility in American life. Achievement in school, poverty planners thought, was directly related to later socioeconomic status. With the help of ESEA funds, schools would help poor students perform like middle-class students. Then they would find good jobs, earn good money, and escape from the world of poverty.[4]

This study of the process of making and implementing educational policy explores whether poverty planners were justified in making these assumptions in developing the educational components of the War on Poverty. It examines why planners initially emphasized an educational solution for poverty and tries to determine whether the ESEA reached its major goal of overcoming that "greatest barrier to progress —poverty." It also briefly considers the case of Headstart, the administration's preschool intervention program, to discover whether early compensatory aid had a greater effect on poor children than aid on the elementary or secondary level.

Investigating the ESEA ultimately raises questions concerning both the method of making policy in government and the dynamics of twentieth-century reform. How systematically do planners, for example, explore assumptions underlying social policy? How realistic are their models of change? Do the requirements of the political process neutralize the intended impact of reform legislation? What capacity does the government seem to have for learning from the experience of its past reform measures?

The ESEA is the vehicle for exploring these kinds of questions and suggests that there are significant problems involved in formulating and implementing social reform measures. For the ESEA never lived up to liberal hopes because policy-makers neither examined their fundamental beliefs nor confronted the nature of the American school system that they hoped to transform, because the political compromises they felt were necessary undermined the chances for successful implementation of the legislation. Since failure never led to a serious attempt to reshape the reform measure, the history of the legislation provides a frustrating commentary on the dynamics of social change in the American political system.

This study has its own bias: that social problems like poverty require the attention of policy-makers, that good will in social planning is hardly enough in the face of rising expectations among disadvantaged groups. Poverty, discrimination, and other social problems all demand solutions formed realistically enough to yield useful information about the process of social change and, hopefully, results.

1. *Public Papers of the Presidents of the United States: Lyndon B. Johnson, 1963-64,* 2:704.

2. *Public Papers of the Presidents of the United States: Lyndon B. Johnson, 1965,* 1:414.

3. Ibid., p. 407.

4. David K. Cohen, "The Schools and Social Reform: The Case of Compensatory Education," p. 3.

Education for Children of the Poor

1

Education as a Solution for Social Problems

The Elementary and Secondary Education Act of 1965 marked a new chapter in the history of American educational reform. Like most reforms, the ESEA had a variety of goals ranging from revitalizing the country's educational system to providing textbooks for parochial school children. But the grandest and most explicit objective of the legislation was to bring education into the front ranks of the nationwide assault on poverty. As Lyndon Johnson carefully explained, there was good reason to give education a crucial role in the War on Poverty. "Very often," he pointed out, "a lack of jobs and money is not the cause of poverty, but the symptom. The cause may lie deeper—in our failure to give our fellow citizens a fair chance to develop their own capacities in a lack of education and training."[1] By allocating federal funds to improve education for poor children, the administration hoped to give them the opportunity to escape a future of deprivation and misery. "With education," Johnson said, "instead of being condemned to poverty and idleness, young Americans can learn the skills to find a job and provide for a family."[2]

In turning to the schools to help solve the problem of mid-twentieth-century poverty, Johnson and administration planners testified to a traditional and tenacious belief in the powers of education. Americans have long expected the public schools to cure a variety of social ills without revolutionizing existing political and economic arrangements.[3] And because schools have been viewed as a major agent of social mobility, many Americans have argued that there is a close connection between education and the eradication of poverty. As Horace Mann, the great Massachusetts reformer, had explained over a century before the ESEA, "Surely nothing but universal education can counterwork this tendency to the domination of capital and the servility of labor. . . . If education be equally diffused, it will draw property after it by the strongest of all attractions; for such a thing can never happen as that an intelligent and practical body of men should be permanently poor."[4]

This broad faith in the powers of education was traditional, but does not explain why Johnson and members of his administration made education such a fundamental component of their attack on poverty. An examination of educational thought in the late forties and fifties illuminates the administration's choices, however. Despite continuing criticism of the American school system during these years, traditional expectations about the responsibilities and capabilities of education expanded. By the early 1960s, liberals, politicians, and educators all agreed that education could deal with newly recognized social problems, so competently had it dealt with other problems growing out of the early cold war.

President Truman gave the first hints of the new responsibility education was to be assigned in postwar America. If the American people lacked adequate opportunities for education, he warned in June 1948, they might well prove responsive to communism.[5] A year later, Truman was more explicit about the connection between the international situation and education. "Education is our first line of defense, the president argued. "In the conflict of principles which divides the world today, America's hope, our hope, the hope of the world is in education. Through education alone can we combat the tenets of communism."[6] The role Truman visualized for education in the cold war was to be, in part, an ideological one, and others agreed with the president. The Educational Policies Commission of the National Education Association (NEA) explained in its publication *Education and National Security*, "The problems which now most urgently require solution are not physical or technical, but moral and social."[7] As the cold war dragged on, however, it became clear that the schools had more than just an ideological role to play in the "war of the classrooms."[8] With the outbreak of the Korean conflict in 1950, Truman linked education with the nation's technological strength.[9] In his 1951 budget message he explained to Americans that "the challenge of communist imperialism requires the full potential of all our people—their initiative, their knowledge, their skills and their ideals. These qualities have given this Nation world leadership and science and industry. Education and research are vital to the maintenance of this leadership."[10] In particular the president emphasized the nation's need for strong elementary and secondary schools. "From the standpoint of national security alone, as well as the enlargement of opportunities for the individual, the Nation needs to see that every youth acquires fundamental education and training which are essential to effective service, whether in the Armed Forces, in industry, or on the farm."[11]

Truman's argument that national security depended on ideological purity and technological expertise, which it was the schools' responsibility to provide, did not convince Congress to pass a federal education bill but did contribute to an extended educational debate over the strengths and weaknesses of the American school system and its responsibilities to students and the nation.[12] Yet, despite the fear that "the United States [was] . . . in desperate danger of falling behind the Soviet world in a crucial field of competition—the life-and-death field of competition in the education and training of adequate numbers of scientists, engineers and technicians . . . the facts . . . [did not really sink] into the public mind" until the launching of Sputnick in October 1957.[13]

Sputnick seemed to provide dramatic proof for those who argued that the Russian schools, which combined quality education with mass education and which successfully inspired students to work to full potential, were more effective than American schools.[14] The United States failed to maintain technological superiority, critics said, because its educational system was inferior. Nourished on progressive principles, schools might be turning out well-adjusted young adults, but they were so poorly trained that four more years of college were necessary to provide them with a broad liberal education.[15] By the time the Science and Education in National Defense hearings opened in the Senate in January 1958, there was substantial agreement that the American school system would have to be improved, and improved quickly, to save the nation. As Chairman Hill warned, Sputnick was "a constant grim reminder that for the first time in the life of our Nation we are looking down the cannon's mouth. The United States truly has reached a historic turning point, and the path we [choose] to pursue may well determine the future not only of western civilization but freedom and peace for all peoples of the earth."[16]

Witnesses testified that the nation needed better-trained teachers, an intellectually rigorous curriculum, and adequate funds for research, teaching institutes, and scholarships for able students.[17] The assumption underlying testimony and debate was that the school system ought to save the country from defeat at the hands of the Russians. As one witness pointed out, "We now face the stark reality that our national survival depends on the success or failure of our educational institutions to provide the intellectual, the scientific, the diplomatic leaders sorely needed to solve complex problems at home and with our neighbors abroad."[18]

The argument that the schools must and could save the country provided the basis for the passage of the National Defense Education Act in 1959. The NDEA provided federal grants to improve science, mathematics, and foreign language programs at the elementary and secondary level, loans and fellowships for college students, and funds for experiments on better teaching methods.[19] But improving the quality of education with federal money, however, was only part of the solution to the problem, as witnesses and critics pointed out.[20] If the United States was to meet the challenges of a technological world, schools would also have to learn to identify talented students and make "special provision" for them. Fortunately, "provision for the needs of the average and the below average . . . has long ago been made."[21] A leading educator, John Gardner, elaborated these points in his book *Excellence: Can We Be Equal and Excellent Too?* (1961): "The sorting out of individuals according to ability is very nearly the most delicate and difficult process our society has to face."[22] Emphasizing talent, Gardner pointed out, was hardly discriminatory:

> Differences in educational opportunity will never be eradicated. They must be reduced in scope and significance. But it would be wrong to leave the impression that stratification of educational opportunity is still a dominant feature of our system. It is not. The vestiges of stratification still exist, but the great drama of American education has been the democratization of educational opportunity over the past century. This has been one of the great social solutions. In emphasizing that much ground remains to be won, we must not belittle the victories already achieved.[23]

Twelve years of debate on the role of schools in American life had led to extensive reexamination of American education, some federal dollars, and a widespread conviction that the school's job was to identify and train talented students. If the schools lived up to newly assigned responsibilities, then, and only then, could the country maintain the technological superiority so crucial to survival in the cold war era. Heavy as these responsibilities for the nation's welfare were, space achievements in the 1960s suggest that the American educational system did succeed in nourishing talent and producing scientific expertise. Though faith in the powers of education were, in this case, justified, there was little evidence that education could be equally successful in dealing with other national problems. Yet the debate of the forties and fifties had created a framework that made it natural to turn to an educational solution again as new social problems surfaced.

For as Sputnick receded into the past, other national problems were becoming visible, and educators were among the first to notice. During the decade of the 1950s while Americans were comparing their schools to Russian schools, important demographic changes were occurring in many American cities and urban school systems. Northern cities were becoming increasingly black as blacks migrated to them and as whites increasingly moved to the suburbs. By the sixties the population of some cities like Washington, D.C., and Newark, New Jersey, was over 50 percent black.[24] These demographic changes rapidly affected urban schools. Whereas a few years earlier few urban school children had been considered disadvantaged, in the first years of the new decade educators estimated that one-third of the public school children in the country's fourteen largest cities were disadvantaged.[25] The racial and economic profile of students in urban schools had obviously shifted during the Sputnick years. The problem facing the cities and the urban schools was that of black poverty.

Confronted with disadvantaged black students, the city schools were clearly failing. Blacks scored far below their white counterparts on achievement tests. Sixty percent of nonwhites who entered school dropped out before finishing. Unlike their immigrant predecessors, poorly educated blacks and dropouts discovered that there were few unskilled jobs for them.[26] Exposing the inadequate education black children were receiving, civil rights activists loudly insisted that the schools wipe out racial differences in achievement as a step toward occupational and economic equality.[27]

Educators appeared genuinely concerned over the school's failure to meet the challenge of deprived children. By the late 1950s superintendents in fourteen cities had begun to develop school programs for them, and the Ford Foundation agreed to supply funds for education projects. A series of conferences on the problems of educating the poor were further indications of spreading awareness that something other than selecting talented students was needed in the schools. In 1962 the Teachers College of Columbia University sponsored a two-week work conference on education in depressed areas. The next year, 1963, the U.S. Office of Education, the Office of Juvenile Delinquency, and the National Institute of Mental Health supported the two-week-long Dedham Conference focusing on education of the poor.[28] Other conferences attracted specialists from various fields to discuss how schools should meet the challenge of poverty. The volume of books and articles on culturally deprived children, the educational term for poor children, grew. Frank Riessman's *The Culturally Disadvantaged Child*, the National Education Association's *Education and the Disadvantaged*, Daniel Schreiber's *Guidance and the School Dropout*, articles by Benjamin Bloom, Martin Deutsch, and Edmund Gordon, all testified to the truth of the observation, "The culturally deprived are now in the spotlight."[29]

Concern was evident and clearly related to both the school conditions and civil rights pressure. But there were other reasons for interest. James Conant's influential book *Slums and Suburbs*, which appeared in 1961, was more explicit than most. "I am convinced," Conant wrote, "we are allowing social dynamite to accumulate in our large cities . . . in slum neighborhoods, I have no doubt that over half of the boys between sixteen and twenty-one are out of school and out of work. Leaving aside human tragedies, I submit that a continuation of this situation is a menace to the social and political health of the large cities."[30]

Fear of disorder and social disintegration, a suspicion that slum-dwellers would be unable to resist the menace of communism, motivated Conant to describe the problems of urban education in urgent tones. The central challenge facing the schools, Conant argued, was how to improve the inadequate school performance of poor students and how to prevent students from dropping out of school into street life and unemployment. Low achievement and dropping out, Conant felt, resulted from the social environment. "One needs only to visit . . . a [slum] school," he pointed out, "to be convinced that the nature of the community largely determines what goes on in the school."[31] But it was foolish to await changes in the social setting to ameliorate the situation. "New housing," for example, Conant said, "works no miracles."[32] Time was short; Conant believed the public school had a central role to play in reshaping the frightening world of city slums. It was both possible and necessary for slum schools to educate its students to hold jobs. "*I submit*," Conant declared, "*that in a heavily urbanized and industrialized free society the educational experiences of youth should fit their subsequent employment.*"[33]

If other educators did not share Conant's vocational emphasis, they did share his concern and hope that the urban school could offer a remedy for poverty. Many of the articles and books in the growing literature of deprivation described the life situation of the poor, rationalized the school's present failure to deal with poor students, and then proposed the favored solution of compensatory education. Drawing heavily on the social sciences, this educational literature was repetitive and timid in tone. Rarely looking below the surface of poverty to discover its underlying causes, it also had an ill-concealed air of superiority when discussing the life style of the poor.[34] But the literature expressed confidence that once more the schools would prove capable of meeting and overcoming a major social challenge.

The National Education Association's 1962 publication *Education and the Disadvantaged American* gave a typical analysis of "the problem of the disadvantaged." "Their cultures are not compatible with modern life," the pamphlet flatly stated.[35] The obvious implication of such a view was that poor people needed more than money. They needed to change their values and their habits, their "culture." In order that no one mistake the damaging (and lower-class) character of this life style, educators described it over and over again. Family structure was unstable, and family members were unable to communicate in a normal fashion. Children suffered severely from this breakdown, since relatives could not give them the toys, physical surroundings, or the attention that the average middle-class family lavished on its children. No wonder, coming from this background, the typical slum child was damaged by the time he reached school. Not only did he lack basic life experiences necessary for learning, he did not even sense that school was important.[36] Once in the classroom, such a child soon realized he could not function and tasted failure. It was not the child's fault, as Martin Deutsch, an expert in child education, noted. "The lower-class child enters the school situation so poorly prepared to produce what the school demands that initial failures are almost inevitable."[37] Time did not improve the situation. The older the child grew, the more each weakness reinforced the others, and the more he was unable to benefit from school. By high school, the poor student was years behind the average middle-class student in achievement and was likely to drop out of school altogether. Unable to wait for future rewards, discouraged by the present, the disadvantaged teen-ager could see no reason for finishing school.[38]

This was "the problem of the disadvantaged," which the pamphlet insisted was quite different from the one that had faced immigrants sixty years earlier. But though the problem was different, the solution was not. The NEA's goal, "practicable and American," was to provide "all people [with] a fair chance to meet the challenges of life." No institution, the pamphlet pointed out, could ensure equal opportunity, but the "school can have a profound influence in this direction."[39] Implicit in this emphasis on opportunity were the ideas that education underlay success, that the structure of society was sound, that education was a "long-range solution" for social problems.[40] The actual means to the goal of providing equal opportunity was compensatory education.

The idea behind compensatory education was simple. Since the home environment was so negative, the school should make up for the child's failure to have enriching family experiences. The earlier the school could reach out to shape the child, the better. Thus, educators encouraged preschool programs that provided small groups of poor youngsters with books, toys, and attention from sympathetic adults. Every teacher was expected to view the child positively, seeing his alien background "not as a judge, but as a student."[41] In this kind of a setting, it was predicted, children could develop the skills, motivation, and self-image necessary for future school success.[42] If possible, teachers were to visit the children's homes and draw parents into the child's school experience.[43]

Compensatory education for older children was similar in

spirit to that recommended for the younger ones. Most compensatory projects in elementary and secondary school stressed reading with extra remedial teachers, specialists, and new reading materials. Changes in classroom methods such as team teaching, ungraded classes, and small-group instruction were encouraged. Guidance counseling was another component of compensatory programs. Enrichment activities featuring trips to museums and other city sights were often suggested as potentially rewarding. Most projects tried to interest parents in the school through home visits and different activities held at school.[44]

By changing the way of instructing poor children, by enriching their experience and expanding services, compensatory education expected to bring deprived children up to the achievement level of middle-class children. Educators stressed, "These disadvantaged children who live in the depressed core of the city—have the same intellectual potential as other normal children. They are not inherently dull or stupid; many are, or would be, bright and alert if their basic physical needs were met, if they were given experiences that would encourage them to want to learn the ways of the middle-class world, if they were carefully and devotedly taught by able teachers who believed in their potential and sought to release it through all the many means of excellent education."[45] If schools could succeed in raising deprived students to the academic level of middle-class students, "then the regular learning procedures of the school which are quite effective for the advantaged children are also likely to be effective for the culturally deprived children."[46] Once deprived children performed like advantaged children, they would eventually obtain jobs and would no longer be a problem.

Embedded in the many descriptions of compensatory education was the objective of teaching lower-class children middle-class habits and values. Most educators believed that poor children's basic problems could be traced to their value systems and their confusing and depressing environments.[47] For the child to succeed in school would mean rejecting his background; the school would encourage the child with its compensatory projects and sympathetic approach. The basic structure and character of the school itself would remain essentially unchanged. Compensatory education did not compensate for the inadequacies of the school so much as for the inadequacies within the child and in his home. Any suggested modifications in the school system were minimal ones, like reducing class size. Not surprisingly, few educators contemplated going beyond these remedies to attack external social conditions.[48]

The belief of educators in the early sixties that compensatory education offered a remedy for poverty was based partly upon the ambitious rhetoric and hopeful view of education growing out of the educational debate of the fifties and partly upon the traditional confidence reformers had had in education as a panacea for social problems. Faced with black failure in the schools, educators of the 1960s were deeply concerned with the problem of helping deprived children escape poverty. Their emphasis lay on providing opportunity, individual mobility, not on group inequality. They gave little thought to some of the difficult issues their belief in compensatory education raised: could education actually overcome the influence of family and neighborhood; did educational success explain social mobility; what other factors contributed to social mobility? As a special-interest group that was zealous in protecting its domain, educators were unlikely to ask these hard questions. Nor were they motivated to examine the existing compensatory education programs to see how well they were, in fact, dealing with the educational difficulties of the poor.

The belief in compensatory education as a partial solution for the problem of poor children was certainly emotionally satisfying but surprising in the face of evidence. Only a few state and local projects, mostly serving blacks, were actually operating.[49] From 1961 on, for example, New York allocated $200,000 annually for local projects on a matching fund basis. California, Connecticut, and Pennsylvania also supported compensatory efforts.[50] The projects initiated a variety of activities; most diverted only a small amount of money for poor children.[51] Returns from programs were just beginning and were not altogether hopeful. Enthusiastic, impressionistic descriptions were plentiful. But as one authority pointed out, "It is clear . . . that the state and local programs for educationally disadvantaged children provided an important testing ground for many different kinds of activities without clearly demonstrating that any were certain to be effective."[52]

In Saint Louis, for example, the Banneker project attempted to improve student motivation and self-confidence and to stimulate teacher expectations. Better motivation, it was hoped, would raise student scores. Activities included assemblies to give students contact with successful people and pep rallies. Spirited efforts were made to draw parents into school activities. At parent meetings, for example, school officials tried to encourage them to help and inspire their children. Home visits served the same purpose. No special changes were made in the curriculum, although reading was emphasized. Despite all these efforts, however, tests indicated that Banneker children did not improve relative to white children.[53] The Higher Horizons Program, initiated in 1959 in New York City and ending in 1962, also tried to motivate disadvantaged children. Curriculum changes, enrichment activities, and remedial teaching all attempted to change the low achievement scores of participating students. Instruction was in small groups. The cost of the programs came to $62 per pupil. Results from this data showed that students in Higher Horizon schools did not perform significantly better on reading and arithmetic tests than students at control schools.[54] On the other hand, the Early Training Project in Nashville, Tennessee, did show small I.Q. differences favoring children participating in summer programs and receiving home visits.[55]

Results from actual compensatory programs could have moderated the enthusiasm of educators who supported them as an approach to poverty. In proposing education as a solution for social problems, educators were reasserting their traditional belief in the schools as an agent of upward social mobility. Yet studies from several disciplines also suggested that this faith ought to be moderated. The relationship between education and upward mobility was not the simple causal one that many educators assumed.

Patricia Sexton considered her 1961 *Education and Income: Inequalities of Opportunity in Our Public Schools* as a breakthrough in educational literature. Sexton sensed an "inertia, indifference, and opposition to an understanding of the Reality of our schools and our society."[56] Rejecting as a myth the belief that education traditionally fostered mobility, she claimed children from the lowest socioeconomic class did not succeed in school and never had.[57] True, a few lower-class children did make it through the school system, but Sexton pointed out that a Russian worker's child had "*twice* as good a chance of going to college as his U.S. counterpart."[58] The typical situation, Sexton suggested, was what her study of the 285,000 students, 10,000 teachers, and nearly 300 schools in Detroit disclosed. Achievement and I.Q. scores had a direct relation to the student's socioeconomic status; poor students had low scores; middle-class students had high scores. Since scores determined a student's program, poor students did not participate in special educational activities.[59] Often they were even excluded from remedial reading classes.[60] Schools were sorting students in a way that reinforced original social and economic distinctions.

Sexton's picture was clear. But why did the well-to-do appear more able than the poor? Not because poor people had limited abilities, Sexton insisted. There was "not a shred of proof," she claimed, that low I.Q. scores indicated inferior abilities.[61] Poor children did badly in school because they were badly taught, because they were relegated to an inferior academic status, because their schools were insufficiently financed. What was responsible for the situation? First, Sexton claimed, too many educators accepted I.Q. scores as a justification for stratification. Second, a large number of people were indifferent to the poor. Many "in and out of schools" believed "preferential treatment *should* be given to upper-income groups."[62] Finally, since school boards were usually controlled by upper-income groups, they allocated rewards as they chose. Poor parents did little to pressure the school boards into changing their policies.[63]

A succession of articles published in the fifties and early sixties disagreed with part of Sexton's analysis. It was not the school that denied its poor students opportunity, the studies suggested, since the student's family background itself had a profound effect on school performance. One such study by Basil Bernstein in the 1958 *British Journal of Sociology* stressed that the family's speech pattern influenced how children learned. The simplified "public" language that the lower-class family used shaped the way the child conceptualized and made formal academic work difficult.[64] Changing the situation would be complicated, necessitating either a modification of the social structure or a change in the structure of speech. The latter solution was both delicate and hazardous. Bernstein concluded, "The integration of the lower-working class into the wider society raises critical problems of the nature of society and the extent to which the school, by itself, can accelerate the process of assimilation."[65]

Other studies highlighted other aspects of the significance of family background. The family, one suggested, provided the stimulating environment that encouraged high aspirations in its children.[66] Family social class appeared to be a vital factor both in explaining a student's school achievement and in determining who would continue into higher education. "Over and above differences in ability, the financial, educational, and cultural differences in ability which are indicated by the occupation of the father clearly play an important role in determining which high school graduates enter college."[67]

Another article in the *American Sociological Review* in 1957 presented complementary data on all high school seniors in Wisconsin. Controlling for the effects of intelligence, the authors agreed that "the present tests lend support to the sociological claim that values specific to different status positions are important influences in level of educational and occupational aspiration."[68]

Sociologist Peter Rossi summarized research on school achievement in 1961. After recapitulating the material on social factors that influence achievement, he turned to investigate in-school factors. The studies he reviewed found teacher contributions to be "minimal," at least in the short run.[69] Research on different curricula was not clear but "failed to reveal that differences among schools and different educational practices contribute a great deal to the scores of students on achievement tests."[70] This kind of a review provided scant support for compensatory efforts and suggested that environmental and family factors prevented poor students from succeeding in school.

Several studies suggested that the social-class composition within the schools did, at least, have an effect on students. In 1959 Alan Wilson published his survey of thirteen California high schools. Wilson discovered students with similar social-class backgrounds and I.Q. scores had different educational aspirations in schools of different social-class composition. Lower-class students in middle-class schools shared the aspirations of their classmates.[71] Natalie Rogoff's impressive study of 1961 supported Wilson's conclusions. Rogoff used data from a national sample of 35,000 high school seniors, combining it with other data such as the size and social-class composition of local communities. Rogoff found that the school's composition clearly influenced aptitude scores and college plans. "No matter how privileged or underprivileged the kind of family from which they came," Rogoff observed, "high school seniors at least double their chances of scoring in the top fourth in aptitude if they attend a school where most of their classmates are from the upper strata."[72]

None of these studies was comprehensive enough to establish the relationship between schooling and social class definitively. But they suggested, despite what educators wished to believe, that family and community factors influenced student achievement more than school factors. Within the school, social-class composition appeared to affect achievement. Yet, the whole idea of compensatory education implied teaching the deprived student separately in his own lower-class school, not integrating him with more-advantaged students.

The belief that the school was an agent of upward mobility rested on the larger assumption that years of education related directly to job possibilities. The increasing number of years of education completed by the general population was regarded as a sign of increased opportunity and mobility. In

1910, for example, only 13 percent of men between twenty-five and sixty-four had finished high school, and 4 percent had gone on to complete college. In 1960, 44 percent of the men from this age group were high school graduates, and 11 percent received college diplomas.[73] But upper-class students still received more education than lower-class students; social inequalities still explained educational inequalities.[74] And as educational levels rose, so too did job requirements. Increased education did not lead to income equality, especially for blacks.[75] The belief that more years of schooling led to mobility was unsubstantiated.[76]

John Folger and Charles Nam completed a study in 1964 weighing the relationship between education and occupation. Using data on non-farm white men between thirty-five and fifty-four in 1940, 1950, and 1960, the authors concluded that although there was some relationship between job and education, it was "declining." "The educational upgrading of the population," wrote the authors, "will very likely continue to be more rapid than the shift in the occupational structure."[77] What then explained mobility? "A Skeptical Note on Education and Mobility," by sociologist C. Arnold Anderson, suggested that upward mobility depended on the number of openings higher up in the social scale.[78] Although education did affect mobility, many of those rising into a higher class did so without the benefits of a good education. Conversely, well-educated workers were likely to lose status if they were not competent in high-status jobs.[79] Formal education did not provide many qualities necessary for job success. Ability and motivation, Anderson felt, explained much individual mobility. "Education," he wrote, "is but one of many factors influencing mobility, and, it may be far from a dominant factor."[80]

Two other impressive works examined the cause of mobility in American life. Natalie Rogoff's 1953 *Recent Trends in Occupational Mobility* and Seymour Lipset and Richard Bendix's 1959 *Social Mobility in Industrial Society* both concluded that mobility was related to industrialism. "The rate of social mobility is high in *all* industrial societies," Lipset and Bendix pointed out.[81] "Economic expansion and industrialization are more significant in determining the extent of social mobility in a given society than variations in political, economic, or cultural value systems."[82]

Mobility did, then, exist, but the significant issues were whether mobility and education were closely related and whether lower-class people got the jobs at the top. Anderson's 1961 study pointed out that some did. Other evidence suggested that most high-status jobs did not go to members of the lower class. Lipset and Bendix noted that between 1771 and 1920 about two-thirds of each generation's successful business leaders came from established families.[83] Bernard Barker showed corroborating evidence in 1961. Fifty-seven percent of the business leaders in 1952 had a college diploma, and another 19 percent had at least attended college.[84] Combined with data suggesting that middle-class students had a greater chance of going to college than lower-class students, the figures supported the idea that lower-class students did not get many high-status jobs and that they had limited mobility and opportunity—that American society was more stratified than was commonly accepted.

Proponents of compensatory education overlooked troubling evidence of this kind which suggested that education was not the central factor in explaining social and economic mobility. The discussions of the fifties that had enlivened the belief in the powers of education supported their new attempt to resolve social problems. Other groups would find it equally easy to adopt the analysis of poverty and the program to deal with it that educators developed.

Concern over property and race was not, of course, confined to educators mobilized by civil rights groups and conditions in urban schools. The early sixties saw a growing interest among intellectuals and liberals in government circles in these problems. Dwight Macdonald's essay "Our Invisible Poor," which appeared in the *New Yorker* in 1962, summarized an expanding body of poverty literature. To Macdonald it was clear that the country's "two gravest social problems" were mass poverty and the race issue.[85] As interest in these issues grew, many people began to agree with educators that the compensatory scheme provided a valid remedy.

John Galbraith's article in *Harper's Magazine* in 1964 shows the eagerness with which liberals adopted the compensatory solution. Galbraith began his discussion by stating, "The elimination of poverty at home and its mitigation abroad are jobs for liberals. They will not be accomplished unless liberalism is a determined faith."[86] Poverty could be wiped out by continuing efforts in "civil rights, education, slum abatement, the rest." But, Galbraith suggested, one further step had great potential. Accepting the assumption that education caused prosperity and ignorance caused poverty, Galbraith maintained, "There is no place in the world where a well-educated population is really poor." The federal government, Galbraith suggested, should set aside funds for education in the hundred poorest areas of the country. Funds would pay for "truly excellent and comprehensive school plant[s]," an "elite body of teachers," and small family grants for food and clothing for school children.[87] Such an approach, Galbraith suggested, offered every indication of succeeding. "Can anyone argue," Galbraith asked, "that youngsters with these facilities and this training would share the dismal fate of their parents?"[88]

Most educators and liberals were prepared to agree with Galbraith. In the early sixties few offered more sweeping solutions for the problems of urban poverty. Job-creation programs, a family allowance system, or a negative income tax plan were occasionally discussed but had few adherents. Such plans were too expensive to be attractive. Compensatory education, on the other hand, did not have to be expensive. It did not disrupt social arrangements. Few educators even visualized far-reaching changes within the schools themselves. And compensatory education claimed to offer a way to meet urban problems by overcoming the effects of the culture of poverty.

Yet the solution of compensatory education raised some significant questions that few liberals or educators confronted. Were the effects of education powerful enough to offset the combined influence of family and neighborhood? Would normal school achievement, the goal of compensatory education, facilitate social mobility for the poor white or black student?

Was equal educational opportunity to change the distribution of social and economic rewards in any substantial way? Clearly, the intent of compensatory education was to increase social mobility; the children of poor parents would rise in occupational status and earn more money than their parents because of compensatory programs.[89] But did this objective mean an important modification of the rates of upward and downward mobility? If so, would the American system tolerate these changes?

The pattern of American social mobility, which shows a constant relationship between social fluidity and stability over time, suggests that significant changes in this pattern might be disruptive. Since 1880, few important alterations in the country's over-all rate of occupational mobility have occurred, for example.[90] Between 30 and 35 percent of families starting in manual positions have usually managed to climb into the middle class, and 70 to 80 percent of the middle class have retained their occupational status (although the system has not been this fluid for blacks).[91] Most upward mobility has been of short range, often stimulated by changes in the economic system, not by additional or better education.[92] Not only has this pattern characterized the American social system but the social systems of other industrialized nations.[93] The mobility from working class to white-collar status is about 31 percent in Sweden, 39 percent in France, and 45 percent in Switzerland, for example.[94] It is true that the American social system has been slightly more open than Europe's, since the movement from the working class and manual class into elite positions in the United States has been relatively high: 10.41 percent of the working class and 9.91 percent of those in manual occupations have moved upward into elite positions, whereas only 4.43 percent and 3.50 percent in similar categories in Sweden and 1.99 percent to 4.19 percent and 1.56 percent to 3.56 percent in France have managed to rise to this level.[95] Yet, significantly, in all three countries, a larger portion of the middle class has won elite status than have members of the working class.[96] Starting high seems to help almost everywhere.

The stability of American rates over time and the essential

similarity of American figures to mobility rates in other industrial countries suggest that there may well be an upper limit to the amount of social openness an industrial society is normally willing to accommodate. Without economic changes or changing fertility patterns, substantial modification of the rate of upward mobility might threaten to displace part of the middle class.[97] Moreover, social scientists have speculated that a highly mobile society may exhibit strain "in terms of . . . combativeness, frustration, rootlessness, and other social ills."[98] If compensatory education were to produce these disruptive results, it would hardly be politically feasible.

Yet central though these kinds of issues were to any effort designed to solve social problems through education, educators and liberals did not investigate them. But their failure to do so was understandable; they were not responsible for drawing up national educational legislation but merely provided the ideas from which government planners could pick and choose. In the course of planning the War on Poverty, it was quite possible that policy-makers would evaluate the ideas of educators and, in clarifying some of the crucial issues that educational ideas raised, reject the favored approach altogether.

1. *Public Papers of the Presidents of the United States, Lyndon B. Johnson, 1936-1964*, p. 114.

2. *Public Papers of the Presidents of the United States: Lyndon B. Johnson, 1965*, p. 365.

3. Henry J. Perkinson, *The Imperfect Panacea*, passim; Rousas J. Rushdoony, *The Messianic Character of American Education*, p. 29; Marvin Lazeron, "Urban Reform and the Schools"; Marvin Lazeron, *Origins of the Urban School*, passim.

4. Quoted in Rush Welter, *Popular Education and Democratic Thought in America*, p. 100; see Lawrence A. Cremin, *The American Common School*, pp. 49-62.

5. *Public Papers of the Presidents of the United States: Harry S Truman, 1948*, p. 289.

6. *Public Papers of the Presidents of the United States: Harry S Truman, 1949*, p. 167.

7. Educational Policies Commission and the American Council on Education, *Education and National Security* (Washington, D.C.: Educational Policies Commission and the American Council on Education, 1951), p. 15.

8. William Benton, *This Is the Challenge*, chap. 3, uses the phrase "cold war of the classrooms."

9. *Public Papers of the Presidents of the United States: Harry S Truman, 1951*, pp. 4, 64.

10. Ibid., p. 94.

11. Ibid., pp. 95–96.

12. Benton, *This Is the Challenge*; Nicholas De Witt, *Soviet Professional Manpower*; C. Winfield Scott, Clyde M. Hill, and Robert W. Burns, eds., *The Great Debate*; *Hearings before the Subcommittee on Research and Development on the Shortage of Scientific and Engineering Manpower*, 84th Cong., 2d Sess., 1956, Joint Committee.

13. Quoted in Benton, *This Is the Challenge*, p. 90.

14. H. G. Rickover, *Education and Freedom*, pp. 35, 181.

15. Ibid., p. 121; on a more popular level, see "Crisis in Education," *Life Magazine* reprint, 1958.

16. *Hearings before the Committee on Labor and Public Welfare on Science and Education for National Defense*, 85th Cong., 2d Sess., 1958, Senate, p. 2.

17. Ibid., pp. 5–6, 11, 24, 46, 150.

18. Ibid., p. 576; for a summary of the difficulties of devising a politically acceptable bill, see Paul E. March and Ross A. Gortner, *Federal Aid to Science Education*, pp. 24–29.

19. Sidney C. Sufrin, *Administering the National Defense Education Act*, pp. 10–12, 16–27.

20. *Senate Hearings*, 1958, pp. 58, 106, 150, 524.

21. Rickover, *Education and Freedom*, pp. 112, 127.

22. John W. Gardner, *Excellence*, p. 71.

23. Ibid., p. 41.

24. Charles E. Silberman, *Crisis in Black and White*, p. 7; Philip Meranto, *The Politics of Federal Aid to Education in 1965*, pp. 22–23.

25. Joe L. Frost and Glenn R. Hawkes, eds., *The Disadvantaged Child*, p. 226.

26. Nat Hentoff, *The New Equality*, p. 178.

27. Meranto, *The Politics of Federal Aid to Education*, p. 31.

28. Charles Philip Kearney, "The 1964 Presidential Task Force in Education and the Elementary and Secondary Education Act of 1965," p. 184.

29. Frost and Hawkes, *Disadvantaged Child*, p. 372.

30. James B. Conant, *Slums and Suburbs*, p. 2. See also Educational Policies Commission, *Education and the Disadvantaged American* (Washington, D.C.: National Education Association, 1962), p. 37. Although the social dangers of deprivation are not often as explicitly stated as they are by Conant, other writers do deal with the issue.

31. Conant, *Slums and Suburbs*, p. 20.

32. Ibid., p. 33.

33. Ibid., p. 2, 40.

34. See, for example, Educational Policies Commission, *Education*.

35. Ibid., p. 11.

36. A. Harry Passow, ed., *Education in Depressed Areas*, p. 87.

37. Ibid., p. 163.

38. Ibid., p. 88.

39. Educational Policies Commission, *Education*, pp. 9, 11.

40. Ibid., p. 36.

41. Frost and Hawkes, *Disadvantaged Child*, p. 352.

42. Ibid., p. 187; Passow, *Depressed Areas*, p. 163.

43. Ibid., p. 37.

44. Harry L. Miller, ed., *Education for the Disadvantaged*, pp. 105–8.

45. Passow, *Depressed Areas*, p. 21.

46. Benjamin S. Bloom, Allison Davis, and Robert Hess, *Compensatory Education for Cultural Deprivation*, pp. 16–17.

47. Frost and Hawkes, *Disadvantaged Child*, p. 176.

48. Ibid., p. 278.

49. Miller, *Current Issues*, p. 98.

50. Edith K. Mosher, "The Origins, Enactment, and Implementation of the Elementary and Secondary Education Act of 1965," p. 74.

51. Ibid., pp. 76–77.

52. Ibid., p. 77.

53. Edward M. McDill, Mary S. McDill, and J. Timothy Sprehe, *Strategies for Success in Compensatory Education*, p. 38; Edmund W. Gordon and Doxey A. Wilkerson, *Compensatory Education for the Disadvantaged*, p. 250.

54. McDill et al., *Strategies*, p. 38; Gordon and Wilkerson, *Compensatory Education*, p. 264.

55. McDill et al., *Strategies*, p. 39.

56. Patricia Cayo Sexton, *Education and Income*, p. xxi.

57. Ibid., p. xvi.

58. Ibid., p. xviii.

59. Ibid., p. 60.

60. Ibid., p. 34.

61. Ibid., pp. 40–52.

62. Ibid., pp. 6–7.

63. Ibid., pp. 7–8. See pp. 234–37 for a discussion of the social-class composition of local school boards.

64. A. H. Halsey, Jean Floud, and C. Arnold Anderson, eds., *Education, Economy, and Society*, pp. 288–92.

65. Ibid., p. 310.

66. Ibid., p. 229.

67. Ibid., p. 230.

68. William H. Sewell, Archie O. Haller, and Murray A. Straus, "Social Status and Educational and Occupational Aspiration," p. 73.

69. Halsey et al., *Education*, p. 270.

70. Ibid., p. 271.

71. Donald A. Hansen and Joel E. Gerstl, eds., *On Education*, p. 139.

72. Quoted in ibid., pp. 109–10.

73. John K. Folger and Charles B. Nam, "Trends in Education in Relation to the Occupational Structure," p. 23.

74. Bernard Barber, "Social-class Differences in Educational Life-Chances," pp. 104, 106.

75. Herb Gintis and Sam Bowles, "The Ideology of Educational Reform," p. 26.

76. See Robert J. Havighurst, Bernice L. Neugarten, and Jacqueline Falk, eds., *Society and Education*, pp. 234–35; William G. Spady, "Educational Mobility and Access."

77. Folger and Nam, "Trends," p. 33.

78. Halsey et al., *Education*, p. 164.

79. Ibid., pp. 174–75.

80. Ibid., p. 176.

81. Seymour M. Lipset and Reinhard Bendix, *Social Mobility in Industrial Society*, p. 76.

82. Ibid., p. 281.

83. Ibid., p. 123.

84. Barber, "Social-class Differences," p. 104.

85. Barton J. Bernstein and Allen J. Matusow, eds., *Twentieth Century America*, p. 505.

86. John Kenneth Galbraith, "Let Us Begin," p. 18.

87. Ibid., p. 26.

88. Ibid.

89. S. M. Miller and Pamela A. Roby, *The Future of Inequality*, p. 119.

90. Peter M. Blau and Otis Dudley Duncan, *The American Occupational Structure*, pp. 98–113; Seymour Martin Lipset, "Social Mobility and Equal Opportunity," pp. 91–92; Stephan Thernstrom, "Poverty in Historical Perspective," in Daniel P. Moynihan, ed., *On Understanding Poverty*, pp. 167–69.

91. Lipset, "Social Mobility," pp. 93, 96.

92. Duncan and Blau, *The American Occupational Structure*, pp. 420, 435; Phillips Cartright, "Occupational Inheritance"; John P. Neelsen, "Education and Social Mobility." Other causes of mobility include urban migration, family size, career starting point, etc.

93. Lipset, "Social Mobility," p. 98.

94. Duncan and Blau, *The American Occupational Structure*, p. 433; Lipset and Bendix, *Social Mobility*, p. 25.

95. Duncan and Blau, *The American Occupational Structure*, p. 434.

96. Ibid.

97. Ibid., p. 435.

98. Lipset and Bendix, *Social Mobility*, p. 285.

2

Education in the Early War on Poverty

As government planners formulated an antipoverty program in late 1963 and early 1964, they agreed that education offered one of the most effective ways of attacking poverty. A January 1964 draft of the president's Message on Education embodied this point of view. Borrowing the imagery of Michael Harrington's *The Other America*, the draft agreed that there were "two Americas . . . an America in the sunlight, a country in which tens of millions share the blessings of unprecedented prosperity . . . [and an] America in shadows, in which many millions share poverty not prosperity." The draft went on to describe education as "the sturdiest lever to raise and move forward this open and democratic society," and to picture educational achievement as a clear promise of economic achievement. Having clarified the link between education and income, the draft message proposed special educational help for poor children, urging Americans to confront "the overriding fact that our schools are especially weak for the children of our slums and depressed rural areas who require the best education and often get the worst."[1]

Although President Johnson never delivered this message, the thinking it represented underlay much of the planning for the poverty program between November 1963 and February 1964. During this period a task force drawn from the Bureau of the Budget and the Council of Economic Advisers, and headed by Walter Heller, the council's chairman, developed a poverty bill with two titles. The first title proposed community action programs, the second, education grants for the poor. In early February 1964, however, a shift in emphasis occurred. A new task force, led by the Peace Corps's forceful director, Sargeant Shriver, dropped most of Heller's legislative plan. The new poverty bill, the Economic Opportunity Act, was a conglomerate measure that retained only some of the emphasis of the Heller bill. Yet the administration's decision to adopt another approach did not reflect the conclusion that the educational solution for poverty was misguided but only that the broader bill would have a greater political appeal. The decision was right. The Economic Opportunity Act passed Congress by early August 1964, and was signed ceremoniously by President Johnson on 20 August. Since the poverty bill created political interest in the kind of educational proposals discussed by Heller's group, however, that solution was not gone for long. It would reappear in modified but more impressive form as the ESEA a year later.

Organizing task forces to draw up legislative programs represented a move away from traditional methods of planning that gave agencies the responsibility for drawing up legislative proposals, leaving final approval to the White House staff and the Bureau of the Budget.[2] This system had given agencies substantial planning power. President Kennedy, anxious to assert personal control over the "sprawling feudalism of government" and to "get things moving," initially decided to create an executive task force to develop the poverty program.[3] His successor was no less interested in shaping legislation. Both men were concerned not only to influence government policy by controlling the planning process more closely but also to bring fresh ideas into government and to coordinate planning. The two relied more and more often on outside task forces and executive groups to make policy. Gradually, these task forces became a means of absorbing agency powers.[4]

Although using task forces to develop administration planning represented an attempt to introduce new thinking into government circles, in this case the results were disappointing. For the most part, the two poverty task forces in 1963 and 1964 stayed close to traditional agency proposals. Probably too much task force time and energy was dissipated in struggling with the vested power of agencies and in plotting congressional strategy to allow the task force to become as creative a factor in government planning as Kennedy and Johnson had hoped.

A careful examination of the task force's deliberations on educational measures illustrates related problems in the planning process and suggests the obstacles to careful formulation of social policy. Despite the different models of educational reform that task force participants held, Heller's group never seems to have explored them. Nor does the group seem to have systematically evaluated research on the general relationship between education and poverty, or more mundane matters such as whether compensatory education programs were successful. When the task force changed as Shriver became the head of planning in 1964, the new group primarily concerned itself with political appeal, not careful evaluation. The new legislative proposal, the Economic Opportunity bill, did not rest on any firmer analytical grounds than the original measure.

The deliberations of the poverty task forces, thus, exemplify many of the intellectual, bureaucratic, and political problems that often play a part in determining the government's response to social problems.[5] But the central question remains why planners were so quick to adopt an educational focus in the first place. First, administration anxieties suggested an urban program aimed at the young, the blacks, and the unemployed. For all these, education seemed to offer the possibility of economic improvement. Second, leading planners, though perceiving education reform from different perspectives, were sympathetic to some kind of educational solution. Their agreement on the importance of education concealed the conflict between their viewpoints.

Administration worry over unemployment and inadequate economic expansion was one of the driving forces behind the attack on poverty. These concerns had troubled Kennedy and his advisers since 1961, when the economy had been at a low point. Though the situation improved, unemployment statistics continued to be disheartening. Walter Heller, Kennedy's leading economic adviser, hoping to reduce unemployment to 4 percent, persuaded Kennedy by the spring of 1963 that a tax cut to stimulate the economy and to create two to three million jobs for the unemployed was necessary.[6] Yet the tax cut would not end unemployment. "Those caught in the web of illiteracy, lack of skills, poor health and squalor would not be able to make use of . . . exits" and opportunities the cut would provide, Heller pointed out. For these unfortunate people, then, new measures focusing "sharply and specifically on removal of the road blocks of poverty" were essential.[7]

Since young people made up an unnecessarily large part of the unemployment rolls, worries about the unemployment rate were also worries about youth. In 1962 when the general unemployment rate was 5.6 percent, the average rate of teenage unemployment was about 13 percent.[8] By the next year the President's Committee on Youth Employment was warning that the youth problem had reached crisis proportions. Recognizing the seriousness of the situation, Kennedy sent the Vocational Education bill to Congress in 1963 and initiated a summer program to persuade dropouts to return to school. Yet, neither effort seemed an adequate solution to the lack of education and skills that these unemployed young people presumably exhibited.

The problem of what to do for black America probably concerned Kennedy most deeply. Although the 1960 census indicated that most poor were whites living in rural or suburban areas, it was the poor ill-educated blacks who were dangerously crowded into decaying urban areas, with an unemployment rate 112 percent that of whites in 1963.[9] It was these same blacks whom Civil Rights movement had made increasingly aware of their plight.[10] Sensing black unrest, Kennedy spent a major part of one cabinet meeting in June 1963 discussing Negro unemployment and asking for staff papers on the problem.[11] The March on Washington two months later further clarified that blacks demanded, and demanded urgently, both civil rights and jobs. For Kennedy, then, the mood of blacks that summer of 1963 was "ominous."[12] Few, including the president, could forget the suggestive events of only a few months earlier when civil rights demonstrations in Birmingham, Alabama, had turned into violent riots. Some response to black demands was clearly in order.

Lyndon Johnson inherited these major administration concerns about unemployment, youth, and race in November 1963, and added the one of time. Presidential elections were less than a year away. Precipitated so unexpectedly to the presidency, Johnson was concerned with establishing an image for his administration rapidly so that he could wage an effective campaign in 1964. The reality of the election made the tentative poverty program an attractive possibility. Initial work had already started on it, and the task force could probably pull its thinking into legislative form quickly. Moreover, the program was not yet publicly identified with his charismatic predecessor and complemented both Johnson's view of himself as a New Deal social reformer and his romanticized picture of his own deprived youth.[13] These factors combined to make the new president favor the work in progress. Two days after the assassination, Johnson informed Heller, "That's my kind of program," and urged him to continue work "full speed ahead."[14]

The government, under the press of related and urgent problems, moved toward the rapid development of an antipoverty program that focused on urban areas with large numbers of young unemployed blacks. There were, of course, many possible alternatives for actions. The interests of Heller's task force members, however, made them immediately sympathetic to some kind of an educational solution. Agreement on an educational focus, however, masked basic disagreements. Early task force deliberations reflected the economist's perceptions of poverty and possible solutions. Later, as David Hackett became more important in task force planning, the sociologist's definition vied with the economist's in a battle largely unnoticed by participants.

The economic analysis was the one first developed by the task force, many of whom were professional economists. Kennedy's initial interest, in December 1962, in the facts and figures of poverty stimulated Walter Heller to assign economist Robert Lampman, a council staff member, to gather relevant data on poverty. Calling his analysis "no nonsense from anybody liberalism," Lampman revised his 1959 study *The Low Income Population and Economic Growth* for Heller's consideration. Stressing that steady economic growth helped much of the population, Lampman pointed out, however, that some groups still remained in poverty. His calculations suggested that even with continuing growth as many as 31.3 millions might be indigent in 1970. Cash assistance programs, Lampman suggested, only reached a small portion of the poor. Going on to describe the statistical attributes of the poor, Lampman showed that poverty groups often exhibited "handicapping characteristics" like color, sex, and low education.[15] Lampman's analysis, which was circulated in several summer memorandums, could and did influence task force members, who saw clear connections between inadequate education and poverty.

A 29 October 1963 memorandum from Michael March, a task force member from the Bureau of the Budget, to his director, Kermit Gordon, illustrates how the task force used Lampman's material. March reported that the poverty task force had met twice, had studied the statistics of low income population, and had discussed the effects of the proposed tax cut. "It has been assumed," March recalled, that "[the tax cut] . . . would not help many of the 20% of the people who are below the poverty line. Among these people low education is heavily associated with poverty. . . . " March's memorandum suggested that the task force interpreted Lampman's statistics as an indication that education was part of the cure for poverty. "The group's consensus," he wrote, "leans toward relying on a wide range of programs. Preventive and remedial programs, such as improved education, training and health services deserve first priority." In fact, March reported that the task force had gone on to discuss possible specific compensatory measures for the poor, such as enrichment programs and rural and slum community school projects.[16]

Walter Heller's own interests reinforced the group's tendencies to perceive poverty as an economic condition with an educational solution. For Heller the problem of poverty ultimately involved the country's long-term economic growth. Although full employment obviously stimulated further expansion, it could not generate an adequate growth rate for the future.[17] Other measures focused on the expansion of human resources, which to Heller was just as important as investing in plant equipment, were necessary. Education was one such measure, and "this acceptance of education," Heller pointed out, "is long overdue."[18] By transforming the unproductive worker into a highly skilled and productive member of the work force, education could contribute to general economic growth. With this view of education as the "essential instrument for achieving higher productivity, technological advance and broad understanding which underlie economic growth," Heller predictably favored federal aid to public schools.[19] "The big pay off will come from basic education," he claimed.[20] In this analysis of education as a tool for economic expansion, Heller seems to have regarded the public school system as essentially sound, though in need of greater financial support.

David Hackett, executive director of the President's Committee on Juvenile Delinquency and Youth Crime established in 1961, also supported an educational solution to poverty, although it differed from that of the economist. During the summer of 1964 Hackett was only informally involved in poverty discussions with Heller's task force. In the fall, however, Hackett came to his President's Committee staff members saying, "I want you guys to think about a comprehensive poverty program." As one staff member recalled, "Heller was supposed to be working in the economics of poverty to prove it existed, look at income distribution. We were to work on programs."[21] In early November Hackett offered his formal suggestions to Heller. By mid-December Hackett had become a leading figure in program-planning, providing the coordinating theme of community action for Heller's group.

Hackett's understanding of the relation between education and poverty stemmed from his work as director of the President's Committee. When President Kennedy had decided to "do something about delinquency" before his inauguration, he had selected Hackett for the job.[22] As Hackett was in the process of investigating what was known or theorized about juvenile delinquency, he met Lloyd Ohlin, a sociologist, who had just written an important book about delinquency with another sociologist, Richard Cloward. "Impressed" with Ohlin, Hackett invited him to come to Washington. Ohlin eventually accepted.[23]

Hackett was sympathetic to Cloward and Ohlin's approach to the delinquency problem, which focused on structural defects in the social system.[24] The two sociologists suggested that lower-class youths turned to crime because unsympathetic institutions frustrated their will to succeed.[25] "Institutional inadequacies generate these [social] problems," Cloward emphasized.[26] Thus, any attempt to prevent delinquency implied changing the social system to make institutions more responsive to the poor and perhaps challenging the power structure itself.

The opportunity theory provided the theoretical underpinning for the work of the President's Committee, which made grants to sixteen communities to work out comprehensive plans to eliminate delinquency. Each program was to identify "many sources of the problem" and to propose "changes in many institutions."[27] As the program coordinator of the President's Committee observed later, "We believed that the answers to lower-class delinquency and poverty lay in a massive reform of institutional practices in schools, social-welfare agencies, and employment services." The coordinator revealed, "We believed with fervor that a combination of refined intellectual understanding of problems, mixed with political 'clout' and new funds would be the magic ingredients in the war on delinquency."[28]

Since Hackett saw an intimate relation between crime and poverty, he perceived his delinquency program as a model for an antipoverty effort.[29] Indeed, some of Hackett's staff felt his early conversations with the Heller task force represented the "kind of situation in which our boss was giving our program away."[30] The boss's program had attractive features for the task force. Hackett had always seen change within the schools as a vital part of any effort to deal with delinquency, and his views generally appeared to support the economists, who saw education as an escape route from poverty.[31] Actually, however, Hackett's emphasis on changing the school system through a combination of "negotiation, cooption and the lure of new funds" diverged from the economists' in seeing the system itself as a problem.[32]

The Ford Foundation's efforts in urban areas also fed into the generalized thinking of the Heller task force. Since the late 1950s the Ford Foundation had been experimenting to improve the social condition of central cities under its Public Affairs Program Director Paul Ylvisaker.[33] A key focus of Ford Foundation strategy was the public school system. "We have placed the Ford Foundation's first bet not on the central business district of the city," Ylvisaker pointed out, "but on its school system, and more on school outlook and methods than on buildings."[34] By holding out the hope of grants, by negotiating with important community leaders, and finally by supporting educational experiments, Ford believed it could bring about change. Ylvisaker, with the weight of the Ford Foundation's money and experience behind him, also participated in task force deliberations in mid-December.[35]

The President's Committee and the Ford Foundation had close ties with each other. Both emphasized "changing the environment, rather than the individual and both recognized education and vocational opportunities as crucial aspects of the environment. Reform, they both believed, must grow out of a much more coherent integration of relevant institutions."[36]

The interests and professional concerns of Lampman, Heller, Hackett, and Ylvisaker all suggested some kind of educational proposal for the poverty program and fitted in with the controlling administration interest in youth, race, and employment. But actually, members of the task force and others involved in the planning effort defined poverty and its relation to formal education differently. As Heller visualized poverty, "Much of the problem and much of the solution was economic in nature."[37] For Hackett, however, poverty resulted from the organization of society that discriminated against the poor. But these views were not the only ones of task force members, who at times slipped into a cultural explanation of poverty as a psychological rather than an economic or social problem.[38] From this perspective the schools were regarded as basically sound but in need of additional compensatory programs to help deprived children overcome the effects of poverty.

That such different perspectives on the relationship between education, schools, and poverty went largely unrecognized suggests serious limitations of the process of developing policy. The initial enthusiasm involved in planning a new program and the general desire to see it implemented seem partially to explain this failure to come to grips with conflicting views. One observer of the task force specifically noted this tendency as the group considered the community action proposal. Although they held quite different strategies for institutional change, the observer pointed out, "few of the participants argued *against* the ideas of others so much as they argued *for* their own."[39]

Certain other aspects of the planning process hindered recognition of significant problems with the educational approach. The task force itself was a group with changing membership, an informal method of operation, and a center of activity shifting from the council to the Bureau of the Budget. The nature of the group was unstructured enough to have encouraged adopting policies without any clear formulation of goals and means.[40] Furthermore, the common ideological framework of most of the task force also explains why incompatibilities and difficulties were never noticed. As Heller realized, "Obviously, we were deep in the realm of social goals and values."[41] Early task force memoirs agreed on the importance of providing opportunity, of letting the poor help themselves.[42] Heller was proposing a tax cut, not a massive increase in social services for the poor.[43] Task force members agreed that education, health, and training were preferable to job creation programs.[44] Even Hackett expected that institutions would willingly transform themselves. As participants later pointed out, radical alternatives were not seriously considered.[45] Finally, the task force had to face financial reality. Johnson wanted the war against poverty to be cheap. These factors all led to ready acceptance of an educational solution that was neither expensive nor threatening to the social order, which was supported by traditional belief in schools as the road to social and economic mobility.

The task force's method of operation also seems to have worked against the careful examination of ideas. Despite its desire for novel ideas, Heller's task force never formulated its own program. Starting by canvassing governmental departments for "imaginative new" suggestions on 5 November 1963, the task force soon found itself flooded with proposals, more than a hundred within the first month.[46] Task force members were busy evaluating and costing out different proposals. Even more important, the task force found itself involved with agencies now pressing to have their pet proposals part of the new program and controversial issues such as who or what department would run the poverty program. This is not to say that the task force had no effect on the shape of the program. It did color the program by its decision to adopt Hackett's proposal of community action as one central theme. But the task force did not create a program; it put one together under various bureaucratic pressures.

The actual education solution adopted by the Heller task force was a measure initially proposed by HEW and reshaped by Bureau of the Budget criticism. The way in which this particular solution was selected and developed illustrates the general kind of problems involved in planning the poverty effort. HEW's first response to Heller's 5 November 1963 memorandum asking for departmental suggestions for the poverty program was typically bureaucratic: revive department legislation. The legislation HEW had in mind was Kennedy's National Education Act proposed in the winter of 1963. On 13 November Francis Keppel, commissioner of education, went over this plan with Wilbur Cohen, the assistant secretary of HEW in charge of legislation. Keppel thought of suggesting two bills to Heller, one offering general school aid for construction and teacher salaries, and the other establishing grants for "experimental and action projects designed to improve educational opportunity and achievements of students attending schools in areas—*both urban slums and rural depressed*—marked by high rates of unemployment and by low per capita income and educational achievements."[47] Keppel's second proposal did not contemplate moving outside the public school system. The commissioner visualized funds for poor students smoothly flowing from Washington to state educational departments and local school districts. Of course, such an allocation of funds would probably mean that urban bureaucrats and substantial members of local communities would control the program.[48]

On 19 November 1963 Cohen sent HEW's suggestions on to Heller in a memorandum that revealed that HEW was making a bid for major control over the new poverty program. "The Department of Health, Education, and Welfare is vitally concerned with the prevention and alleviation of poverty," Cohen wrote. "All of our programs are directed—in one way or another—towards the conservation and development of human resources and the opening of opportunities for more satisfying individual and community life."[49] Cohen's list of proposals offered a traditional HEW program of improving social security benefits, providing vocational rehabilitation for the disabled, meeting the needs of the aged, and supporting work relief and training programs.

Although Cohen included Keppel's poverty grant plan to improve educational opportunity and achievement, he warned that the task force should not think that HEW had moved away from "our strong support for the portions of the 1963 proposals relating to teacher salary increases and urgently needed school construction."[50] This was not the case at all, and it appeared that HEW was as eager as ever to get a general aid bill that now could be rationalized in terms of poverty. Poverty conditions made construction and salary aid even more necessary, Cohen suggested. Arguing that over-crowding and unhealthy conditions were characteristic of poor schools, and that teacher salaries and experience had a direct relation to educational attainment, the assistant secretary did admit federal aid would help all schools; still, "enactment would be particularly beneficial in economically and educationally deprived areas where teacher salary increase and school construction needs are especially urgent and severe. The urgency of enacting legislation to meet these needs should be given great emphasis in the instant program to widen participation in prosperity."[51] HEW's strategy was clear. For the following two and a half months, the department would be fighting to get a general aid to education bill. And the task force would be on the defensive.

William Capron, an economist and one of the leading members of Heller's task force, and Michael March, from the Bureau of the Budget, evaluated the HEW package on 21 November 1963. Disliking the heavy emphasis on welfare-type programs, they reported that the suggestions were "quite light on the really useful programs relating to youth." They felt the best bet was the grants proposal of $180 million for school projects in poverty areas. Initially underestimating HEW's determination to get general aid, the two task force members felt there was "great merit" in the idea of diverting all the funds HEW wanted for general aid "into a really significant anti-poverty program."[52]

Even though the task force considered HEW's educational suggestions to be limited, it surprisingly made the educational grants proposal into a major part of its program. Accepting a proposal it defined as limited may have been part of a task force attempt to prevent the more traditional but less attractive educational aid measure from being incorporated into the program. HEW was after all a huge and powerful department with strong ties to educational associations and various interest groups, whereas the task force was only a temporary, shifting group. Incorporating some of the HEW package into the new proposal no doubt made it easier to reject the rest. Then, too, the task force centered its discussions around Keppel's suggestion because it fit into their own ideological framework. Task force members believed that "the incidence of poverty among adults is overwhelmingly dependent on their employability. . . . Employability in turn is basically dependent on the amount and quality of education . . . received in childhood and youth."[53] Such factors prevented judging the proposal itself in terms of task force expectations.

In early December 1963 much of the task force's energy was devoted to an attempt to pull the poverty effort together into a coherent and attractive piece of legislation. Central though the education theme was, it did not provide a new look or unify the program as the task force desired. Nor did the theme protect the task force sufficiently from other departments wanting the task force to include their own programs. As December wore on, David Hackett played an increasingly important part in task force deliberations and provided the answer to the dilemma.

In early November 1963, when Hackett had suggested the community action concept to the task force, he visualized a few demonstration areas experimenting with planning and implementing community action programs. A month later Hackett sent Heller a memorandum of almost forty pages in which he expanded upon his original ideas. Hackett again urged establishing local demonstration projects. More important, he now included his ideas about how planning the attack on poverty should proceed. "There is a clear need for a broad study of all programs pertaining to poverty," Hackett stated a few days later. To ensure careful planning, Hackett suggested bringing together a series of task forces to analyze the needs of different groups of the poor and then work out the program. Hackett pointed out that there would have to be a thorough study of existing government programs, which were often poorly coordinated, overlapped, and occasionally did not even reach the poor. Finally, Hackett advised setting up a cabinet committee to "give the project the prestige of a federal undertaking at the highest level . . . [and to] act as a coordinating structure to implement the findings" of the different study groups.[54]

Some of Heller's task force were sympathetic to aspects

of Hackett's plan. Bureau of the Budget members were dismayed by poor planning and bureaucratic inefficiency in government, and one of them, William Cannon, pushed Hackett's ideas. By mid-December the task force had agreed to establish a ten-year poverty program with a modest beginning. Community demonstration areas were to receive funds to plan and to coordinate comprehensive antipoverty programs in their communities, as Hackett had suggested. The task force was also sympathetic to the idea of establishing a cabinet committee or council.[55] But the thorough process of multi-level planning that Hackett proposed does not seem to have become a part of task force thinking. For the task force had more concerns than providing for good planning. One of Heller's assistants provided a clue to the task force's enthusiastic response to Hackett's ideas. "This may be the way to really make something out of this poverty program," he wrote.[56] Community action was new and could give a distinctive look to the poverty program. The concept also could coordinate the different elements of an attack on poverty. Finally, the proposal provided a way for the task force to escape departmental pressures. Each community would select and coordinate its own programs.[57]

The decision to incorporate community action into the poverty program gave it a new look but did not signify an end of the education focus. As a memorandum of 18 December 1963 indicates, the task force visualized a composite package including community action, health and welfare programs, and funds for education, "along the general line proposed by Galbraith."[58] The decision to bring these elements into one program and to consider the kind of planning suggestions offered by Hackett offered an ideal opportunity for policy-makers to evaluate each of their tentative proposals. The moment was equally favorable for an examination of the distinct models of change now embodied in the program. Hackett's concept of community action implied reforming institutions; the educational grants proposal, on the other hand, was vague about expected changes. Yet, little clarification of views seems to have occurred.

Disagreements over the nature of the educational grants

proposals continued to occupy the time and energy of task force members in the Bureau of the Budget and HEW into January 1964. First, HEW feared that community action was becoming too important in the over-all program and was jealous. As Cohen pointed out, "I would make the community action program the second string to the bow rather then the first string."[59] Then, too, HEW's Secretary Celebrezze was causing trouble. Celebrezze continued to insist that HEW needed a general aid bill that would include the educational grants proposal. The Bureau of the Budget disagreed. As a January memorandum pointed out, "It must be recognized that the elementary-secondary education bill may go down the drain, and the Administration would not only lose this significant education measure but also a key element in its attack on poverty."[60]

But there were other "far reaching" differences between the task force and HEW, as a series of January memorandums revealed. Budget Bureau task force members found HEW's educational grant plan "restrictive" because it was tied too closely to the traditional educational power structure of state and local public authorities, and because HEW favored automatic formula grants to the states. These features were "undesirable limitations" from the bureau's point of view, and the HEW plan was "too much a competitor of the new poverty program."[61] What the bureau sought was a more flexible approach pinpointing "federal resources to a limited number of high poverty projects" selected by the commissioner of education, not by the states as HEW desired.[62] The projects themselves should be focused on individuals with special educational needs, with priority going to projects under the community action aegis. Public schools, too, could sponsor projects, as HEW had insisted, but so should universities, private agencies, and other units of local government.[63]

The bureau's criticism of the HEW plan suggested some awareness about the problems facing the proposed legislation. Policy-makers obviously feared that the cautious public school system might use federal funds to undercut the spirit of the new program. They also recognized that present school programs were "inadequate in most school districts in terms of meeting special problems of individual children."[64] These insights stimulated their wish to move outside the system. Yet, bureau members do not appear to have incorporated their insights into any organized theory about the nature of the public school system or the character of the educational bureaucracy that might make it unsympathetic if not hostile to the poor.[65] The failure to develop these issues meant bureau planners were able to agree that all that was needed was "additional services . . . provided through Federal aid for demonstration action-type projects."[66] In any case, practical matters appear to have been uppermost. Task force planners wanted to include parochial children in the bill and, thus, favored private project sponsors. If money went only to public schools, parochial students might never participate in these activities. As a 14 January memorandum concluded, "Provision should be made for projects *outside* the framework of the public school system as the best means of providing services for children irrespective of their regular attendance at public or non-public schools."[67]

In response to the bureau's criticisms, HEW revised its proposal.[68] By the end of January 1964 a compromise emerged to become the second title of the community action bill. HEW finally dropped general aid in favor of the educational grants proposal. But in return for such a concession, HEW had won several of its major points. The new bill contained a complex automatic formula that determined the amount of state allocation. But HEW had been less successful with project selection. State education departments now lost the power to determine criteria for selecting project proposals and awarding grants to the commissioner of education. And the new title did represent some attempt to escape public school orientation. Local and welfare agencies were to advise and assist in the development of projects. Community action agencies had to approve special education programs. But the most significant victory of HEW emerged from the process of negotiation. The public school would develop plans and administer the program. This meant the local school system, representing the local power structure, would make the vital decision of how to spend project money.

HEW's victory on this point exemplified the agency's influence and even more the task force's planning failure. Many
of these administrative arrangements favored by HEW would
reappear in the ESEA the following year.

In all the discussions over the educational proposal, there
had been much discussion about administration and implementation but little about the bill's educational content or
purpose. The goal of the title, "Educational Improvement in
Low Income Areas," was "to encourage and assist in the
development of programs to meet the special educational
needs of children and youth in areas with high concentrations
of low income families."[69] In the first year of operation $140
million was allocated for this purpose. Projects were to be "of
sufficient variety, scope, and size as to give reasonable promise of substantial progress toward meeting the special educational needs of young people."[70] The bill did not define key
terms like "reasonable promise" and "substantial progress."
No evidence exists to indicate that the task force ever considered what these terms meant either. The title's purpose
was, thus, vague, and success would be hard to measure.

The bill did suggest some typical compensatory programs suitable for funding, however. These included strengthening instruction in reading and mathematics, providing
guidance counseling and services for students, and supporting after-school study centers and cultural enrichment
programs. The Bureau of the Budget had originally tried to
broaden the scope of activities to include programs for health
care and special programs for handicapped children, the
talented, and children of migrant workers.[71] The effort to
widen services failed, and had not represented a different
approach to the poor in any case. Bureau members did not
question the effectiveness of the compensatory solutions in
meeting special educational needs of poor children, although
several compensatory projects like New York's Higher Horizon project and the Banneker project in Saint Louis already
suggested that these kinds of programs yielded few measurable academic results.

The title did convey again the sense that something was
wrong with education for poor children. The grant set aside

15 percent of the funds for teacher training and research, demonstration projects to develop "new or improved methods" of teaching the poor, and migrant programs.[72] Still, most of the title's money did not stimulate curriculum or organizational changes but encouraged doing more of the same kind of things schools were already doing. The title suggested that planners expected that money alone could transform public schools into effective institutions for the poor.

The compensatory solution the title proposed was weak, the view of educational change, vague. Nor did the title represent an effort to gain knowledge about the educational process for deprived children. The title established a committee to review and evaluate projects funded by the title. But since there were no provisions for reports from local areas, and since educational goals were imprecise, this provision would probably yield little useful information for later policy-makers.

By the end of January 1964 the task force was ready to go ahead with a poverty bill that had a community action title and an education title. The draft bill was hardly a victory for rational social planning, and Hackett himself was displeased. In a memorandum of 23 January he criticized the bill's failure to provide for a thorough examination of problems before developing action programs, its failure to emphasize planning on the federal level, to study existing programs, and to emphasize innovation.[73] His criticism certainly pinpointed the weakness of the education title, which proposed an inadequate compensatory solution and offered no clearly conceived concept of educational change.

Alternatives to the education title had certainly come to the task force's attention. Willard Wirtz, secretary of labor, had been a vocal critic of the task force plan. Since Wirtz saw poverty as a lack of income, he argued that the War on Poverty should stress employment. Community action programs promised few jobs. Furthermore, Wirtz feared that the bill would give local educators and welfare workers too much authority. He urged a poverty program that would be an enlargement and redirection of existing agency programs.[74] The task force rejected Wirtz's arguments because the tax cut was expected to provide jobs, because agency domination of the poverty programs was undesirable.[75]

Wirtz did not oppose education; he merely warned it would pay off only in the long run. In fact, he made a series of penetrating speeches dealing with educational reform far more thoroughly than the task force apparently did. At an AFL-CIO convention on 8 November 1963, for example, Wirtz suggested that a war on ignorance would necessitate building schools with living quarters for the poor, since poor children needed to escape the environment of poverty. Wirtz also called for more training for teachers of deprived children. Such measures, Wirtz pointed out, would have the advantage of making education into a real business and solving unemployment as well.[76] On 20 December 1963 Wirtz spoke at the University of Michigan. "The school system is no longer preparing enough people for the jobs that need to be done," he warned. "The job needs have changed, the educational system hasn't."[77] In his speeches Wirtz went to some of the central issues, such as the relation between education, the home environment, and poverty, and the nature of the school system. But the task force disregarded these insights.

The task force had not only failed to come up with a carefully thought out bill to attack poverty, it had also failed to please the president. Dissatisfied with the group's delay in putting a poverty program together and its failure to resolve departmental rivalries, and realizing the need for aggressive leadership, Johnson appointed Sargeant Shriver, head of the Peace Corps, to lead the effort on 1 February 1964.[78] The evening after his appointment Shriver asked Charles Schultze, assistant director of the Bureau of the Budget, to describe the Heller task force's approach and its plan. During an all-day meeting including department representatives, White House staff, and other experts on 4 February, Shriver observed departmental disagreements over the community action emphasis. Willard Wirtz attacked community action, arguing once more that the War on Poverty must emphasize job creation and training, which would bring immediate results. Other voices joined Wirtz to urge a multifaceted attack on poverty.[79]

A shift in emphasis away from reliance on community action and formal education was primarily motivated by political, not intellectual, considerations. Shriver recognized the obvious fact that the poverty program must justify itself almost immediately if Congress was to reappropriate funds the next year.[80] Furthermore, the November election was fast approaching, and the president needed an achievement for his campaign. Johnson and the news media had already begun to create expectations in the public. Shriver found the Heller task force bill too modest in its reliance on a few community action programs and educational grants. Both titles would take too long to get going and would disappoint both the president and the country. As Schultze noted on 8 February 1964, Shriver was beginning from scratch, looking for easy-to-start programs with "relatively quick payoffs." Finally, Shriver sensed the hunger of the departments and agencies for their share of the poverty program. Departmental pressures had partly immobilized the Heller task force. Shriver was willing to expand the program to include the departments. As Schultze also pointed out, Shriver "has obtained papers from the various departments on possible programs and is now about where we were three months ago—completely at sea."[81]

Shriver quickly gathered a new group of advisers around him that included department representatives like Daniel Moynihan, assistant secretary of labor, and James Sundquist, undersecretary of agriculture. His chief aide was civil rights expert Adam Yarmolinsky, on loan from the Defense Department. Scores of outsiders were consulted. The members of Heller's task force found themselves thrust out of the principal decision-making process, although at first they did not realize it. On 8 February 1964 Charles Schultze thought he had persuaded Shriver to go along with the Bureau of the Budget's limited project-oriented approach, which concentrated funds.[82] But his hopes were dashed when antipoverty efforts spilled out in many directions as the month continued.[83]

To the community action proposal, the new task force added provisions pushed by agencies like the rural loan title, and the title establishing a National Service Corps, now called VISTA. Under the influence of Labor Secretary Wirtz, the group incorporated the Youth Conservation Corps and the Neighborhood Youth Corps in the bill. Shriver was trying to put together a broad bill that would reach many people and that promised to get them into jobs quickly.[84]

As these programs were being added to the new poverty bill, education lost its prominent place in the antipoverty effort. Shriver disliked the community action-education package from the start, feeling it would not go over in Congress.[85] School bills traditionally ran into trouble in Congress. Nor did Shriver wish to channel money through the public school system. Grants to schools would not bring quick, visible pay-offs. Shriver favored federal control, not local control. As the Bureau of the Budget's Bill Cannon reported on 13 February 1964, "Shriver still appears to be highly distrustful of [the] willingness or ability of local people to do a proper job."[86] As six weeks went by, training measures began to assume importance. Adam Yarmolinsky recalled, "We decided that the Poverty Program should concentrate on preparing and training the poor to get and hold better jobs. . . . It was this decision which led to a heavy emphasis not only on Community Action, but also on the Job Corps, and other vocational and pre-vocational training programs."[87] For the new task force, education became no more important than other approaches.[88]

Shriver's first thought was to assign $200 million to the community action title for educational projects sponsored by both public and private groups. Competition for funds might jolt the public school system into being more responsive to the poor.[89] A 13 February 1964 memorandum reported, "Keppel has agreed . . . to let Shriver call the shots on his program, but HEW will probably resist the other features of the current approach."[90] Since Shriver offered Keppel's Office of Education the opportunity to develop education programs under the community action title, the commissioner supported the new measure. Keppel had decided in any case that the educational grants would not pass Congress alone. Moreover, the Shriver plan had the advantage of offering money to public and private schools, which Keppel favored.

Church-state issues were of major importance in working out the educational components of the community action title in a satisfactory political form. But as the effort to de-velop a solution to the church-state issue proceeded, the specif-ic educational grants proposal disappeared. The 24 February draft bill listed some educational activities like preschool and guidance counseling as examples of possible community action projects.[91] But since so many new training and health activities were now included in the program, the amount of money available for education dwindled.[92] When members of the task force realized Congress might make suggestions into legislative requirements, they dropped the list of sug-gested activities.[93]

The final Economic Opportunity Act sent to Congress in mid-March 1964 had six titles establishing many programs aimed at different age groups. As Shriver had hoped, the bill offered everyone something, even if the offering were not new. Shriver countered the accusation that the Economic Oppor-tunity Act was old hat by asserting that the programs had proven themselves through experience. They were not just the result of "some theatrical new ideas that somebody has."[94] Administration witnesses in hearings insisted that the bill represented a rational, coordinated plan to wipe out poverty even though the planning process had been disorganized and hurried.

The bill proposed to "eliminate the paradox of poverty . . . by opening to everyone the opportunity for education and training, the opportunity to work, and the opportunity to live in decency and dignity."[95] Although the bill retained an educational emphasis, aid for schools no longer spearheaded the attack on poverty. The shift to training was clear. Title I allocated $412 million for the Neighborhood Youth Corps, work training programs, and one of the new bill's major of-ferings, the Job Corps. These programs aimed at salvaging young people already out of school. The Job Corps, which set up boarding schools to offer basic education and training, would presumably have an immediate impact. There was some thought that the Job Corps would be a rival to the public schools, but nothing much came of this. Job Corps centers later focused on character-building and -training, not on developing an approach to education that might succeed with the poor.[96] In Title II community action programs were eligible for a total of $345 million to coordinate community efforts, including education, in the fight against poverty. Education of all kinds would not receive as much money under Title II as it would have in the $200 million grants proposal.

Shriver's task force presented a bill that did not specifically try to encourage the school system to reach out to poor children, nor did it establish viable educational alternatives to public schools. Critics of the bill pointed out these weaknesses during hearings and highlighted the fact that the Shriver task force had thought no more about major educational questions than had the Heller task force.

Hearings opened in the House on 17 March and in the Senate on 7 June. In both hearings committee members wondered why the bill did so little with formal education. Perkins, chairman of the House subcommittee, stated that a massive attack on education on the elementary and secondary level was necessary.[97] In the Senate, Representative Freylinghuysen pointed out, "It is my very strong feeling that if we have this kind of defect in our educational system, if the children of the slums, if this is what we are aiming at, are not receiving the quality of education that they should and the Federal Government must therefore take them out of their environment and put them somewhere else to learn to read and write, then what we should be worrying about is the adequacy of the schools they have been at."[98]

In the House, Attorney General Robert Kennedy agreed that the school system needed reform. Poor children had inferior schooling. "The local community . . . must face up to the problems," he said.[99] The federal government should spur local communities, indeed, require "them to do that in order to get help and assistance of the Federal Government; otherwise in my judgment the money is wasted."[100] Kennedy came closest to presenting a coherent picture of school reform through the Economic Opportunity Act. In the Senate, however, Shriver claimed, "This office is not being created or proposed . . . to give advice about what ought to be done about public education. After all, that is the Commissioner of

Education's responsibility at the Federal level."[101] The difference of opinion between the two men betrayed how little thought had gone into the whole problem of how education, formal or informal, related to the goals of the poverty program.

Yarmolinsky later recalled that the task force spent only a week talking about general questions. After that attention centered on practical matters, as it had in the Heller task force.[102] So it was, perhaps, no surprise that Kennedy and Shriver disagreed in hearings on matters that were never discussed.

Yet, the fact that the task force did not explore intellectual issues does not excuse its failure to ask the one vital question. Did education have much to do with eliminating poverty?

No one asked such a question during the hearings. There is no suggestion that anyone ever asked the question in the process of working out the attack on poverty. Policy-makers assumed that formal education provided an exit from poverty because they were sure education led to a job. They were imbued with a sense of confidence about the entire anti-poverty effort. As Shriver emphasized in House hearings, "This country, with its enormous productivity, the mobility of its people, and the speed of its communications, has both the resources and the know-how to eliminate grinding poverty. Furthermore, we now have a greater understanding of the complex causes of poverty, what makes people poor and what keeps them that way, too often from generation to generation."[103] Heller echoed Shriver's faith: "All that is required is the will to do the job and the specific ways to strike at the stubborn roots of poverty."[104]

Policy-makers and Congressmen just never looked at the evidence of what schools did. Studies were scattered, but they suggested that schools confirmed children in their socioeconomic class and that outside factors were far more important to achievement than schools were. Compensatory education projects had inconclusive results with poor children. Various studies showed that the relation of formal education to economic growth and jobs was far from the simple one that Heller believed.[105] Education and socioeconomic status had some relationship but not enough to support a major offensive in the War on Poverty. Real experiments, too, indicated that it was not easy to reform the outlook and practices of the school establishment. The Ford Foundation's Grey Area Program had tried to stimulate changes within the school system with its funds. The foundation negotiated with city school systems about the kinds of programs to initiate in the public schools. But little thought went into the mechanics of change. When city superintendents were lukewarm about reform and school personnel misunderstood or resisted different approaches, the Ford Foundation did not know what to do.[106] New York's Mobilization for Youth tried pressure tactics on the school system. The school system resisted.[107] In Boston the school department was eager to absorb money for programs, but they were "hardly bold and experimental." Most were "simply extensions of schemes already in operation in the system."[108]

It is hard to escape the conclusion that Daniel Moynihan reached. Moynihan felt that the government just did not know what it was doing when it worked out significant parts of the poverty program.[109]

To blame the task force for its failure to establish a firm foundation for social policy does not mean that social policy can only proceed on the basis of proven theory. But planners should look at available evidence before proceeding with programs that proclaim ambitious social goals and that arouse expectations. And they should plan their measures so that they yield useful information to guide future social programs.

The task forces did consider some alternative courses of action. Shriver's task force replaced formal education with job training and rejected a job-creation program that could cost as much as $4 billion yearly.[110] Michael Harrington and writer Paul Jacobs reminded Shriver's group that there must be far-reaching changes in the social structure to alleviate poverty, but no one heeded their advice.[111] Other possible approaches to the poverty problem were never considered. Promising alternatives included measures like housing programs for the poor, the elimination of educational requirements for jobs, subsidy programs such as a family allowance system, or a negative income tax plan. Many of these plans would be expensive. The negative income tax proposal, one expert estimated, could cost between $2 and $5 billion a year.[112] When Yarmolinsky looked back on these planning days, he remembered, "The rejection of an income strategy was assumed to be politically unavoidable."[113]

Many options were excluded for budgetary reasons. The total poverty budget was only $962.5 million. Of this amount $462 million came from transferring budget requests from other areas to the Economic Opportunity Act. The War on Poverty was not to be an expensive handout but a handup.

The press of events also explained why the two task forces never seriously entertained alternatives. The time was right for an attack on poverty, and Johnson urged the task forces on to rapid solutions. Shriver explained in House hearings, "I cannot really justify or explain, perhaps in detail why it turned out to be timely now to do it. There is simply the fact that people are interested in doing it now. . . . Fifteen or twenty years from now they might not continue to be. But now they are."[114] One Shriver task force member emphasized, "We haven't got time to study; we have to act."[115]

Kennedy and Johnson had both been dissatisfied with traditional methods of formulating policy through the traditional bureaucracy. They were groping for a more innovative, intelligent method of planning in their use of executive task forces. But the experience with the two poverty groups suggested that it was not easy to develop consistent policy within the task force framework. The task forces did not have a clear idea of their function or an established power base. Task force members relied on the departments for suggestions. Although task forces can be a conduit for new ideas, in this case they did not feel free to develop their own plans, and adopted ones that were offered to them. Moreover, the task forces were unable to resist the pressure that powerful departments could exert.

Task force planning had, however, produced a poverty bill and expectations. The War against Poverty could be won through attacking several fronts at once. Although formal education did not have a central role in the Economic Opportunity Act, it presumably represented one of the most hopeful ways of overcoming the problem. As Johnson himself maintained, "When we consider these problems, when we study them, when we evaluate what can be done, the answer almost always comes down to one word: education."[116]

The poverty bill left unfinished education business. California's Governor Pat Brown pointed out in poverty hearings in the House, "The bill before you makes no separate provisions for the sort of massive assault on illiteracy which I am convinced must be made before the poverty program can succeed. I support this program as a beginning of the end. I am confident that the administration enters the battle in the same spirit."[117] The next attempt to organize an educational attack on poverty would revert to the familiar methods of legislative planning within the departments, and would provide another opportunity to consider substantive intellectual issues and an opportunity to decide whether the educational solution of 1963-64 would be revived or rejected.

1. Draft of "Message on Education to Accompany 1964 Legislative Program," 16 January 1964, General Counsel Files, HEW.

2. Harold Seidman, *Politics, Position, and Power*, p. 77.

3. Arthur M. Schlesinger, Jr., *A Thousand Days*, p. 681.

4. Ibid., p. 77. See James L. Sundquist, ed., *On Fighting Poverty*, p. 7, for a discussion of Kennedy's dissatisfaction with piecemeal programs. See also William D. Carey, "Presidential Staffing in the Sixties and Seventies," p. 45.

5. See Walter Williams, *Social Policy Research and Analysis*.

6. Margaret S. Gordon, "U.S. Manpower and Employment Policy," p. 1314. Walter W. Heller, *New Dimensions of Political Economy*, p. 20.

7. Heller, *New Dimensions*, p. 20.

8. U.S. Bureau of Labor Statistics, *Employment and Earnings*, p. ix.

9. Samuel H. Beer and Richard E. Barringer, eds., *The State and the Poor*, p. 316.

10. Stephen M. Rose, *The Betrayal of the Poor*, p. 84.

11. John C. Donovan, *The Politics of Poverty*, p. 23.

12. Schlesinger, *A Thousand Days*, p. 968.

13. Donovan, *Politics*, p. 22; Lyndon Baines Johnson, *The Vantage Point*, p. 73.

14. Quoted in Sar A. Levitan, *The Great Society's Poor Law*, p. 18.

15. Alice M. Rivlin, *Systematic Thinking for Social Action*, pp. 10–11; Rivlin points out how primitive the data at the disposal of government planners in 1963 were. Rose, *Betrayal of the Poor*, p. 76. See also Richard Blumenthal, "The

Bureaucracy: Antipoverty and the CAP," in Allan P. Sindler, ed., *American Political Institutions and Public Policy*, pp. 143–44.

16. Memorandum from Michael S. March to the director, "Progress Report on the 'Selective Service' and 'Opportunity' Projects," 29 October 1963, General Counsel Files, HEW.

17. Walter W. Heller, "Comment of a Policymaker," p. 41.

18. Edward S. Flash, Jr., *Economic Advice and Presidental Leadership*, p. 190; Walter W. Heller, "The Economic Outlook of Education," p. 48.

19. Heller, "Economic Outlook," p. 50.

20. Heller, *New Dimensions*, p. 110.

21. Quoted in Beryl A. Radin and Richardson White, Jr., "Youth and Opportunity," pp. 167–68.

22. Quoted in ibid., p. 44.

23. Ibid., pp. 47–52.

24. Ibid., p. 49.

25. Richard A. Cloward and Lloyd E. Ohlin, *Delinquency and Opportunity*, pp. 98, 103–4, 120.

26. Quoted in Radin and White, "Youth and Opportunity," p. 36.

27. Quoted in Sundquist, *On Fighting Poverty*, p. 11.

28. Ibid., p. 56.

29. Richard Blumenthal, "Community Action," p. 7.

30. Quoted in Radin and White, "Youth and Opportunity," p. 259.

31. Ibid., p. 200.

32. Ibid., p. 69.

33. Sundquist, *On Fighting Poverty*, p. 36.

34. Quoted in Daniel P. Moynihan, *Maximum Feasible Misunderstanding*, p. 41.

35. Rose, *Betrayal of the Poor*, p. 90.

36. Peter Marris and Martin Rein, *Dilemmas of Social Reform*, p. 2; Blumenthal, "The Bureaucracy," p. 135.

37. Heller, *New Dimensions*, p. 20.

38. William M. Capron and Burton A. Weisbrod, "Preliminary Draft," 2 December 1963, Bureau of the Budget files. This draft discusses the sources of poverty: "Cultural deprivation lies at the root of much poverty. Children brought up in broken families, children accustomed to living on relief, children reared in family and community environments in which the importance of education is deprecated and hope for escaping poverty is smothered—such children are prime candidates for adulthoods in poverty, as the vicious cycle continues."

39. Blumenthal, "Community Action," p. 30.

40. Radin and White note that this was true of planning within the President's Committee. See Blumenthal, "The Bureaucracy," p. 146.

41. Heller, *New Dimensions*, p. 20.

42. See memorandum from Walter W. Heller to the secretaries of Agriculture; Commerce; Labor; Health, Education, and Welfare; the director of the Bureau of the Budget; the administrator of the Housing and Home Finance Agency: "1964 Legislative Programs for 'Widening Participation in Prosperity'—An Attack on Poverty," 5 November 1963, Bureau of the Budget files.

43. John C. Donovan, *The Policy Makers*, pp. 86–87; Eugene Keller, "Social Priorities, Economic Policy, and the State," pp. 615–16.

44. See memorandum from William Capron and Michael March, "Comments on the HEW and Labor Department proposals for the human conservation or antipoverty program," 21 November 1963, Bureau of the Budget files.

45. See Sundquist, *On Fighting Poverty*, pp. 36–37. Blumenthal does show, however, that there were those believing in more radical methods of change in Hackett's group of "guerrillas" but that the deficiencies in approach were not clearly recognized ("The Bureaucracy," pp. 137–41).

46. Levitan, *The Great Society's Poor Law*, p. 17; "Major Issues Involved in HEW Legislative Program for 1964," 8 December 1963, General Counsel Files, HEW.

47. Memorandum from Francis Keppel to Wilbur J. Cohen, "Office of Education Legislative Program for Calendar Year 1964," 13 November 1964, General Counsel files, HEW.

48. See Stan Dropkin, Harold Full, and Ernest Schwarcz, eds., *Contemporary American Education*, pp. 292–98, 305.

49. Memorandum from Wilbur J. Cohen to Walter Heller, "1964 Legislative Programs for 'Widening Participation in Prosperity—An Attack on Poverty,' " 19 November 1963, Bureau of the Budget files.

50. Ibid.

51. Ibid.

52. Michael S. March and William Capron, "Comments on the HEW and Labor Department Proposals for the Human Conservation or Anti-Poverty Program," 21 November 1963, Bureau of the Budget files.

53. Ibid.

54. Radin and White, "Youth and Opportunity," pp. 259–62.

55. Ibid., pp. 262–63; Blumenthal, "The Bureaucracy," pp. 146–49.

56. Quoted in Johnson, *The Vantage Point*, p. 74.

57. Sundquist, *On Fighting Poverty*, pp. 21–24.

58. See "Agenda for meeting December 18: HEW, BOB and CEA," Bureau of Budget files.

59. Memorandum from Wilbur J. Cohen to Theodore Sorensen, "Legislative Program to Attack Poverty," 26 December 1963, Bureau of the Budget files.

60. Memorandum from Hirst Sutton to Kermit Gordon, "Unresolved issues concerning education project grants," 8 January 1964, Bureau of the Budget files.

61. Ibid.

62. Memorandum with attachment to Lee White, "HEW proposal for special education projects to improve and strengthen elementary and secondary education," 14 January 1964, Bureau of the Budget files.

63. Memorandum to White, "HEW proposal," 14 January 1964.

64. Ibid.

65. See Blumenthal, "Community Action," p. 15, for a discussion of how task force participants avoided clarifying the idea of class conflict when they developed the community action proposal.

66. Memorandum to White, "HEW proposal," 14 January 1964.

67. Memorandum from Sutton to Gordon, "Unresolved issues," 8 January 1964.

68. Wilbur Cohen to Phillip S. Hughes, 27 January 1964, General Counsel Files, HEW.

69. Draft bill, 30 January 1964, Sec. 201, Bureau of the Budget files.

70. Ibid., Sec. 201.(b)(4).

71. See memorandum to White, "HEW proposal," 14 January 1964.

72. Draft bill, 30 January 1964, Sec. 209.(a).

73. See Radin and White, "Youth and Opportunity," p. 265. These authors see

a mid-January shift in task force planning due to presidential pressure and see Hackett's disapproval as a result of the shift. This author feels the task force never implemented Hackett's ideas wholeheartedly, in any case. See Sundquist, *On Fighting Poverty*, p. 24.

74. Sundquist, *On Fighting Poverty*, p. 24.

75. Robert A. Levine, *The Poor Ye Need Not Have With You*, p. 50.

76. *New York Times*, 9 November 1963.

77. Ibid., 20 December 1963.

78. Weeks, *Job Corps*, p. 64.

79. John Bibby and Roger Davidson, *On Capitol Hill*, pp. 230–31.

80. Sundquist, *On Fighting Poverty*, p. 36.

81. Memorandum from Charles Schultze to Kermit Gordon, "Some notes on unfinished business," 8 February 1964, Bureau of the Budget files.

82. Ibid.

83. Sundquist, *On Fighting Poverty*, p. 91.

84. Adam Yarmolinsky, personal interview with the author, 21 June 1971.

85. Sundquist, *On Fighting Poverty*, p. 36.

86. Memorandum from William Cannon to Walter Heller and Kermit Gordon, "Shriver Poverty Program," 13 February 1964, Bureau of the Budget files.

87. Adam Yarmolinsky, "The Origin of 'Maximum Feasible Participation,'" p. 19.

88. Yarmolinsky interview.

89. Samuel Halperin, personal interview with the author, 3 March 1971.

90. Memorandum from Cannon to Heller and Gordon, "Shriver Poverty Program."

91. Levitan, *The Great Society's Poor Law*, p. 34.

92. Sundquist, *On Fighting Poverty*, p. 40.

93. Levitan, *The Great Society's Poor Law*, p. 35.

94. *Hearings before the Select Subcommittee on Poverty on The Economic Opportunity Act of 1964*, 88th Cong., 2d Sess., 1964, Senate, p. 74.

95. House Resolution 10440, sec. 2.

96. Christopher Weeks, *Job Corps*, pp. 96–102; Fred R. Harris, ed., *Social Science and National Policy*, p. 87.

97. *Hearings before the Subcommittee on the War on Poverty Program*, 88th Cong., 2d Sess., 1964, House, p. 452.

98. *Senate Poverty Hearings*, 1964, p. 180.

99. *House Poverty Hearings*, 1964, p. 312.

100. Ibid., p. 312.

101. *Senate Poverty Hearings*, 1964, p. 109.

102. Yarmolinsky interview.

103. *House Poverty Hearings*, 1964, p. 20.

104. Ibid., p. 26.

105. See Ivar Berg, *Education and Jobs*, for a discussion of the relation of formal education to jobs and economic growth and for a full citation of evidence.

106. Marris and Rein, *Dilemmas*, pp. 462–63.

107. Ibid., pp. 67–69.

108. Stephan Thernstrom, *Poverty, Planning, and Politics in the New Boston*, pp. 137–39.

109.   Moynihan, *Maximum Feasible Misunderstanding*, p. 170.

110.   Levine, *The Poor Ye Need Not Have*, p. 219.

111.   Sundquist, *On Fighting Poverty*, p. 38.

112.   Levine, *The Poor Ye Need Not Have*, pp. 207–8.

113.   Sundquist, *On Fighting Poverty*, p. 36.

114.   *House Poverty Hearings*, 1964, p. 100.

115.   Quoted in Robinson O. Everett, ed., *Anti-Poverty Programs*, p. 55 n. 33.

116.   *Public Papers of the Presidents of the United States: Lyndon B. Johnson, 1963–1964*, 2:916.

117.   *House Poverty Hearings*, 1964, p. 1387.

The Passage of the Bill

During the hearings on the Economic Opportunity Act in the spring and early summer of 1964, administration spokesmen sold the proposals to Congress and the public as a major attack on the roots of poverty. Yet privately, men like Francis Keppel, commissioner of education, and Anthony Celebrezze, secretary of HEW, realized that the Economic Opportunity Act was not a vigorous attack on either the educational deficiencies due to poverty or the weaknesses of the public school system. HEW was already working on a school aid bill during the hearings; but since Keppel felt the bill had a poor chance of passing the eighty-eighth Congress, he intended to wait until the eighty-ninth Congress, meeting in 1965, before presenting new legislation for consideration.[1] By July 1964, however, Keppel was ready to admit openly that the poverty bill was limited and that a more massive educational attack on poverty would be necessary.[2]

The main contribution of the poverty hearings to the eventual passage of an aid to education bill was the argument witnesses developed that inadequate education and poverty were linked. As Secretary Celebrezze recalled, "We found, no matter in which direction we went, we always ended up with the problems of education. We had to educate . . . [the poor], we had to retain them . . . [yet] we weren't doing a thing for primary and secondary education."[3] If an education bill borrowed the politically persuasive rationale from the Economic Opportunity Act, it might successfully ensure the passage of federal aid to education. Although the supporters of federal aid had long pointed to the shortage of teachers and classrooms, to the inability of local areas to pay for education, the major issues of race, religion, federal control, and distribution of funds interacted to defeat one bill after another.[4] The Kennedy administration's recent failures to pass federal aid dramatized the necessity of developing an entirely new context for legislation. But though the proposals that the administration had sent to Congress in 1961 and 1963 and that HEW had given to Heller's Task Force in 1963 suggested HEW's early interest in improving education for the disadvantaged, they also indicated how reluctant HEW planners were to give up the principle of general aid.

Education had been "the one domestic subject that mattered most to John Kennedy," although his freedom to propose legislation was, of necessity, limited by his religion.[5] As a presidential candidate who was determined to show that his Catholicism would not shape his presidential actions, Kennedy had supported federal aid for both public school construction and teachers' salaries but argued that aid to parochial schools was unconstitutional. The Educational Task Force appointed by the president-elect supported this stand in its report released in January 1961 and advocated general aid for public schools only.[6] The lines of a dramatic battle over aid to education were forming. Since the task force report had rejected general aid for Catholic schools, Cardinal Spellman of New York announced the report "unthinkable." Kennedy grimly rejoined, "He never said a word about any of Eisenhower's bills for public schools only, and he didn't go that far in 1949 either."[7]

The specific proposals for the education bill in 1961 and legislation in 1963 were developed by Ted Sorensen, "the mainstay of the development of most of . . . the [educational] ideas" during Kennedy's administration, and assistant secretary of HEW, Wilbur Cohen.[8] The first title of the bill sent to Congress in early 1961 proposed to funnel $2.3 billion to the states over a three-year period to be used for public school construction and salary aid, with the added stipulation that 10 percent of the grant should be used to develop programs addressing the needs of urban and other economically distressed areas. Parochial schools were to receive nothing. Title I's political appeal was enhanced, however, by being joined to the popular impact program that had distributed education funds for construction and operating expenses to school districts with federal bases since 1950. Because so many federal bases were located in the South and because so many House members came from areas that received impact funds, the administration hoped to win over supporters to the more controversial general aid title by the extension of impact aid.[9] In an attempt to head off religious opposition, Kennedy's message on education pointed to the "clear prohibition of the constitution" to general aid for private schools.[10]

Before hearings even began, however, it was clear that the administration bill would have troubles in Congress, and not merely religious ones. Archbishop Atter, chairman of the administrative board of the National Catholic Welfare Conference, the major Catholic interest group, warned the administration on 1 March that the Catholic hierarchy would oppose the administration bill unless it incorporated a loan program for private schools.[11] Another veiled warning came from Adam Clayton Powell, chairman of the House Education and Labor Committee, who kept open his option of adding an amendment denying federal aid for segregated schools to any education bill. Despite premonitions of trouble, however, the religiously uncompromising bill passed the Senate in May by a vote of 49 to 34. Several amendments on the "issues" were rejected during debate. One had proposed loans for private schools, another attempted to withhold funds for segregated schools, and still another moved to ensure federal funds for segregated schools.[12] All were defeated.

The House had always been the graveyard for federal aid to education. The 1961 package survived hearings and went to the Rules Committee on 20 June. There James Dulaney, Democrat from New York, held the vote that would determine whether the committee would report the bill to the House floor or not. Dulaney, a Catholic favoring some kind of aid for parochial schools, hoped that financial help might be forthcoming in the form of a loan program. Two months earlier, Kennedy had finally acted upon the hierarchy's hint that long-term low-cost loans for Catholic schools would compensate for the "failure" to win general aid. An HEW brief had informed the president that although grants to parochial schools were unconstitutional, low-interest loans probably were not.[13] In his April message to Congress, the president had, therefore, proposed an extension of the NDEA of 1958, which made loans (in certain categories) available to nonpublic schools. This extension would indicate that the Constitution did not deny parochial schools all aid but only general aid. Congress had responded to the presidential message with its possibility of compromise and was considering an extension of the NDEA. Dulaney, however, was fearful of voting to send the administration bill alone to the House, suspecting that this would result in eventual defeat for the NDEA proposal. When it became apparent that there was little possibility of joining the two approaches or voting on the NDEA first, Dulaney joined the Republicans and southern Democrats on the Rules Committee and voted to table the bill on 18 July.[14]

Although the administrations's bill seemed dead, Kennedy did not want to admit defeat. Secretary of HEW Abraham Ribicoff suggested possible compromises that would enable the administration to claim some significant achievement in education and "would defer the controversial issues until a later date."[15] Adam Clayton Powell led the effort to salvage a compromise bill excluding teachers' salaries by bringing it to the House floor on "Calendar Wednesday." By a vote of 242 to 170, however, the House refused even to consider the compromise. The educational effort of 1961 had been a debacle, although the ever popular impacted areas program sailed through the House a week later.[16]

In describing the education failure, newspapers and editorials suggested that the religious issue had killed the bill. But, as Kennedy himself was aware, the administration's inability to pass federal aid was more complex than the papers reported. The religious question was a dramatic one, but, in fact, roll calls revealed that most Catholic members of the House had voted in favor of considering the compromise bill; in the Rules Committee two of the three Catholics had supported the administration. Republicans opposed to federal aid and southern Democrats fearful of upsetting race relations had joined forces to make general aid impossible. In the House, for example, the southern Democrats and Republicans had ruined the chances of a compromise bill. Seven of the eight negative votes in the Rules Committee were cast by Republicans and Dixiecrats. "That's who really killed the bill," the president argued, "just as they've killed it for fifty years, not the Catholics."[17]

The complex interaction of issues and political forces had defeated federal aid to education, but the administration itself bore some responsibility for the failure in 1961. During that crucial year relations between the congressional committees and HEW were so far from cordial that an involved party recalled "bad feeling between the Committee and the Department." The new commissioner of education, Dr. Sterling McMurrin, gave ineffective support to proposals that he had not helped develop, and Secretary Ribicoff was unsuccessful in dealing with education lobbies. Although the secretary did not neglect them, "he generally offended them. They felt that he told them he could handle the legislation and didn't need their help."[18] Perhaps even more serious, the administration had called upon neither liberal Republican congressmen nor Catholic educators to aid in planning its legislative program. Nor had it responded to the possibility of compromise through the NDEA loan package with much enthusiasm. McMurrin had refused to take any official stand on the action, and Secretary Ribicoff and the president were both evasive.

When it became clear how thorny the path of federal aid was, the president was unwilling to jeopardize his entire legislative program and perhaps his political future by a last-ditch fight for federal aid.[19]

Within the administration legislative failure set in motion an attempt "to reassess the situation." As Secretary Ribicoff admitted in an October memorandum to the president, "The passage of any broad-scale education legislation will be a most difficult task. . . . I am convinced that there is not a full committment to education in this Nation." Ribicoff thought that grants for construction or teacher salaries were out of the question and advised postponing any new legislative attempt until 1963, when "specific programs designed to provide assistance to specific phases of education in this country" could be presented.[20] Although Kennedy did ask for aid for elementary and secondary education in his 1962 message to Congress, essentially he agreed with Ribicoff's memorandum.[21]

Within the administration, however, efforts in 1962 were focused on finding a fresh approach for federal aid. The Bureau of the Budget circulated a paper in October 1962 that elaborated on the theme of education and economic growth, an approach, however, that the authors Rashi Fein and Michael March acknowledged did "not mean that other reasons for supporting Federal aid to education are no longer valid."[22] The paper stimulated a lively internal debate. Peter P. Muirhead, assistant commissioner for progress and legislative planning, thought the paper had identified an "underutilized appeal" but was sure that "the resolution of the deep-seated problems surrounding Federal aid to education will require a great deal more in the way of political effort and political leadership than merely new approaches or more appealing 'packages.' " Wilbur Cohen agreed that the new rationale was more of "an academic exercise than . . . any particularly new or valuable contribution to the solution of our legislative dilemma." He found the report's emphasis on special aid for slum areas to be politically hazardous. As Cohen was aware, the report reiterated the conclusions of Kennedy's 1961 Task Force on Education, which had proposed special educational efforts aimed at urban slum schools. This suggestion had been reflected in the 1961 bill, which had set aside money for problems of urban education. But although Cohen had been instrumental in developing the 1961 legislation, he felt that the Bureau of the Budget report had not pursued "this approach in apparent awareness of the pitfalls which have befallen our efforts for greater equalization." Large grants for urban education, he argued, would have "rough going in Congress" unless rural areas in the South received comparable amounts.[24] A few weeks later Cohen had decided that the themes of economic growth and social welfare would make an education package "if anything, less appealing," and suggested that an emphasis on national security and big power competition for world markets would be more appropriate.[25]

Others, however, favored combining a social welfare emphasis with an emphasis on economic growth as the basis for a new federal program in education. Such an approach would mean that the education bill could be presented as a means of aiding "people . . . rather than . . . institutions . . . thus hopefully minimizing the public-private issue." Why then should not the same support be given to human resources as was given to physical ones? "Why shouldn't slum children be entitled to education to the same degree as children of middle- and upper-class families?" But though there was disagreement over the merits of the proposed approach, there was substantial support for the report's suggestions of developing an omnibus education bill. Separate bills, as members of the administration knew only too well, succeeded in "dredging up in passionate form the issues of public school versus private and segregation versus desegration."[26]

The National Education Improvement Act that Kennedy sent to Congress in 1963 indicated that the debate on a new context for federal aid had never been entirely resolved. The message that accompanied the bill, which sought aid for all levels of education, utilized a number of arguments in support of federal aid. Better education, Kennedy told Congress, was "essential to give new meaning to our national purpose and power." Yet if Kennedy stressed an old theme and one that Cohen had found most appropriate, he also stressed the fundamental importance of education to economic growth. "Recent research," the president stated, "has shown that one of the most beneficial of all . . . investments is education." The social welfare theme was there in the references to ignorance, illiteracy, and unskilled workers, the "waste of human resources," that existed in the United States.[27] In the specific proposal for elementary and secondary education, however, the debate was reflected little if at all. Asking for a four-year program of $1.5 billion, Kennedy pointed once more to the needs for public school construction and better teacher salaries. Although the bill did propose "initiating pilot, experimental or demonstration projects to meet special educational problems, particularly in slums and depressed rural and urban areas," this emphasis was still secondary to the argument in favor of general construction and teacher salary aid.[28] This title, upon which Congress never acted, would be revived as the vehicle by which HEW hoped to control the poverty program later that year.

A new and effective context for elementary and secondary education aid, then, still eluded administration planners, who continued to think in terms of general aid for teachers' salaries and construction aid. But it was becoming increasingly clear that the old approach could not win the approval of Congress. In some respects, however, 1963 offered some hope for the passage of future education legislation. A breakthrough of sorts, occurred when the National Education Association (NEA) decided not to oppose federal construction aid to private colleges, which the omnibus bill proposed.[29] Although aid to higher education had never created the same kind of religious frenzy that aid to public secondary education had, the new stance of the NEA was hopeful. Then, too, the Office of Education had had, since December 1962, a new and vigorous commissioner, Francis Keppel. Kennedy had appointed Keppel knowing well that Keppel believed that "no frontal attack should be made on any of the major educational groups but rather emphasis should be placed on developing a consensus on the role of the Federal Government in education."[30] By 1963 Keppel was hard at work trying to "neutralize the inside fighting in the educational world" and had opened direct communications with Catholic interest groups. As Keppel recalled later, "They wanted me to have—*they* being Sorensen, and I'm perfectly sure he was reflecting the president—wanted me to have a direct communication line to the Catholic Church, which the Office of Education had never had before."[31] By mid-1964 prospects looked even more hopeful with the passage of the Civil Rights Act, which, in Title VI, forbade racial discrimination in any program receiving federal funds. The explosive question of whether segregated schools in the South would get federal aid seemed answered at last.

Yet, if the prospects for federal aid to education appeared better by 1964 than they had in the previous three years, they were far from sure. Even though the experiences with legislation in the early 1960s had made administration planners sensitive to the subtleties of the issues, there was no certainty that the arguments developed in poverty hearings that poverty and inadequate education were inextricably linked would be convincing enough to neutralize the old issues of religion, federal control, and money and to calm the passions that school bills seemed to create. Nor was it certain that HEW would give up its favored general aid approach, which it had presented in 1961 and in 1963 to Congress and in 1963 to the Heller Task Force.

Indeed, the summer and fall of 1964 saw the search for legislation that could avoid political defeat continue in HEW and the Office of Education. Even though the poverty hearings suggested a new rationale, planners hesitated. They were still attracted to the department's traditional type of school bill offering public schools general aid for construction and teacher salaries, despite its disastrous history. In his 5 June 1964 memorandum to Cohen, Philip des Marais, deputy assistant secretary of HEW, considered this familiar alternative. He thought perhaps a large electoral victory for Johnson might make a general aid bill feasible even though this type of legislation had so often failed in the past.[32] Des Marais realized, however, that the form of the bill would have to have the kind of content that could attract public attention. On 11 June 1964 Peter Muirhead, assistant commissioner of education, sent Keppel a memorandum that weighed a bill offering general aid against a bill focusing aid on poor children. Muirhead was undecided which alternative to choose.[33]

The poverty approach, of course, had definite possibilities and was natural in the context of Great Society legislation. HEW had had some interest in the approach since 1961. The Heller task force had already developed an education title for its poverty bill in December 1963 and January 1964. But administration planners were not alone in exploring the poverty theme. On 20 February 1964 Senator Wayne Morse, chairman of the Senate Subcommittee on Education and Labor and a key figure in the fate of education bills, introduced a bill in the Senate to provide local educational agencies with assistance for the education of children from needy families and in areas of high unemployment. Morse argued that the presence of poverty affected the ability of local areas to support education adequately just as did the presence of federal installations. He thus offered his bill as an amendment to the popular impacted areas bill (PL 815-874). Although Morse did not think his bill had much chance of passing the eighty-eighth Congress, he planned to hold hearings on it and publicize its rationale. Initially, HEW gave Morse little sympathy or aid. Asked by Morse to give an opinion on the proposal, Secretary Celebrezze brusquely rejected the senator's approach on 2 March 1964. Although he acknowledged the relationship between poverty and inadequate education, Celebrezze insisted that the efforts under the Economic Opportunity Act along with the passage of a general aid bill would be sufficient to deal with poverty problems.[34]

By June 1964, however, HEW had realized that Morse's bill offered real political possibilities even though the department was not yet convinced the bill represented the most effective political approach and was hesitant to adopt it. Morse held his hearings on 29 and 30 July 1964. Appearing before Morse, Commissioner of Education Keppel now acknowledged that the educational possibilities under the Economic Opportunity Act were limited.[35] Yet, although HEW was privately considering the idea, Keppel insisted that Morse's proposal needed much more study. He did not object to the poverty rationale, but pointed out that there were troublesome administrative questions and few reliable guides to the bill's cost. Moreover, Keppel did not like the way the bill distributed funds.[36] Clearly, these kinds of considerations would have an effect on any bill's political chances. Promising that HEW would weigh Morse's proposals carefully, Keppel indicated, however, that the administration could not support the bill at that time and admitted that he still had lingering thoughts of revising the educational grants proposal.[37] Morse was annoyed by the administration's cold shoulder, and told the commissioner, "I am aghast to understand an administration that is given an opportunity to come forward to support a bill but which says to the subcommittee this morning through you, we are going to stall."[38]

Keppel explained later what effect the hearings had on HEW. "The central point that he (Morse) made was, if we wanted this bill to pass, it would be wise to hitch it up to a piece of legislation that has plenty of Congressional support (namely, the Impacted Areas Bill) and to the problems of the poor." His advice was excellent, and not unlike Kennedy's strategy in 1961. What was new was the emphasis on poverty.[39]

By 17 September 1964 a bill giving the disadvantaged educational priority was finally beginning to shape up.[40] Although the bill was far from final form, during this month a group in the Office of Education, guided by thinking of Wilbur Cohen and Charles Lee of Senator Morse's staff, began the essential task of working out the formula for distributing funds.[41] As Cohen knew, the allocation formula was "the crux of the political, financial, and methodological problem[s]" in any legislation.[42] The formula of Morse's bill was unwieldy and complicated, and the group rejected it. But other methods of allocating money raised the specter of congressional division and failure. One favored method of computing school aid was based on the number of children in school. But if only public school children were counted, Catholics objected; if all children in school were counted,

public school interest groups objected. Cohen had long strug-
gled with this problem, but "either in policy or in mathematics
or in allotment or in financing—there was seemingly no perfect
solution."[43] And yet, some solution had to be found to avoid
another religious conflict, as Cohen knew and as LBJ had
made clear when he told them, "By the way, Wilbur, be
sure that whatever you do you don't come out with something
that's going to get me right in the middle of this religious
controversy. I don't want to have the Baptists attacking me
from one hand and the Catholics from another."[44]

Cohen was also sensitive to the necessity of finding a formula that gave a good rural-urban distribution of money; the
seeming blindness of the 1962 Bureau of the Budget paper
"Education and Economic Growth" to this problem had led
him to reject its suggested emphasis on slum schools as being
politically impossible. Money would have to go to the urban
and rural areas where poverty existed and where, more important, there were the congressional votes necessary for the
passage of a school bill.

As the group grappled with these problems, Cohen found
inspiration in the work he had done on income and welfare
in the fifties at the University of Michigan, which had sensi-
tized him to the ways in which income levels indicated educational, poverty, and welfare problems. Here was the solution to the formula dilemma. " 'Look,' " said Cohen, " 'why
not substitute all of these controversial, complicated things
for two thousand, three thousand dollars, whatever figure you
want as the income determinant, and then you will be giving
money for disadvantage[d] children, and the disadvantaged
children want to go to public school or parochial school.' "
Income figures existed, moreover, "not only by state and by
counties, but by other political subdivisions in the tapes of
the Census Bureau."[45] With this breakthrough, work on the
formula was finished by 13 November. The final formula
distributed funds to states based on the total number of children from families on welfare and from families with an annual income under $2,000 and on the state's average per pupil
expenditure. As Cohen had planned, ordinary census data
yielded most of this material.[46] Furthermore, and this was a

matter of vital strategic importance, the formula allowed immediate computations on the amounts each congressional district could expect to receive.[47] This would be a strong asset in persuading Congress to pass the bill. The money issue with its related religious complications seemed solved.

By the beginning of November 1964, the work of drafting an actual bill began.[48] During the month Keppel explained in detail why planners, following Wilbur Cohen's lead, had finally chosen the impacted areas approach. An emphasis on giving money to the needy child rather than the school offered a good chance of avoiding the whole religious question, which focused on whether federal aid should go to parochial schools. Avoiding a religious controversy was politically fundamental in Keppel's opinion as it was in Cohen's and the president's. Moreover, the poverty theme was politically popular, as the passage of the Economic Opportunity Act indicated. As Keppel pointed out, "It is not easy to oppose a combination of the existing impacted areas program and an added program for the poor."[49] Of course, since the bill did not offer general aid, none of the major interest groups would be entirely satisfied. Yet, as Keppel noted, the bill offered each group something that made opposition difficult. Similarly, four of the five titles of the bill contained funds for other groups than the poor and thus had a similar effect of disarming opposition. Finally, the formula emphasized the priority of urban and rural areas with their essential congressional votes. In Keppel's mind, clearly, the political issues had been the predominant ones in developing the bill and selecting the impact approach. But the concern with political strategy left little time for considering whether the content of the bill was educationally sound. Never did Keppel or other planners examine evidence suggesting that education did not provide an exit from poverty, that compensatory education was unproven, that local school boards were inflexible and disinterested in the problems of the poor. Ironically, the very skills that led to a bill that Congress could accept contributed to the development of a bill resting on fragile intellectual and practical foundations.

During the months of deciding how to formulate a school

aid bill, HEW had enjoyed the president's vigorous support. Upon coming to the presidency in 1963, Johnson had unequivocally committed himself to the passage of federal aid to education.[50] With the expansion of the National Defense Education Act and several education measures in progress during the winter and spring of 1964 and Keppel's reluctance to work with the Eighty-eighth Congress on elementary and secondary school aid, Johnson never presented a bill in 1964. But he continually renewed his pledge to do something about education. When his presidential campaign got under way in the late summer and early fall, he made the passage of an education bill into a major issue.[51] As Keppel said of Johnson, "Education was one of his real interests—genuine interests."[52] Education, Johnson felt, had made his own rise from poverty possible.[53] From a political viewpoint the president judged that Americans were interested in education and finally ready to support an education bill.[54]

In his speeches Johnson consistently tied the improvement of education to the goal of creating a Great Society.[55] His theme, repeated over and over, was that the nation must offer each child the best education he could take if the country were to realize its own possibilities.[56] It was now time for a revolution and breakthrough in education, Johnson affirmed.[57] "Unless we act," he warned, "our educational system is going to be deficient, and it will really crack under the pressure."[58] Acknowledging that there were stumbling blocks obstructing the passage of a federal aid bill, he insisted that they must be overcome.[59] Personally, Johnson saw no reason why a compromise over religious issues could not be worked out as it could over other issues.[60] This delicate task he left to Keppel with directions to avoid a church-state controversy.[61] Finally, Johnson emphasized the relationship between a school aid bill and the War on Poverty. In a succinct November policy paper, the president stated, "Our war on poverty can be won *only* if those who are poverty's prisoners can break the chains of ignorance."[62]

Johnson triumphed at the polls on 4 November 1964. His victory spurred on planners developing the school aid bill. As November passed, the impact approach received some criticism. On 20 November Kermit Gordon, director of the Bureau of the Budget, discussed the drawbacks of the impact formula. It spread funds too widely. "It is unlikely that such an approach would effectively provide sufficient funds in many districts to accomplish significant results," Gordon noted.[63] The Bureau of the Budget felt that the bill needed at least $5 to $10 billion, not the meager $1 billion planned.[64] In response to this criticism, HEW added provision for extra grants for some local educational agencies. Generally, however, the impacted areas approach was there to stay as was the $1 billion figure. No one had given the bill serious criticism during the months of planning. After Thanksgiving, Johnson gave his approval to the proposal and told HEW to begin drawing up the legislation in detail.

So finally HEW dropped general aid to education for a poverty-oriented school bill. But the selection and development of the legislative vehicle had not been the only political task to accomplish. As work went on in HEW on the bill, Keppel was negotiating with the major interest groups over how to resolve the religious issue. The National Education Association and the National Catholic Welfare Conference were the two most important groups. The NEA, with its insistence on excluding parochial schools from federal aid, and the National Catholic Welfare Conference, with its equal insistence that they be included, had interacted to kill many a federal aid measure; but Keppel now hoped to lead them into a coalition supporting the new bill.

Keppel's personal ties with the two groups were good, since he had consulted them in 1962 and 1963 over the passage of Kennedy's omnibus education bill.[65] By 1964 both were finally willing to compromise over elementary and secondary school aid. There was, Keppel observed, "a genuine desire on everyone's part to solve the educational problem of the children."[66] The defeat of Kennedy's school bills in 1961 and 1963 clearly suggested to the interest groups that no federal aid bill could pass without some religious compromise. The defeats of Kennedy's bills had also convinced the administration that it, too, must avoid too rigid a stand over aid to parochial schools.[67] Furthermore, a Protestant presi-

dent could afford to be more relaxed on the religious issue
than a Catholic president could be. Keppel hoped his new
approach would satisfy Catholics and Protestants alike. One
of Keppel's colleagues recalled the commissioner's reasoning.
" 'Suppose,' he [Keppel] said, 'that a Federal-aid program
could be put together in which the money would go to the
public schools but the services it purchased would be available to all pupils, no matter where they went to school,
whether in public institutions or nonpublic. The benefit would
be to the pupil, not to the school.' "[68] Keppel explored these
sensitive issues with the groups. But "the details of the legislation . . . were never discussed in an organized fashion at
these meetings," he remembered. "It was rather a matter
of sensing moods, of feeling out how far the several groups
would be willing to go."[69] Keppel's strategy was successful.
The interest groups felt, as one member of the NEA said,
that Keppel "got the emotion out of the issue," and the commissioner got an indication of what the groups would accept.[70]

LBJ's tremendous electoral victory gave the final push to
religious cooperation. Catholics now feared the revival of a
Kennedy-type bill that would give federal funds only to public
schools.[71] They also realized that direct aid to Catholic
schools could lead to a court battle that "would only delay
aid to education and heighten acrimony."[72] As for the NEA,
it sensed that HEW might ignore its advice during the crucial
stage of implementing the bill if it now opposed the administration's effort.[73] On 16 December 1964, therefore, the NEA
announced that it would accept aid for parochial students.[74]
As Keppel remarked, "In a nice way, the administration in
effect said, Do you dare oppose this one? In fact the parties
did not, and actually they gave generally favorable testimony
when asked their views by the Committees of Congress."[75]

The final bill represented, then, a favorable resolution of
the religious issue. By focusing on the needs of poor children, Title I established that local school districts must include parochial children in their special services and arrangements for deprived children. In the second title parochial
students were to have the use of library materials and books

that the title funded. In Title III supplementary educational services were to be available to parochial and public school students alike. As Keppel had planned, "By proposing a package of legislative programs, not including 'general aid' as usually defined," he had provided "a middle way through the church-state conflict which has stalemated aid to lower education in the past."[76]

At the same time that Keppel and other members of HEW were making substantive decisions about the form of the ESEA during the summer and fall months of 1964, Johnson's task force on education, headed by John Gardner and made up of thirteen members mostly from the academic and business world, had been working on a report of the nation's educational needs. Unlike the Heller task force, this group did not develop a bill. That delicate political task belonged to HEW. But the task force did have a role to play in aiding the passage of the bill.[77] Publicly, Johnson claimed that the function of all his task forces was to help identify major problems and suggest legislative programs.[78] In actuality, the education task force did not contribute any new insights into educational problems or much material for the bill.[79] Nor did it treat with the substantive issues like religion or funding, which occupied so much of HEW's attention.[80] Keppel admitted that the task force, "didn't have anything to say about the political combination that made up the ESEA —call it if you want to be a little more sardonic, the 'House of Cards.' "[81]

The task force apparently existed to give an attractive identity to Johnson's educational program. One of its members, David Reisman, agreed that the task force was a legitimizing device.[82] Comments made at an Austin press conference by Secretary of Labor Willard Wirtz and HEW Secretary Celebrezze on 14 November 1964 reinforce this interpretation. The two secretaries told newsmen that Johnson would structure most of his 1965 legislative program around the task force reports. They also indicated that the programs were far from being formulated.[83] This, of course, was untrue. The education bill, at least, had been in the works for weeks. But it would do the bill no harm to have people believe that the distinguished task force was responsible for the legislation when, in fact, it was a department bill.[84] Since the administration never released the task force report, no one had the opportunity of comparing it with the final bill.

The ESEA was sent to Congress in early January 1965. So convinced was Johnson that the time was now right for a school bill, that he decided to start his 1965 legislative program off with the ESEA and Medicare. The momentum created by the passage of these two would provide impetus for the rest of his program, the president reasoned.[85] Johnson, who realized that he was in his honeymoon period with Congress, had thought out this legislative strategy carefully. For, as he admitted, "I worked like hell to become President, and I'm not going to throw it away." Echoed Wilbur Cohen, "I never worked so hard in my life [as] between February of 1965 and June of '65."[86]

The ESEA, so many months in process, was how under the scrutiny of Congress and the public. Polls revealed that public opinion supported federal aid to education with funds for both Catholic and public schools. In 1961 only 36 percent of the respondents had thought private schools should share federal funds. Two years later, 44 percent of the respondents had favored this alternative. Now in early 1965, the majority, 51 percent, felt both sectors ought to receive some federal aid.[87]

The bill established two noble goals: "to strengthen and improve educational quality and educational opportunities" in the nation's schools. Title I was the heart of the bill where most of the money was concentrated. Focused on the children of poverty, Title I recognized their "special educational needs . . . and the impact that concentrations of low income families have on the ability of local educational agencies to support adequate educational programs." It was "the policy of the United States to provide financial assistance . . . to local educational agencies serving areas with concentrations of children from low income families," the title declared, so that these agencies could "expand and improve their educational programs by various means (including where necessary the construction of school facilities) which contribute particularly to meeting the special educational needs of educationally deprived children."[88] Local areas could use ESEA funds for many kinds of projects, if they helped meet the special needs of educationally deprived children from poor areas and were of "sufficient size, scope, and quality to give reasonable promise of substantial progress toward meeting those needs." Control of funds lay with the public agency.[89] Local educational agencies had various responsibilities. They were to formulate projects and programs that the state education agency would send on to the commissioner of education for his approval according to "such basic criteria as the commissioner may establish," to include parochial school children in special services and arrangements, and finally to make an annual report to the state on its programs.[90]

The other four titles of the bill, generally relating to the goal of improving educational quality, did not distribute money according to the poverty formula of Title I. In Title II grants were established to provide library books and other materials for the use of private and public school children. Title III set up supplementary education centers to furnish educational programs and services unavailable in the local school, to conduct experimental programs, and to serve as models for regular schools. Both children and adults could be involved in center activities. Title IV sought to support regional centers of research, and the last title gave funds to state departments of education to be used for the purpose of making them stronger, more efficient, and responsive.

Despite the new framework, Title I of the ESEA was, in several respects, similar to the education title that Heller's task force had supported the year before. No fresh thinking had taken place about the educational content of the 1965 bill; even the same phrases recurred to describe the bill's purposes. Each bill, recognizing the special educational needs of poor children, proposed programs of sufficient size, scope, and quality to meet these special needs in areas with a high concentration of the poor. Neither title defined the key phrases. But the programs to be funded were clearly compensatory in nature.

Both bills had similar administrative arrangements. Although the commissioner of education could draw up requirements for programs, substantial powers remained at the local level. In actuality this meant that in small school districts the school board, and in large districts the school board and the superintendent, would control funds.[91] Sociological studies had established the nature of the educational system, showing that school board members were generally better educated and richer than the average citizen, that their selection by nonpartisan elections or by appointment meant that they were less pressured by low-income groups, that they closed many of their meetings to the public.[92] In larger areas where the superintendent and the board shared power, it was recognized that the presence of an established bureaucracy was a factor inhibiting change.[93] But although planners at both times sensed the nature of the educational bureaucracy and recognized that local power structures had long ignored the poor and were educationally conservative, they feared that the local control issue could defeat their bills. So they had chosen to give local areas substantial and important powers. But more than fear now underlay this decision. Keppel and other departmental planners thought that federal funds could instigate reforms in attitude and practice, could infuse the whole educational structure with a desire for change. In this faith they were similar to other poverty planners who believed that it was possible to produce reform by cooperation, cooptation, and funds. But HEW planners, like the others, underestimated the difficulties of institutional reform within the federal system.[94] The different titles of the ESEA, in fact, allocated most or all money on an automatic formula basis, leaving the Office of Education with only the powers "to coax and cajole localities" to change their practices.[95]

In some ways, however, the ESEA did represent some advance over the Heller bill. Title I offered far more money for educating the poor than Heller's bill had. And, as a package, the bill did try to combine research and better administration with aid. Title V, for example, had funds for strengthening state departments of education. Title IV, acknowledging inadequate data about the process of education, proposed grants for research. Title III sought to stimulate imaginative school programs. But these last three titles had minimal funding. More important, the essential questions underlying the educational approach still remained unasked: did education contribute directly to ending poverty; did compensatory education work; were local power structures likely to change? Samuel Halperin, deputy assistant secretary for legislation in HEW, indicated why planners of the ESEA never thought of such questions. "The first task of the Administration's legislative team . . . was to devise a bill which was politically viable." Moreover, vagueness would ease political passage. "In time, one reasoned, the legislative process would remedy any imperfections or omissions in the original ESEA concept."[96]

The president and HEW were satisfied with the bill, however, because it met the top priority; the legislation had a good chance of passing the new Congress. The recent election had given the Democrats control of Congress. Senate Democrats increased their liberal majority with a gain of two seats. In the House, where education bills so regularly died, Democrats won thirty-eight new seats. If liberal Republicans voted with northern liberal Democrats, the education measure would pass. The House Subcommittee on Education and Labor, always a trouble spot for federal aid legislation, saw the addition of five Democrats and one Republican favoring federal aid.[97] The future, therefore, looked promising for the ESEA when the House subcommittee began its hearings on 22 January 1965. Nevertheless, the administration was realistic enough to realize that old passions and arguments might still erupt to destroy the bill. As Laurence O'Brien wrote to the president, "The greatest danger to this bill is that enactment will be stalled enough for religious and racial problems to arise."[98] Representative James Dulaney, who had cast the deciding vote in 1961 to table Kennedy's education bill, approved the ESEA in an interview for avoiding a "discriminatory" approach but ominously threatened to "be against it" if the bill were amended to exclude aid for parochial children.[99] With memories of Kennedy's defeats still fresh, the administration decided to take no chances. The legislative strategy called for hurrying the bill through the House, discouraging all amendments, and then maneuvering the Senate into passing an identical bill to avoid the need for a House-Senate conference.[100] Key congressional leaders, Morse and Perkins, agreed with this plan and helped make the administration's strategy a reality.

In accordance with the theme of haste, hearings in the House were compressed into a two-week period. Lest he be accused of rushing, Chairman Perkins suspended the ruling that limited subcommittee members to five minutes of questions for each witness and expressed his concern that everyone have the opportunity to examine the bill and witnesses thoroughly. Nevertheless, he reminded the subcommittee that it had a full schedule and warned against wasting time.[101]

Secretary Celebrezze and Commissioner Keppel led off with testimony supporting the bill. Describing the legislation as a major innovation, Celebrezze suggested that its goals were to break the cycle of poverty and to pull the poor into the economic mainstream. The educational problem that he described was largely one of inadequate financing for schools in poverty districts, and the solution was, of course, federal aid.[102] The bill offered, Celebrezze suggested, "fundamental and eminently sound solutions to problems of very long standing."[103] Keppel supported Celebrezze with a short explanation of certain aspects of the proposal. His written statement echoed Celebrezze's claim that the bill was both new and imaginative and that its focus was on breaking the pattern of "paralysis that poverty breeds."[104] The brief picture he gave of compensatory efforts indicated that "heartening results" could be expected from the bill.[105] The $1 billion of aid in Title I, he asserted, indicated that the solution was massive enough "to make a real difference."[106] He went on to mention the necessity of escaping from the standard pattern of educational structure and warned, "It is well we face the issue frankly, interfaith cooperation is essential."[107]

In the days that followed, a stream of witnesses supported the administration's contention that the bill was both necessary and expedient. So favorable were these witnesses that Charles Goodell, Republican from New York and leader of opposition to the bill, accused a group of city superintendents of just wanting money. "I have heard very few comments," he noted sharply, "beyond this from you gentlemen as to any concerns you have over what goes with the money."[108] Goodell's point was that federal control would be the inescapable companion of federal aid. Claiming that he was not opposed to federal aid as such but merely wished to clarify the legislation's intent, Goodell rejected the administration's verbal support of local autonomy as false.[109] Celebrezze's crisp comment, "You call it control. I refer to it as objectives of the legislation," made no difference to Goodell's attacks.[110] Implicitly, Goodell's line of questioning illuminated the problems of trying to channel reform from the federal level to the local, while maintaining some semblance of local freedom. Yet, Goodell approached the issue intent on arousing traditional fears rather than exposing the problems of reforming through the political system. He was interested in the bill's defeat, not the problem of reform. But his attacks received little support from the witnesses appearing before the subcommittee.[111] Probably Goodell was right. School people wanted money and realized that the "reform" bill would actually leave substantial power in their own hands.

There was more enthusiasm for Goodell's criticism of the religious arrangements the bill proposed. Claiming to be confused about the way parochial students would participate in the bill, Goodell asked administration spokesmen and witness after witness whether certain situations were likely if the bill was passed, and whether they were constitutional. Would a public school teacher, for example, be able to teach in a private school?[112] Under Title II were not books actually going to parochial schools, not to the children?[113] Was it possible that the supplementary education centers, established by Title III, might fall under parochial control?[114] Debate over these issues became heated and tangled as administration spokesmen and witnesses gave contradictory answers. It was obvious that there were wide areas of disagreement over the kinds of arrangements that the bill proposed and their legality. At Goodell's insistence, Keppel returned to clarify the bill's intent and to correct an aide's "slip of the tongue."[115] Keppel changed the record but failed to satisfy Goodell, who accused him of being evasive.[116] Yet, Goodell himself was unable to unglue the religious compromise that Keppel had pasted together. Despite the confusion of the debate, major interest groups claimed there was no church-state conflict in the bill. It had their backing. Keppel had done his work well.

Goodell, however, did raise some important educational issues, although he seemed more interested in wrecking the administration proposal than in exploring the bill as a realistic social measure. Pointing out that a good deal of educational research indicated that the child's early years were the most fruitful for educational intervention, Goodell observed that the bill did not emphasize the preschool years. Instead, the bill appeared to focus on children between five and seventeen.[117] Other witnesses stressed the same point.[118] HEW's choice of the five- to seventeen-years age group had been pragmatic. This span of years represented the traditional school period, and states wanted to work with this familiar group for which they were equipped.[119] To Goodell the administration merely replied that the bill did not exclude preschool programs; furthermore, money was already set aside for young children under the Economic Opportunity Act.[120] The age factor did not become a serious issue.

John Brademas, Democrat from Indiana, expressed other doubts more pertinent to evaluating the bill as a measure of social policy. Both Celebrezze and Keppel had mentioned breaking the poverty cycle. Brademas asked a series of questions about the feasibility of such a goal. First of all, he wondered whether there would be enough trained teachers to implement the program. Keppel was "optimistic."[121] More important, how could Congress be sure that spending money would really improve the quality of education?[122] Keppel assured Brademas that the reporting provisions would measure the bill's progress.[123] But Brademas went deeper into the central issue. He asked how much was really known about educational programs for the poor.[124] Was there "hard evidence" to justify the bill's approach?[125] The conflicting answers Brademas received indicated the uncertain basis for the legislation and highlighted the need for substantial research. On the one hand, Dr. George Bloom, (*not* Dr. Benjamin

Bloom) an authority on early education from the University of Chicago, told Brademas, "I would say clearly we do not know everything, but we do know enough actually to implement a great deal of educational practice in this area."[126] On the other hand, Arthur Singer of the Carnegie Corporation noted, "I think there has not been a lot of advance in understanding the problems of education for . . . disadvantaged people."[127] Brademas concluded that money should be concentrated not on Title I but on research.[128] Yet, although Brademas had raised a vital question, he did not raise enough doubts about the bill's foundations to cause any loss of support. Few representatives, including Brademas himself, considered that ignorance should impede passing federal aid to education.

Other witnesses had provided a different perspective to Brademas's concerns but were equally ineffective in diverting the legislation from its ultimate goal of passage. Although most school superintendents testified that pilot compensatory programs were either planned or in operation and, thus, indicated local concern for the poor, a few questioned this interest. The superintendent of Washington, D.C., admitted that local people "may need some stimulation" to be aware of the poverty problem.[129] Pittsburgh's superintendent agreed, saying, "School people have not developed attitudes, techniques, and materials to find the true starting point for disadvantaged children and to promote successful educational progress. Lack of funds, know-how, and custom prevent school people in communities having concentrations of disadvantaged from offering compensatory education."[130] An NAACP representative spoke up for the poor, saying that power and special interest groups did not serve the poor's best interests.[131] Yet, when a Rutgers professor suggested that there should be restrictions on the way money would be spent so that the school systems would not use it "any old way they care to," Perkins gave the significant reply. If such suggestions were heeded, "we would never pass the bill, looking from a realistic viewpoint."[132]

The function of the House hearings was clearly to hurry the bill toward eventual passage and to smooth over divisive issues that had wrecked school aid in the past. It was too much to expect this aspect of the political process to deal with the substantive issues that planners had neglected earlier. Yet, vital questions had been asked if not answered. The subcommittee voted to send the bill to full committee by a vote of 6-0. The disgruntled but powerless Republicans boycotted the meeting.

Senator Wayne Morse, Democrat from Oregon, presided over the Senate hearings, which began four days after those in the House. Morse compared his hearings to a seminar. "We study together, to try to find out what the facts are about the very important education problems which confront us," he reminded his fellow senators.[133] Morse's comparison was apt. The tone of the sessions was courteous. Little time was spent on the political issues of federal control and aid to parochial schools. Major weaknesses of the legislation's assumptions emerged. But despite the seminar approach, Senate hearings had no more effect on the substance of the legislation than had House hearings. But Morse did succeed in the most important task, that of following the administration's strategy of keeping the bill largely intact to avoid what could be a fatal collision with the House in conference.

Administration spokesmen repeated presentations they had given in the House. Almost at once, questions from Peter Dominick, Republican from Colorado, began to expose the administration's concept of the mechanism of reform. "It is your feeling, then," he asked Secretary Celebrezze, "that more funds and better facilities will upgrade educational opportunities for children of poor families." Celebrezze quickly replied, "There is no doubt about it in my mind."[134] Realizing that his answer implied that money was, by itself, a sufficient lever for change, Celebrezze hastened to add that he meant "the prudent expenditure of money for specific purposes where you see a deficiency."[135] Yet, a later HEW memorandum indicated that despite a lack of evidence about the relation between spending and education, "it may . . . be assumed that quality of education has a direct relationship to expenditure level."[136]

Several subcommittee members suspected that spending money was all the administration had in mind and that it would not work.[137] One concern was that money would be misspent. Both Dominick and Robert Kennedy suggested that local school boards were all too capable of using funds for their own purposes.[138] Kennedy, still influenced by the President's Committee on Juvenile Delinquency's concept of the schools as obstacles to opportunity, pointed out that the schools had actually participated in creating deprivation: "If you are placing or putting money into a school system which itself creates this problem or helps create it, or does nothing, or little, to alleviate it, are we not just in fact wasting the money of the Federal Government . . . investing money where it really is going to accomplish very little, if any good?", he asked. Keppel's reassurance that the school system was in the process of change and Celebrezze's comment that this was the price of democracy did little to alleviate Kennedy's concern.[139]

Another series of questions reflected Kennedy's skepticism about the spending approach and his interest in planning, which also dated back to his involvement with the President's Committee. Money without knowledge was useless, he warned. "Unless there is a meaningful program developed at the local level, which is really tested and checked by you, I don't think this program is going to be effective."[140] But despite his skepticism about setting up programs without knowledge or information, Kennedy's comments led only to a stiffening of evaluation requirements, not to a reconsideration of the proposal or a decision to run it on a careful experimental basis.

The radical critique of the bill offered by Kennedy was balanced by a conservative critique proposed by Roger Freeman, an authority on school financing. His testimony was the most straightforward criticism of the bill given. Denying poor children were necessarily deprived, he asked whether it was true that state and local officials treated the poor unfairly. "No evidence is being advanced for such charges except that there is a correlation between low family income, low educational achievements, and unemployment. That correlation does not by itself prove what the cause of the trouble is, where it all starts, and how it can be corrected."[141] Freeman touched on an administration nerve. Earlier in the hearings, Keppel had been entangled in the problem of defining educational deprivation, which he did largely in terms of the poverty environment, though he admitted that an educationally deprived child was not necessarily poor.[142] Keppel later resorted to studies correlating low income and low achievement.[143] But as Freeman pointed out, the two were not necessarily causally related. In his opinion different types of schools definitely did not produce different achievement patterns. "We must look elsewhere for the cause," he said, suggesting his own view that genetic differences underlay educational deprivation.[144] Such a conclusion was unacceptable to the liberal subcommittee. Morse thanked Freeman and dismissed him.

Senate hearings had clearly raised fundamental questions about both the strategy of reform and the basic assumptions of the bill. Yet the administration proposal emerged from hearings with only minor modifications. Evaluation requirements were strengthened and public school control over funds clarified. A new clause encouraged the dissemination of research results to teachers and administrators. Such changes were cosmetic. Clearly no one saw the function of hearings as one of creating a well-planned sound bill. Though inadequacies emerged, no senator or representative thought that they were important enough to obstruct the real functions of the process: creating legislative history that might affect how the bill actually operated and making pragmatic adjustments necessary to pass the bill. Subcommittee members generally shared the administration's desire to dispose of the ESEA hastily. The fact that the moment was right for federal aid to education was far more important than the fact that the bill might represent the wrong approach to the problem.

Congressional debates in late March and early April covered much of the same ground as the hearings while exposing some of the political compromise that had been made to ensure the bill's passage. In the House, Goodell once more emphasized that Title I's focus on children from five to seventeen skipped the promising early years between three and five.[145] But Republican Albert Quie's amendment to change the terms of Title I to cover only children from three to seven failed.[146] The religious question flared up in the first day of debate with tempers becoming so heated that representatives were shouting at one another across the aisles. It became clear that the bill was still vague on what services would be available to private school students.[147] The *New York Times* reported, "Some Democrats, believed to be lined up to support the bill, looked puzzled as they listened to the debate."[148] Even the leaders of the debate were confused. As Representative Cahill, Republican from New Jersey, pointed out, no matter what the services were, which were provided under the child benefit theory, the parochial school child would not get equal treatment.[149] Republican Robert Griffin of Michigan perceived that "the discussion we have had this afternoon, which has consumed most of our time, may be some indication that this bill does not avoid that religious issue."[150]

Prolonged discussions ranged around the formula. Each congressman had a clear stake in how much money his state could expect. Since the allotment a state would receive was based not only on the number of deprived children but also on the average amount that state spent on each pupil's education, rich states would get more money than poor states with an equal number of poor children.[151] Although the bill's supporters argued that education was more costly in wealthy states, Mrs. Green, Democrat from Oregon who offered an unsuccessful formula amendment, remarked that there was a fairer way to divide funds if one really wished to help culturally deprived children.[152]

Debate in the House, therefore, illuminated some of the religious and monetary compromises that the developers of the bill had made, but only rarely did the House's attention stray to educational goals or issues. As the administration feared, old questions were still foremost even if they were neutralized by the desire for aid and the compromises in the bill. Under the firm guidance of Adam Clayton Powell, who limited debate in the last hours of House consideration, significant amendments were ultimately defeated. The atmosphere was tense, however, as Powell wielded his authority.

Rules Committee Chairman Howard Smith gruffly observed, "This bill has been treated like it was just dropped from heaven, that it is sacred and must not be touched."[153] But delays might be fatal in the view of the administration and its supporters. Few were sure the ESEA would survive congressional examination and the graveyard of the House. Yet, the strategy of control and speed succeeded. On 29 March the bill passed the House triumphantly by a vote of 263 to 153.

The breakdown of the vote suggested the ways in which the administration's legislative strategy and events had succeeded in neutralizing the old issues. Ninety-eight percent of the northern Democrats and 37 percent of Democrats from the South voted for the ESEA; certainly, the 1964 Civil Rights Act had not solved the race issue. Still, more southern Democrats favored aid to education in 1965 than had in 1961; their lukewarm support ensured that the Democratic party could pass the ESEA unaided. Of the Republicans, only 27 percent supported the education bill. But an examination of both Republican and southern Democratic votes suggested the administration's allocation formula had done its work. Those from urban areas, now assured of their share of the funds, were those voting for federal aid. Finally, the religious issue had been defused as Catholic Democratic House members gave entusiastic support to the administration even if their Republican co-religionists did not.[154]

As Senator Morse remarked when debate opened in the calm atmosphere of the Senate on 7 April 1965, even the opposition agreed on the needs of lower-income children.[155] The new rationale had indeed won friends and disarmed foes. Morse, interested though he was in poverty, relentlessly pushed the bill through the Senate with as little controversy as possible. Warning against amending the bill and thus necessitating a House-Senate conference, he assured his colleagues, "Were great matters of principle at stake . . . I would not hesitate to go to conference; but the major issues on the bill have been resolved." Clearly it was political issues like constitutionality that Morse thought were major. Reminding the hesitant that they could change the bill the next year, he told the senators that Johnson wanted the bill passed quickly.[156] Much of the criticism in the Senate centered around accusations of administration railroading.

None of the bill's basic problems were resolved in the Senate. Senator Dominick saw the commitment to overcoming cultural deprivation as incomplete. He therefore offered several amendments to focus all five titles on this problem instead of just the first.[157] Morse deflected such attempts by warning of the hazards of a joint House-Senate conference, which in the past had resulted in no bill at all. Moreover, he implied that Dominick misunderstood that the bill after all had more than one aim.[158] True, on the one hand Title I concentrated on the deprived. Yet, on the other hand, the rest of the bill offered benefits to a wide range of ages and people.[159] Even under Title I, 95 percent of the nation's counties were eligible for funds. The bill was in some ways a general aid bill, Morse suggested.

Morse countered the inevitable demands for modifying the formula by claiming that it cost more to educate students in rich states than in others. Robert Kennedy supported Morse, pointing out that New York would pay more in taxes than it would receive from the bill.[160] Near the end of the debate Senator Ralph Yarborough, Democrat from Texas, exposed the problems inherent in this position. What states spent on education, he commented, reflected not only the costs of education but also its quality. Differences in the cost of living were not so great as the differences in federal grants to be awarded under the proposed bill.[161] Despite such arguments the formula amendments, like all the others, failed. The bill passed on 9 April 1965 by a wide margin of 73-18. All of the northern Democrats and 75 percent of the southern Democrats supported the bill. All but four of the opposing votes came from the Republicans, yet a majority of their fellow party members had cast their votes for education. Success had come at last.[162] The entire legislative process had taken less than three months.

Federal aid was now a reality. Not surprisingly, the three days of Senate debate, like debate in the House, had pointed out but not resolved some of the uncertainties of the bill.

In the Senate, Morse defended conflicting provisions and perplexing issues when they were noticed. As a politician, he was committed to passing federal aid to education, to glossing over problems in the bill. As he candidly admitted, "Let us face it. We are going into Federal aid for elementary and secondary schools in the bill through the back door."[163]

It probably did not occur to Morse that the bill he supported so ably might not help deprived children escape from their lives of poverty. Morse concentrated on getting federal aid to education passed quickly, as Johnson and HEW planners desired. The bill that planners had developed was an attractive political measure. They finally had created an education bill that could leap the hurdles of hearings and debates in Congress. Troubling questions, although raised, never had to be answered. Congressmen wanted the bill.

The political success of the bill was, however, self-defeating. So intent were planners on developing the political framework for the legislation that they never questioned whether the goals they established were feasible. The ESEA was a political masterpiece, but it rested on the liberal faith of planners. The next few years would reveal whether faith was enough of a justification for social policy.

1. Francis Keppel, personal interview with the author, 22 June 1971. In the House conservative Republicans joined with southern Democrats to make a voting majority. Eugene Eidenberg and Roy D. Morey, *An Act of Congress*, p. 35.

2. *Hearings before the Subcommittee on Education of the Committee on Labor and Public Welfare on Expansion of Public Laws 815 and 874*, 88th Cong., 2d Sess., 1964, Senate, p. 93. (Hereafter cited as *Morse Senate Hearings*.)

3. Anthony Celebrezze, *Oral History*, Lyndon Baines Johnson Library, pp. 10–11.

4. Frank J. Munger and Richard F. Fenno, Jr., *National Politics and Federal Aid to Education*, p. 74.

5. Theodore C. Sorensen, *Kennedy* (New York: Harper & Row, 1965), p. 358.

6. Philip Meranto, *The Politics of Federal Aid to Education in 1965*, p. 58.

7. Quoted in Sorensen, *Kennedy*, p. 360.

8. Wilbur Cohen, *Oral History*, John F. Kennedy Library, reel 4, p. 13.

9. Munger and Fenno, *National Politics*, p. 168; Keith Ellison, "John Kennedy and the 1961 Federal Aid to Education Bill," p. 3.

10. Alan F. Westin, ed., *The Uses of Power: Seven Cases in American Politics*, p. 24.

11. Meranto, *The Politics of Federal Aid*, p. 60.

12. William T. O'Hara, ed., *John F. Kennedy on Education*, pp. 18–20.

13. Ibid., pp. 18–19.

14. Sorensen, *Kennedy*, p. 361.

15. Memorandum from Abraham Ribicoff to the president, "Possible Proposals and Procedures on Education Legislation," 20 July 1961, Theodore Sorensen papers, Subject File, John F. Kennedy Library.

16. Munger and Fenno, *National Politics*, p. 168.

17. Quoted in Sorensen, *Kennedy*, p. 362; see Munger and Fenno, *National Politics*, pp. 156–58.

18. Mrs. Richard Bolling, *Oral History*, John F. Kennedy Library, pp. 35, 58; Ellison "John Kennedy and Federal Aid," p. 26.

19. Westin, *The Uses of Power*, pp. 41, 68; Ellison, "John Kennedy and Federal Aid," pp. 25–26.

20. Memorandum from Abraham Ribicoff to the President, 6 October 1961, Presidential Office Files, Departments and Agencies, John F. Kennedy Library.

21. O'Hara, *Kennedy on Education*, p. 22.

22. "Education and Economic Growth," October 1962, p. 10, roll 20, HEW files, John F. Kennedy Library.

23. Memorandum from Peter P. Muirhead to Wilbur Cohen, "Education and Economic Growth," 31 October 1962, roll 20, HEW files, John F. Kennedy Library.

24. Memorandum from Wilbur Cohen to Reginald E. Conley, "Comments on Fein-March Paper on Education and Economic Growth," 31 October 1962, roll 20, HEW files, John F. Kennedy Library.

25. Memorandum from Wilbur Cohen to Reginald E. Conley, "Budget Bureau Education Legislative Proposals," 14 November 1962, roll 20, HEW files, John F. Kennedy Library.

26. "A New Federal Program in Education," 7 November 1962, Sorensen Papers, Subject File.

27. O'Hara, *Kennedy on Education*, p. 155.

28. Ibid., pp. 166–67.

29. David K. Cohen et al., "The Effects of Revenue Sharing and Block Grants on Education," pp. 97–98.

30. Memorandum from Ralph A. Dungan to the president, 19 November 1962, Presidential Offices Files, Departments and Agencies, John F. Kennedy Library.

31. Francis Keppel, *Oral History*, John F. Kennedy Library, pp. 8, 13.

32. Memorandum from Philip des Marais to Wilbur Cohen, "Further Comments on Office of Education Position Paper—Elementary and Secondary Education," 5 June 1964, General Counsel Files, HEW.

33. Memorandum from Peter P. Muirhead, "HEW Legislative Program for 1965," 11 June 1965, General Counsel files, HEW.

34. *Morse Senate Hearings*, 1964, p. 7.

35. Ibid., pp. 93, 100.

36. Ibid., p. 94.

37. Ibid., p. 100.

38. Ibid., p. 97.

39. Department of Health, Education, and Welfare, Office of Education, "History of the Office of Education" (unpublished, Lyndon Baines Johnson Library), appendix, p. 14.

40. Charles Philip Kearney, "The 1964 Presidential Task Force on Education and the Elementary and Secondary Education Act of 1965," p. 121.

41. Ibid., p. 236. Personal communication from Wilbur Cohen to the author, 22 March 1976.

42. Cohen, *Oral History*, reel 4, p. 16.

43. Ibid., pp. 13–14.

44. Ibid., p. 15.

45. Ibid., pp. 14–15.

46. James L. Sundquist, *Politics and Policy*, p. 212.

47. Jerome T. Murphy, "Title I of ESEA," p. 39.

48. Kearney, "Task Force," p. 237.

49. Memorandum from Francis Keppel, "Education Program and Messages," undated but before 2 December 1964, General Counsel files, HEW. Cohen letter, 22 March 1976.

50. *Public Papers of the Presidents of the United States: Lyndon B. Johnson, 1963–1964*, 1:58, 189.

51. Ibid., 2:1318.

52. Francis Keppel, *Oral History*, Lyndon Baines Johnson Library, p. 11.

53. *Public Papers: Lyndon B. Johnson, 1963–64*, 1:372, 183.

54. Ibid., 2:371, 397.

55. Ibid., 1:706.

56. Ibid., 2:706, 780, 916, 1430, 1318.

57. Ibid., p. 1430.

58. Ibid., p. 1344.

59. Ibid., p. 1431.

60. Eric F. Goldman, *The Tragedy of Lyndon Johnson*, p. 299.

61. Eidenberg and Morey, *An Act of Congress*, p. 77.

62. *Public Papers: Lyndon B. Johnson, 1963–64*, 2:1563.

63. Memorandum from Kermit Gordon to Secretary Celebrezze, Secretary MacNamara, Secretary Wirtz, and Mr. Shriver, "Meeting on Education and Training Programs," 20 November 1964, Bureau of the Budget files.

64. *Congressional Records*, 91st Cong., 2d Sess., 1970, p. 8494.

65. Kearney, "Task Force," pp. 212–13.

66. Eidenberg and Morey, *An Act of Congress*, p. 84.

67. Stephen K. Bailey and Edith K. Mosher, *ESEA*, p. 34.

68. "History of the Office of Education"; Wayne O. Reed, *Oral History*, Lyndon Baines Johnson Library, p. 13.

69. Eidenberg and Morey, *An Act of Congress*, p. 84, and Keppel.

70. Kearney, "Task Force," p. 215.

71. Eidenberg and Morey, *An Act of Congress*, pp. 85–86.

72. Memorandum from Douglas Cater to the president, 19 December 1964, Executive File, Le/Fe2, Lyndon Baines Johnson Library.

73. Eidenberg and Morey, *An Act of Congress*, p. 62.

74. Ibid., p. 64.

75. Ibid., p. 84, and Keppel interview.

76. Memorandum to the president, 1964, Executive File, Le/Fa2, Lyndon Baines Johnson Library.

77. Kearney, "Task Force," pp. 82–83.

78. *Public Papers, Lyndon B. Johnson, 1963–64*, 2:729.

79. Kearney, "Task Force," pp. 277–80.

80. Ibid., p. 247.

81. Keppel, *Oral History*, LBJ Library p. 12.

82. Kearney, "Task Force," p. 176.

83. *New York Times*, 15 November 1964.

84. See, for instance, *New York Times*, 8 November 1964. HEW later claimed, "The Presidential task force prepared the basic outline for legislation." See Department of Health, Education, and Welfare, Office of Education, "History of Title I ESEA" (Mimeo, June 1969), p. 1.

85. Goldman, *Tragedy of Johnson*, p. 284.

86. Quoted in ibid., p. 259. Wilbur Cohen, *Oral History*, reel 3, p. 16.

87. George H. Gallup, *The Gallup Poll: Public Opinion 1937–1971*, 3:1712, 1804, 1939, 1928.

88. Public Law 89-10, Sec. 201. The parenthetical expression was changed after committee hearings to read "(including preschool programs)."

89. Ibid., Sec. 205.(a)(1).

90. Ibid., Sec. 205.(a).

91. Roald F. Campbell, Luvern L. Cunningham, and Roderick F. McPhee, *The Organization and Control of American Schools*, p. 188.

92. Ibid., pp. 176, 167; Patricio Cayo Sexton, *The American School*, p. 29.

93. Robert L. Crain and David Street, "School Desegregation and School Decision-Making," p. 79. For a recent analysis of what is known about the educational power structure, see Frederick M. Wirt and Michael W. Kirst, *The Political Web of American Schools*, pp. 67–77, 79–88.

94. Mark G. Yudof, "Title I and Empowerment," p. 11.

95. David K. Cohen, "Politics and Research," p. 220.

96. Samuel Halperin, personal interview with the author, 3 March 1971, and Jerome T. Murphy, personal interview with the author, 25 February 1971; *Congressional Record*, 91st Cong., 2d Sess., p. 8492.

97. Eidenberg and Morey, *An Act of Congress*, pp. 48–49.

98. Memorandum from Laurence O'Brien to the president, 8 March 1965, Executive File Le-Fa2, Lyndon Baines Johnson Library.

99. Quoted in Munger and Fenno, *National Politics*, p. 71.

100. Meranto, *The Politics of Federal Aid*, p. 123.

101. *Hearings before the General Subcommittee on Education of the Committee on Education and Labor on Aid to Elementary and Secondary Education*, 89th Cong., 1st Sess., 1965, House, p. 135.

102. Ibid., pp. 63–64.

103. Ibid., p. 66.

104. Ibid., p. 83.

105. Ibid., p. 88.

106. Ibid., p. 83.

107. Ibid., pp. 90, 84.

108. Ibid., p. 605.

109. Ibid., p. 175.

110. Ibid., p. 148.

111. Ibid., p. 235 for example.

112. Ibid., p. 275.

113. Ibid., p. 269.

114. Ibid., pp. 1745–46.

115. Ibid., p. 1749.

116. Ibid., p. 1737.

117. Ibid., pp. 155, 353.

118. Ibid., pp. 339–40.

119. Keppel interview.

120. *House Hearings*, 1965, pp. 155, 158.

121. Ibid., p. 141.

122. Ibid., pp. 141, 350.

123. Ibid., p. 141.

124. Ibid., pp. 141, 350.

125. Ibid., p. 262.

126. Ibid., p. 351.

127. Ibid., p. 1214.

128. Ibid., p. 1215.

129. Ibid., p. 202.

130. Ibid., p. 240.

131. Ibid., p. 1188.

132. Ibid., p. 654.

133. *Hearings before the Subcommittee on Labor and Public Welfare on the Elementary and Secondary Education Act of 1965*, 89th Cong., 1st Sess., 1965, Senate, p. 2.

134. Ibid., p. 480.

135. Ibid., p. 481.

136. Ibid., p. 1187.

137. Ibid., p. 896.

138. Ibid., p. 895.

139. Ibid., pp. 511, 513.

140. Ibid., pp. 902–3.

141. Ibid., pp. 2765–66.

142. Ibid., pp. 501, 510.

143. Ibid., p. 893.

144. Ibid., p. 2768.

145. *Congressional Record*, 89th Cong., 1st Sess., 1965, pp. 5768, 5770.

146. Ibid., pp. 6016–20.

147. Ibid., pp. 5743–50; 5754–55; 5757.

148. *New York Times*, 25 March 1965.

149. *Congressional Record*, 89th Cong., 1st Sess., 1965, p. 5978.

150. Ibid., p. 5761.

151. Ibid., p. 5965.

152. Ibid., p. 5965.

153. Quoted in Bailey and Mosher, *ESEA*, p. 65.

154. Meranto, *Politics of Federal Aid*, pp. 4, 91–97.

155. *Congressional Record*, 89th Cong., 1st Sess., 1965, p. 7297.

156. Ibid., pp. 7307, 7671.

157. Ibid., pp. 7526–28; 7687.
158. Ibid., pp. 7308, 7535.
159. Ibid., pp. 7545, 7687.
160. Ibid., p. 7561.
161. Ibid., p. 7620.
162. Meranto, *Politics of Federal Aid*, p. 93.
163. *Congressional Record*, 89th Cong., 1st Sess., 1965, p. 7317.

4

Implementation

The president was jubilant at the passage of the ESEA, which he declared was "the most significant education bill in the history of Congress." At a reception to celebrate the bill's success, Johnson told the assembled congressmen, "You take it from me. I worked harder and longer on this measure than on any measure I have ever worked on since I came to Washington in 1931—and I am proud of it." He reminded his listeners of the bleak years since 1945 when school legislation had failed as the same issues divided legislators again and again. Finally all that was over, and, the president pointed out, responsibility for the bill lay with the executive. "We must carry on and we must administer it," the president said. "I have a very keen sense of . . . obligation to each of you . . . to make certain that the program is carried out swiftly and efficiently."[1]

As Johnson suggested, attention within the government now turned to the problem of administering the legislation. But the ESEA did not get under way as quickly or as efficiently as the president had hoped. A month before Congress passed the bill, an extensive reorganization of the Office of Education began.[2] The objective of this upheaval, which left some members of the bureau actually unable to find their new offices, was to force the Office of Education to break with its timid past so that it could assume the new responsibilities and image that Keppel thought necessary and that the new legislation would demand. But momentary confusion and delay was one result of reorganization. Nevertheless, work on the essential task of drawing up regulations and guidelines to help state and local officials understand the provisions of the ESEA did begin in April. Since developing guidelines was a delicate and crucial task, the job took several months. During this period Keppel and other members of the Office of Education held a number of meetings with state and local officials to discuss tentative guidelines and to make necessary adjustments in them. The meetings informed officials of the act's purposes, calmed fears of federal control, and provided a forum for bargaining between federal, state, and local authorities. Bargaining with those who would actually receive federal money was a necessary part of ensuring compliance and fit in with Keppel's view of reform filtering down from above. But meetings also took time. Thus, in some cases, local districts began planning projects before operational guidelines actually became available in December 1965. Another month passed until the guidelines were ready for distribution in final form.[3]

This was not the only delay in getting the ESEA into operation, since Congress took several months to vote funds. Because the appropriations bill did not pass until 23 September 1965, money did not get to some areas until April 1966, almost the end of the school year and a year after the president signed the bill. During the first year of operation, Title I only reached 2,500,000 children in summer programs.[4] The next year 9,000,000 children, not all of whom were disadvantaged, participated in Title I projects.[5] By 1969, 20,000 Title I projects were operative, although HEW estimated that only about half of the severely disadvantaged children on the elementary level were involved.[6] Yet although the ESEA did not reach all needy children, it now touched millions of poor students and their schools as no other federal education program had. The question was how effective this contact was.

Underlying the new federal aid approach was the confidence that Title I programs could improve the academic performance of deprived children and that the act could be smoothly administered. As federal funds flowed into local school districts, this confidence began to fade. Problems plagued the program. By 1970 there was widespread skepticism about the ESEA and claims that Title I had "failed" educationally and administratively. Evidence on the legislation piled up. Unfortunately, since there was no national statistical study on the operation of the ESEA, it is impossible to give a definitive picture of the way the act was implemented nationally. Nevertheless, piecemeal evidence is plentiful. Congressional hearings on the ESEA held in 1966, 1967, and 1969 yielded impressionistic pictures of it in action. The comptroller general, the HEW Audit Agency, and the Office of Education all issued numerous reports on Title I's implementation in the states. The largest evaluation of Title I, published by the Office of Education in 1970, investigated the operation of the ESEA in 4,000 elementary schools. In addition to these official studies, which often presented some kind of statistical data, the National Advisory Council on the Education of Disadvantaged Children, composed of twelve individuals appointed by the president, evaluated the administration and academic achievements of Title I and reported to both president and Congress each year. Finally, private organizations like the NAACP, the Washington Research Project, and the Center for Urban Education in New York City carried out and published independent studies of the ESEA. Academic case studies eventually supplemented the picture provided by nongovernment organizations.

The evidence accumulated in these different pieces of research suggests that curiously enough the problem areas were those that critics of aid to education had envisioned for so many years. Opponents of school bills traditionally insisted that federal aid would create difficulties in the relations between federal, state, and local authorities and would embroil them in struggles over money, race, and religion. The great triumph of 1965 had been to muffle the critics by skillful bargaining with the important interest groups and by basic compromises in the bill. Yet, the triumph was, in part, responsible for the act's unsatisfactory administration. Harold Howe II, commissioner of education from 1966 to 1968, observed the connection between the political process and the act's implementation. The "ESEA was the only type of federal activity in education which was likely to be politically viable in 1965," Howe pointed out. "I doubt that anyone could have dreamed up a series of education programs more difficult to administer and less likely to avoid problems in the course of their administration."[7] But problems in administration resulted not only from the political compromises made to secure the bill's passage in 1965 but also from the positive model of reform that planners held. Accepting the necessity of yielding to local control, planners, in any case, preferred to work through the familiar power structure. Keppel and others hoped that federal funds, accompanied by basic program and target criteria established by a now-rejuvenated Office of Education, would stimulate reform on each level handling Title I money and would make disadvantaged children a top educational priority. Commissioner Howe latter suggested the model that original planners had in mind in 1964 and 1965. The ESEA, he said,

> was money aimed at helping states and local school districts bring about new levels of activity, changes in programs, different kinds of services. This money was not designed to pick up the going costs of institutions as they were but instead to bring about changes in those institutions so that they would be more up-to-date and thus serve certain groups better (particularly those children who happened to come from poor families). The objectives were institutional change, curricular change, organizational change, with an idea to helping the elementary and secondary schools meet the problems of modern America.[8]

If some of the problems in the ESEA's implementation can be traced to political compromise and the model of reform held by Keppel and his colleagues, others lay entirely outside the control of HEW planners. The period of 1964 and 1965, with its visions of the Great Society, had been, perhaps, years of consensus. But this consensus disappeared under the strains of the country's frustrating Vietnam involvement, deep divisions within the black community, race riots, and violence. All these factors affected the implementation of the ESEA, and all contributed to a change of mood that was increasingly critical of Great Society legislation and skeptical about its goals.

One of the problems plaguing the operation of the ESEA has been money. Originally, HEW planners were primarily concerned with the way in which money would be allocated, since there was a traditional controversy over the issue in school aid debates. From the first days of drafting the bill, a group within HEW had searched for an appropriate formula that would channel funds to the urban and rural areas where poverty was most severe. If the bill was to have any impact on poverty, they reasoned, concentrating money on the poor was vital.. At the same time it was also essential to distribute funds widely enough to attract significant congressional support. The final formula was complicated but successfully met the political criteria. It determined the funds available to local areas on the basis of several computations. First, for each school district, administrators calculated the number of children both from families earning less than $2,000 and also from families on welfare. A district needed a minimum number of 100 poor children or 3 percent of the total number of children to qualify for aid. Then the number of children was multiplied by the average amount of money the state spent on educating each child, and divided by two. The final figure indicated how much federal money the district could expect under Title I. Because a district needed so few poor children to qualify for funds, most would receive some. On the county level 95 percent of the country's counties would be eligible for Title I money. But, as several Congressmen pointed out in the hearings, the formula had several disadvantages. Funds were spread too widely, and rich industrial states with high educational expenditures would receive more money than poor rural states who needed it most.

Inequities in the way the formula operated quickly became apparent. In the 1966 House hearings, a knowledgeable witness pointed out the obvious flaw in the distribution of funds: "It seems inconceivable," he said, "that many (90-95%) districts are seriously affected by poverty."[9] Wealthy districts with good teachers and facilities already had enough to help the few poor children living there, he argued. The formula cheated poor districts, which faced not just one problem but all the interrelated problems typical of poor communities, by awarding them less money to work with. A 1970 HEW survey supported such an analysis with figures showing that poor children actually were clustered in a few areas. Of reported low income children 80.6 percent lived in only 31.8 percent of the country's public school districts (which had at least 300 pupils enrolled in school). Yet, obviously, the ESEA did not concentrate funds in this way.[10] What the operation of the formula actually did, then, was to enable some districts to spend more on helping poor children than other districts could. Again the HEW survey gave some figures. High-expenditure districts could spend an average of $257 per target child, whereas low-expenditure districts spent only an average of $149.[11] That this was a serious problem which jeopardized an effective delivery of services was clear: 46 percent of the nation's poor children went to school in low-expenditure districts.[12] The third HEW annual report on the act summed the situation up: *"Under the legislatively prescribed formula Title I funds . . . do not flow to school districts and their disadvantaged students proportionally to their needs."*[13]

During the next few years other inequities in the formula emerged. The formula had used 1960 census data to calculate the number of the nation's poor children. By 1967 and 1968 the census figures were no longer applicable. Using out-of-date data became more and more a problem for the central cities, where migration brought additional poor children needing special services into the public schools each year. Yet, these new children were not counted in the formula allocations, and cities were faced with the prospect of diluting services or excluding a growing number of children from Title I aid. Out-of-date census data, however, favored other areas with a decreasing poverty population. In one prosperous

Long Island community, for example, the small group of poor were relocated outside the district after 1960. But the school district was eligible for Title I aid and found the offer of free money too tempting to reject. One official revealed that the major objective of those districts was to make sure that all Title I funds were utilized.[14]

Keppel and his colleagues in the Office of Education had made what they regarded as a necessary compromise over the formula. They compromised again over the total amount of money to be allocated for Title I when they agreed to the $1 billion figure that Johnson favored. Realizing the money could represent only an initial attack on the problem of ignorance and poverty, they assumed that appropriations would increase dramatically over the first few years and would reach $3 or $4 billion by 1968-69.[15] But as Johnson, who had been such a staunch supporter of the ESEA, became entangled in the Vietnam war, he kept the program going at its $1 billion figure. Representative Hugh Carey recognized what was happening as early as the 1966 hearings. "We are being forced to make a choice here between books and bullets," he said. "The first parts of the bill last year were based upon the assurances from the highest possible sources that there would be more money next year."[16] A colleague agreed with Carey that program increases were "immoderately moderate."[17]

What became clear within the next year, however, was that although some liberals complained, the administration's priorities had shifted. Much as Johnson wished to be remembered as the education president and as the president who had eliminated the blight of poverty, the war in Vietnam absorbed his attention and a larger and larger share of the yearly budget. In 1966 defense requirements ate up $54.2 billion, several billion more than the Defense Department had estimated. Only a year later, defense spending had increased by $16 billion, and the climb upward would continue.[18] As defense costs escalated, administration officials and congressmen sparred over education appropriations. The administration was obviously eager to hold down education spending, although domestic spending as a whole continued to grow.[19]

In the 1967 House hearings Chairman Perkins argued with this course of action. "I just don't see how we can afford to dilute and cut back our program at this time," he said.[20] In response Commissioner Howe stated that there had actually been no cutback but merely a smaller increase in funding than expected.[21] Senator Morse also complained that year that the administration failed to honor congressional authorizations and had stabilized its appropriation requests.[22]

But congressional protests were ineffective, and partial funding continued. By 1969 there was only an average of $113 available for each deprived child, although Secretary of HEW Robert Finch admitted that between $538 and $805 per child was required. John Brademas, Democrat from Indiana, observed in House hearings that year, "We have in fact not been spending increasing sums of money or really very large sums of money at all, at least as seen in the perspective of the enormity of the problem."[23] Senator Javits made a similar point in the Senate and asked a compelling question: Was there *any* national priority for education?[24] There did not seem to be. The Vietnam war had become a priority and an obsession. Its requirements meant that education spending was stabilized at a lower figure than planners had ever anticipated, that programs were poorly funded, and that many children never were reached. And when questionable reports of the effectiveness of the ESEA began to trickle into Congress, there was little likelihood that more money would ever become available, war or no war.

Another less obvious effect of the war, only indirectly related to education money, slowly became clearer as the nation's entanglement in the conflict dragged on. The euphoric and hopeful mood of 1964 and 1965 that underlay the passage of poverty legislation evaporated. The liberal majority, which had so cooperatively passed essential legislation, dwindled and divided over foreign involvement.[25] Lackluster reports of the outcome of reform legislation contributed to the growing congressional and public skepticism about the Great Society. Public sympathy and support for what could become expensive social programs disappeared.[26] Reform was on the defensive both in Congress and in the country.

But money was not the only problem and had not been the only political issue that had caused defeats of earlier school bills. Nor was it the only difficulty that would plague the ESEA in operation. ESEA planners had realized there must be some resolution of the religious question if the bill was to satisfy both parochial and public school interest groups, for only with their advance backing could the ESEA pass Congress. The religious arrangement planners worked out was acceptable. The ESEA did not give funds directly to private schools but instructed local school districts to include parochial students in "special educational services and arrangements (such as dual enrollment, educational radio . . . television . . . mobile educational services and equipment), to the extent consistent with the number of educationally deprived children" enrolled in private schools.[27] Planners hoped that parochial schools, which educated 15 percent of the nation's children, might receive between 10 to 13 percent of ESEA funds.[28] Specific arrangements for parochial school children, however, were left to local public and parochial school officials to work out.

The fears of those who had opposed aid to Catholics were unfounded. There was no holy war in American school districts nor was there a Catholic attempt to absorb the public school system. But the expectations of administration planners were dashed. Poor Catholic children did not participate in Title I programs in proportion to their numbers. In its 1966 report the National Advisory Council already perceived the problem.[29] Pursuing the issue in the 1969 report, the council studied seventeen communities and concluded that only a few offered parochial students "genuine" opportunities to take part in Title I activities.[30] In the 1969 House hearings the superintendent of Roman Catholic schools in Brooklyn gave one specific example that supported the over-all picture the National Advisory Council had described. The superintendent pointed out that 15 percent of New York City's deprived children attended parochial schools, yet these children received only 4 percent of Title I services.[31] Independently, the Center for Urban Education in New York City, a regional educational laboratory funded under the act, provided additional figures that supported this picture. Despite the proportion of deprived children in parochial schools, New York's school budget for the 1967-68 school year set aside only $2,877,000 for programs for these children but $49,371,000 for children in public schools. Less was spent on programs for parochial students than was budgeted.[32]

There were so many initial complaints over the question of private school participation that the Office of Education commissioned two Boston College professors to do a study on private schools and Title I. The professors investigated ten large, ten medium, and ten small school systems between 1966 and 1968. Although their study showed "a wide range of differences in almost every aspect that has been considered," it revealed underlying reasons why Catholic and other private school children often did not get the Title I services they needed. To avoid a church-state controversy in Congress, the bill had determined that activities for private school children were to take place customarily in the public schools.[33] Furthermore, public school officials would administer funds and own equipment. The result of this arrangement was twofold. On the one hand, Title I activities were often scheduled at times when it was difficult or inconvenient for Catholic children to attend. In one New England city with 45,000 children attending parochial schools, for example, only sixty-five participated in Title I after-school programs in 1966-67. Since young children could not attend late afternoon activities, none of these children were in the first three grades, where educators thought compensatory programs were most helpful.[34] State laws forbidding the busing of private school pupils also made Catholic participation in Title I programs difficult in many states. On the other hand, because public school authorities often did not consult their Catholic counterparts in planning projects, they could and did use Title I money in public schools to reduce class size or to provide teacher training. Such expenditures were legal under the legislation but were of no value to parochial school students.[35]

The Boston College study pointed out that the minimal involvement of Catholic children in Title I projects was due not only to public school control but also to the bewildering variety of Catholic authorities operating Catholic schools. Frequently, no one person could speak for all the Catholic schools in his area. The report concluded that this factor "posed problems of communication" between public and Catholic school officials.[36] In one midwestern school system, for example, public officials were not even sure whom they should contact in Catholic schools.[37]

The ESEA had provided indirect aid for Catholics and had given local public school authorities the task of actually providing needy Catholic children with the Title I services. Too often the public schools took the responsibility lightly. As one Title I coordinator commented, "Involving people takes time," and he just did not have that time.[38] In the 1969 House hearings Catholic school superintendents made a plea for tightening the law to ensure adequate Catholic participation. Although the subcommittee was sympathetic to the superintendents, their plea was ultimately ignored. Title I funds did not go to many Catholic children who bore the burden of poverty.

The question of whether segregated schools in the South were eligible for federal aid had given the fatal blow to many an education bill since 1945. After passage of the 1964 Civil Rights Act, which allowed the government to terminate federal funds going to segregated institutions, the issue was submerged, and planners did not have to deal with it in writing the bill. The race question did not surface during the debate over the ESEA. But in the final vote in the House, 54 of the 57 Democrats voting against the bill were from the South as were 15 of the 17 Republicans.[39] The only opposing Democratic votes in the Senate were from the South. As these southerners realized, there was a distinct possibility that ESEA funds might be used as a weapon to force desegregation. This was indeed Keppel's hope. In a 13 April 1965 memorandum to Secretary Celebrezze, Keppel pointed out that the act "makes possible a new approach in handling civil rights problems in education." Rather than lose the vast sums of federal money, Keppel felt that poor southern school districts would think it worth their while to comply with desegregation guidelines drawn up under Title VI of the 1964

Civil Rights Act. Keppel did not expect radical changes immediately, but pictured the Office of Education prodding local officials to move toward desegregation as fast as their communities would accept.[40]

During the spring of 1965, as HEW was setting the framework for the administration of Title I, it also grappled with drawing up desegregation guidelines to make formerly *de jure* segregated southern schools eligible for ESEA funds. By April HEW's *General Statement of Policies* was ready. It described the three kinds of desegregation procedures that were the conditions for federal funds. A district without open signs of segregation needed only to file an Assurance of Compliance with the department. Districts with court orders to desegregate were expected to provide HEW with a copy of their final court order as well as a Compliance Report that provided information on the racial composition of schools and the methods the district was using to desegregate them. For those districts still segregated but without a court order, HEW required an Assurance of Compliance, an initial Compliance Report, and voluntary desegregation plans. These plans could provide for desegregation by forming non-racial school attendance zones, by establishing freedom of choice, or by offering a combination of these possibilities.[41] HEW took a firm initial stand on the necessity of ending segregation. The guidelines gave the South only three years to achieve desegregation in all twelve grades.[42]

HEW's initial determination to stimulate desegregation through Title VI of the Civil Rights Act was given tremendous support by the passage of ESEA, which turned federal school aid from a trickle to a flow. There were several unanswered questions, however. The first was whether the promise of funds would be sufficient to induce southern districts to begin the process of desegregation. Another was whether the threat of a fund cutoff would discipline a district that was either making only token efforts to desegregate or misusing funds. The last was whether under the free-choice plan ESEA funds might not be used to reinforce segregation. Since Title I emphasized that services should be focused on deprived children, school districts in the South with freedom-of-choice plans might use federal money to encourage poor black children to stay in their segregated schools. If this situation emerged, one social reform would be manipulated to block another.

The question of whether southern districts were interested in federal funds was answered during the summer of 1965. In early July, three months after the act's passage, the commissioner of education had received only 352 desegregation plans as the prerequisite to ESEA money. Two weeks later 1,800 school districts, over half of the segregated districts in the South, had replied. But by the end of the month the office had returned 700 plans for revision and was exerting pressure on the 400 school districts that had not yet sent in any plans. By 17 August 200 districts still had submitted nothing to HEW. Keppel stepped up pressure by informing state superintendents and congressional delegations of his intention to begin fund cutoffs at the end of the month. To aid districts without any plans, HEW developed a special model that needed only the appropriate signatures.[43] On 31 August, Johnson announced the "deeply encouraging" results of the summer's efforts. He noted "the heartening evidence of Governors, school officials, and other citizens to assume that respect for the law remains a vigorous force everywhere in the country." And he proudly related the figures. "One week ago," he said, "there were 172 school districts which had taken no action to meet the requirements of the Civil Rights Act. Today the figure is 135—and it is shrinking rapidly."[44] By the end of the effort all but a "handful" had sent their plans.[45]

Plans for desegregation were, of course, not the same as desegregation. Only time could tell whether Title I would be the lever to encourage desegregation or not. Although some border states like Kentucky desegregated their schools, disquieting signs began to appear that in many places ESEA funds were being used to maintain racial separation.[46] The National Advisory Council reports of 1967 and 1968 both noted this misuse of Title I money. Council member Sidney Marland warned the House Subcommittee on Education and Labor in 1967, "These are my words to say somebody had better get on the stick and find a way for the distribution of these funds to avoid segregating children by means of the compensatory education program."[47] As the U.S. Commission on Civil Rights in 1967 pointed out, "Under free choice . . . improvement of substandard Negro schools itself inhibits desegregation."[48]

In 1967 testimony before the Senate subcommittee, Jean Fairfax of the NAACP Legal Defense Fund and M. Hayes Mizell of the South Carolina Community Relations Program of the American Friends Service Committee described how southern districts used ESEA funds to strengthen segregation. Their examples, they claimed, were typical of the kinds of complaints they heard. In Lincoln County, Georgia, for instance, Negro schools began to serve pupils free lunches when freedom of choice was initiated. Title I funds paid for the lunches, which served as the bribe for students to stay put. In another case ESEA money bought trailers to relieve overcrowding for the Negro South Warren School in North Carolina. Yet, a white school only one-half mile away had vacant desks, and black children could have found space there.[49] Mizell turned to the situation in South Carolina, which he knew well. There ESEA funds also aimed to improve black schools, with the result that "many children elect to return to the [segregated] school because, among other reasons, it seems that the Negro school has significantly improved."[50] Other evidence supported this picture for South Carolina. The South Carolina Department of Education reported that 74 percent of the children receiving Title I services from 1966 to 1969 were black. Black children were, of course, poor, but the director of the ESEA program acknowledged that much of the state's Title I money was being used to make black schools comparable to white schools.[51] As Mizell concluded, the "ESEA is, in effect . . . shoring up the otherwise floundering Negro school."[52]

Children who moved into integrated schools sometimes found an unexpected punishment: they lost out on their Title I funds. Although the Office of Education tried to handle the situation by issuing memorandums in April, July, and August 1966 and February and March 1967 which stated that services could "follow the child," Mizell felt that the memorandums had "not been adequately implemented," and were "therefore depriving the Negro youngsters of valuable academic programs."[53] Interviews in three counties in Georgia and four in Alabama confirmed this general picture, revealing that services did not follow the child to his new school in all the Georgia counties and one of the Alabama counties.[54] Southern experience with Title I funds suggested that funds alone were insufficient to force changes in local attitudes and habits.

HEW, of course, had the authority under the Civil Rights Act to cut off funds from districts that were using them to enforce segregation. Many southern school districts probably felt as one school board member did in a Virginia County where 95 percent of the black students attended segregated schools: "As long as the school system was receiving Federal funds, the board thought it was in compliance with Federal requirements." Even Mizell admitted that he thought there was no "conspiracy to utilize the ESEA Title I funds to preserve segregation."[55]

Some action was necessary, however, to show southern districts that real desegregation was expected. But HEW felt terminating funds was a drastic remedy that would mean that thousands of poor children did not get the educational help they needed. The administration did not favor it. Moreover, each decision to cut off funds entailed compiling a detailed legal case against the district no matter how glaring the racial discrimination. These complicated bureaucratic requirements for termination procedures, David Seeley, head of HEW's compliance system, ruefully noted, meant that "thirty-five million people had to be brought . . . [in] and convinced for the routine case."[56] These kinds of feelings along with the formidable bureaucratic procedures strengthened the tendency of the department to negotiate or do nothing with uncooperative southern districts, despite the general desire to foster desegregation. By February 1967 Commissioner Howe had only cut off funds from thirty-four southern districts although he had initiated proceedings against 157.[57] In 1969 the Civil Rights Commission estimated that only one-eighth of the school districts in southern states were completely desegregated.[58]

Threatening to cut off funds had failed as a technique for promoting desegregation, and the South knew it. HEW tacitly acknowledged defeat when the secretary and the attorney general announced on 3 July 1969 that government efforts to encourage desegregation would thenceforth be through the courts and not through administrative proceedings and the threatened termination of funds.[59]

In the infrequent case when the Office of Education withheld funds, the action could backfire. In Anadilla, Georgia, for example, the school district lost $200,000 in federal funds in 1969. Except for $25,000 all this money had been used for black students in black schools. The community managed to raise the $25,000 for the white schools, but the money going to the black was just gone so far as the white community was concerned. In 1968, when HEW cut off ESEA funds in Coahoma, Mississippi, because the school board did not submit a suitable desegregation plan, seventy-one teachers were fired. Most of the seventy-one were black and had been hired with Title I money. David Seldon, president of the American Federation of Teachers, suggested, "This occurrence which fires only black teachers and black personnel being paid from Federal funds, is hardly accidental. It is simply a cruel form of reprisals."[60] Black teachers and black children lost out, not whites. HEW, though acknowledging the truth of such observations, claimed in this kind of a case that the permanent gain of integration "far outweighs the temporary loss of Federal programs which comparatively few Negro children must suffer."[61]

Jake Ayers of the Mississippi Freedom Democratic Party pointed to the inevitable result of the government's policy. Faced with the possible loss of benefits for their children, Negro parents were likely to keep quiet.[62] Since HEW mainly depended on public complaints to find out what was happening in southern schools, the failure of blacks to inform HEW about the way ESEA was being used was important. Without it HEW could not even form an accurate picture of southern compliance.[63] Information that states sent on to HEW on the operation of ESEA was imprecise. There were, for example, no required breakdowns on the racial composition of individual Title I projects but only over-all break-downs.[64] HEW had no quantitative way of discovering whether their funds maintained segregation. All too often it appeared from testimony and studies of civil rights organizations that they did.

HEW officials had focused their attention initially on desegregation problems in the South. As it turned out, the first big test of HEW's authority to pressure school districts to desegregate by withholding funds took place in Chicago. Examples of *de facto* segregation abounded in the North as the cores of central cities turned into black ghettos. But although segregation existed in both the North and South, there was no legal basis for efforts to overturn *de facto* segregation that had grown up informally. Nor was there wide public support for combatting this kind of segregation, even though in some states like New York the state board of education did push local school systems toward integration.[65] It was not surprising that the Office of Education had not formulated a policy to deal with the *de facto* situation.[66] But by the end of August 1965 HEW had received complaints of discrimination against fifteen northern school districts, and the Office of Education temporarily held up action on funds for these communities until they could investigate the charges. Keppel was reluctant to move, but the new secretary of HEW, John Gardner, was eager. As an associate recalled, he "seemed to have no trouble in deciding to go ahead."[67]

The decision was made to start with Chicago. On 4 July 1965 the Coordinating Council of Community Organizations, an energetic civil rights group, had sent massive, well-documented evidence charging both the Chicago School Board and Superintendent Benjamin Willis with consciously maintaining segregation.

In actuality it was Willis, Chicago's superintendent for the past thirteen years, who held most power in his hands and who had been responsible for most racial decisions.[68] In September the Office of Education investigating team began its work in Chicago. Not surprisingly, it found Willis uncooperative. Meanwhile, Congress passed its appropriations bill for the ESEA, and reports began to circulate on how Superintendent Willis planned to use his funds. Willis had chosen three target areas. Two of the three were white and included areas with a median yearly income of $8,000. Willis had also implied that he would use some of the money to buy mobile classrooms, disparagingly called "Willis Wagons" by those who realized that the classrooms were a method of avoiding desegregation.[69] Angry at this intended uses of ESEA funds, Keppel sent a letter on 30 September to the Illinois state superintendent. "Complaints of discrimination . . . have been filed with regard to the Chicago system," he wrote. "Some of the complaints are very complex and may require analysis over some period of time. The preliminary investigation of certain of the complaints, however, indicate probable noncompliance." Keppel indicated that until these complaints were cleared up, Chicago would not receive the $32 million in federal funds it expected.[70]

Keppel had hoped to solve the problems in Chicago quietly, but his hopes were shattered. Illinois's state superintendent demanded more information on the charges than the Office of Education had. Mayor Daley was furious at the interference with his city. On 3 October, when both he and the president were in New York, Daley spoke to Johnson. Johnson set Keppel and other HEW officials straight when he returned to the Capitol. The president's interest in providing opportunities for blacks did not include HEW use of muscle that might be politically embarrassing. Undersecretary of HEW Wilbur Cohen flew to Chicago immediately to free the funds.[71] Cohen did win a few desegregation concessions, but Illinois Representative Pucinski was right in describing the negotiations as "an abject surrender by Keppel—a great victory for local government, a great victory for Chicago."[72] The incident was certainly a great defeat to HEW's hopes to use fund cutoffs as a weapon against the North or South. HEW's publicized failure imbued the Office of Education with a strong sense of caution and sparked the hopes of those seeking a way around desegregation guidelines.[73]

It was hardly surprising that HEW found itself unwilling to force desegregation with Title I funds. The department lacked information, cooperation, and both administration and public backing. Congress, too, after the moment of consensus in passing the Civil Rights Act in 1964 and the Voting Rights Act of 1965, found itself once more divided over the race issue. In 1966 and 1967 there were attempts to amend the ESEA so that the commissioner of education could not deny a district suspected of noncompliance under the Civil Rights Act new funds until hearings had been held. Hearings meant delay while the suspected districts continued to receive federal money. In 1966 this amendment failed; but the next year it passed the House, and southern senators threatened a filibuster unless it was inserted in the Senate bill. The filibuster was avoided only when Secretary Gardner promised Senator Russell of Georgia and other southern senators that HEW would not cut off funds without giving at least six months' notice to the district.[74] Despite this concession, still another attempt to weaken HEW's enforcement powers took place in 1968 and in following years. HEW, sensitive to such attacks, could not push too hard for desegregation through Title I. The HEW evaluation report released in 1970 showed that Title I had indeed failed to bring racial mixing. The report indicated that in elementary grades at least 83 percent of Title I children were in classrooms where 90 percent or more of their classmates were of one race.[75]

Yet, other factors also contributed to the floundering efforts to desegrate public schools. In 1963, when administration planners had first considered poverty legislation, the race issue had been a major concern. The March on Washington, with its slogan of "Freedom Now," was clear warning that the black community demanded equal participation in American life. Martin Luther King's dream was one of an integrated society where blacks enjoyed equal job opportunities, equal legal rights, and integrated education.[76] But, as planners knew, the black community enjoyed few of these rights. In December 1963, for example, only 30,798 of the 2,901,671 black pupils in the Old South attended schools with white children. That year northern civil rights groups were trying to overturn *de facto* segregation in 75 cities in 18 states.[77] In October civil rights groups in Chicago staged a successful school boycott—successful in that 225,000 children stayed out of school while 8,000 adults protested at city hall.[78] Other cities followed suit; in February 1964 there were 364,000 absent from school in New York City.[79]

The War on Poverty and the ESEA had been an attempt to alleviate black pressure and to respond to the demands of the black community. But, as one black author commented in *Ebony* in August 1965, "Everywhere white opposition has braked the desegregation speed of the Great Society program and controlled its impact."[80] Local white groups had rapidly organized efforts to maintain their white neighborhood schools.[81] As the Chicago incident indicated, HEW found it difficult to press for its goals. Chicago was, in fact, a symbolic event for both white reformers and black civil rights groups. It had been Chicago civil rights groups who had protested Willis's superintendency, called for a five-day school boycott, and pressed ultimately for federal action.[82] But the result of federal action had been failure; the Office of Education did not even investigate complaints about *de facto* segregation for the next two years.[83] The possibility of King's dream was fading, and blacks knew it. Shortly after the resolution of the Chicago incident, a planning session took place for the proposed White House conference on the civil rights acts to be held the following summer. The session made it clear that blacks were keenly disappointed not only that the White House had caved in to Mayor Daley's pressure but that there were serious divisions among the civil rights groups themselves. As Daniel Moynihan observed, they had been unable to bring about any show of unity "*in effective demands on the administration.*"[84] By the final conference in June, delegates arrived to cries of "Uncle Toms" from militant pickets. The black movement was split.[85] As black writer Louis Lomax observed, "Roy Wilkins failed, James Farmer failed, Martin Luther King failed, Whitney Young failed. And Lyndon B. Johnson failed." Now, "wild, new, strange voices have moved into the leadership vacuum and we are headed for bloodshed and chaos."[86]

Absent from the June conference on civil rights was SNCC. As Stokely Carmichael, soon to be chairman of the organization, had stated a month before the conference, "Integration is irrelevant. Political and economic power is what the black people have to have."[87] Carmichael's statement suggested the slogan which would, that summer, replace "Freedom Now": "Black Power."[88] Black power, of course, meant a rejection of integration as a goal, as CORE made explicit in July when its convention rejected nonviolence and adopted Black Power rather than integration as the group's official policy.[89] As some civil rights groups moved left, others stayed in the center. The day after CORE's decision, the convention of the NAACP once more espoused integration and attacked the concept of Black Power. The Southern Christian Leadership Conference and the Urban League both clung to the old ideals.[90] As the black civil rights movement splintered, black ministers warned in the *New York Times* against "expanding our energies in spastic or ill-tempered explosion without meaningful goals." Explained Bayard Rustin, " 'Black Power' not only lacks any real value for the civil-rights movement, but its propagation is positively harmful. It diverts the movement from any meaningful debate over strategy and tactics, it isolates the Negro community, and it encourages the growth of anti-Negro forces."[91] Although Black Power groups might well disagree with Rustin's analysis, the collapse of the civil rights coalition was clearly harmful to efforts to implement the ESEA. Though the NAACP might continue to push for desegregation in the southern schools, civil rights groups no longer spoke with the authority of one voice. Disagreement on strategy and goals meant that blacks were unable to effectively pressure HEW and Congress to pursue desegregation. As Kenneth Clark later observed, black separatism was "a contributing factor in retarding the process of desegregation of the public schools."[92] Nor could the groups press firmly for increased funding for all black schools. Indeed, the disappearance of effective black pressure left government planners and administrators ever more vulnerable to white backlash in Congress and ever more on the defensive about their reforms.

The inequalities in the distribution of money and in the participation of Catholics and blacks in Title I services were problems plaguing the implementation of the ESEA. They stemmed from external factors over which planners could have no control and from the political compromises of 1964 and 1965 that planners had made. Although the decision to compromise had been pragmatic, the planners' vision of change within the system had also supported the idea that, in any case, compromises would not damage the bill's objectives. The way planners approached the issue of federal control shows the way in which they posited a fruitful relationship between compromise and reform. But as the ESEA began to operate, the limitations of this relationship became increasingly clear.

Opponents of federal aid had long argued that aid to education would have so many strings attached that the federal government would end up by running local schools and by deciding what should be taught. To calm these fears, the policy-planners worked out an arrangement that left substantial power and freedom at the state and local level. But they also wanted change on every level of the education ladder. Thus, they pictured an Office of Education, invigorated by reorganization and new obligations, creating the major outlines of the program and giving advice on the ESEA's operation. The states would receive Title V funds to bolster their education departments. With their power to pass on project applications and their desire to share in the federal bounty, state education departments would select projects carefully and ensure responsible local compliance. Accurate state reports sent to Washington would then enable federal officials to gauge the act's progress and to feed back helpful information to state and local communities so that they could better administer Title I. In this model, however, the greatest power and responsibility for the act obviously lay with local areas. Here projects were conceived and operated. Here federal money was actually spent. Here were the needy children. And here, too, were the schools, planners theorized, that would reshape themselves in order to help the poor. The bill giving local areas extensive freedom and power was, thus, a test case first for the planners' over-all theory of reform and compromise, and second for the theory of local control.

The test case failed. The Office of Education was never rejuvenated, and states were lax in fulfilling their supervisory role. Local school boards and superintendents, many studies suggest, showed little responsibility or initiative in their dealings with children of poverty. Local schools operated with only minimal changes. The relationship the bill's developers had constructed proved to be as much a mirage as were their hopes of eliminating poverty through education.

Those opposing federal aid had always maintained that the Office of Education held enough power to force its will on local communities. Actually, the Office of Education was traditionally weak; and though planners of the ESEA hoped to invigorate the Office, they changed the situation very little. At first glance the duties that the legislation assigned to the Office of Education seemed significant. The commissioner of education, for example, distributed money to local areas. But allocations were set by law, and this power was, therefore, insubstantial. More important than control of the purse, the commissioner could determine "basic criteria" for the projects funded under the act. Even in establishing basic guidelines, however, the Office of Education had had both to consult with state and local officials and to modify the criteria. Then, once it had developed the ground rules, the office had only tenuous control over the actual projects funded. States were obligated to send project applications to the office for approval before they received funds. But since these applications were only two-page letters of assurances by the state that local projects conformed to law, the Office of Education had no real opportunity to influence local projects or enough information to take action on what might be inadequate projects.[93]

The actual operational authority given to the Office of Education, then, was meager. The National Advisory Council reports of 1966 and 1969 concluded that the Office of Education had "found no way except through issuance of basic criteria and through exhortation to try to ensure sound projects or to secure revision of projects of low quality."[94] Most officials in the Office of Education found this approach congenial. They had not planned the bill. Keppel's reorganization had not infused the office with any new sense of mission.

As one official pointed out, "Other than making sure states got their money and making sure it was spent, there was no role for the Office of Education. I don't know anyone around here who wants to monitor. The Office of Education is not investigation-oriented, never has been and never will be."[95]

Moreover, federal officials were very eager to maintain friendly relations with states and local communities in this new experiment with federal aid. The desire for good relations was one factor that explained the office's hesitant race policy. In addition, administrators constantly feared that Congress would accuse the Office of Education of trying to control education and supplant the ESEA with a block grant to states allowing them to spend funds as they wished.[96] A block grant would rob the Office of Education of even its power to establish criteria or pass approval on projects. This fear was not without foundation. In 1967 Republican Albert Quie led a spirited attempt in the House to substitute a block grant for Title I. Although Quie's attempt failed, the threat remained real for policy-makers.

Generally, then, the Office of Education shied away from imposing its point of view on the states. Not until 1969 did it even carry on a review of Title I's operation in the states, and then did so only under pressure.[97] Although the act required states to evaluate their programs periodically and to report them to the commissioner of education, no one pushed this requirement. Massachusetts, for example, never fulfilled its obligations under the law.[98] The Office of Education feared arousing the states to cries of federal control. Nor did it think many states had a trained staff that could carry out an evaluation. Finally, the Office of Education was hesitant to push for evaluations, realizing that these might show the act was not working and, thus, would provide the enemies of federal aid with political ammunition.[99]

Even if the Office of Education did not require states to furnish detailed information on the ESEA, the office knew in a general way how it was operating. By 1971 the HEW Audit Agency had carried out audits in forty-one states to determine the ways in which they were spending Title I money.[100] As the National Advisory Council said in its 1971 report,

these audits clearly showed instances of "naivete, inexperi-
ence, confusion, despair and even clear violations of the
law."[101] The second audit report of Massachusetts, for instance, found that the state did not even have written guidelines for its own audits on local communities and had audited
local areas irregularly or not at all. Because of poor management, Massachusetts had failed to use over $1 million a year
of Title I money.[102] The HEW Audit Agency forwarded such
findings to the Office of Education. But until 1970 the Office of
Education never even filed a suit against a state for noncompliance with the ESEA. Even then the office did not withhold funds.[103] Instead, it urged states to take corrective steps.
Superintendents felt free to ignore such gentle pressure.[104]
Massachusetts's Title I director said, the Office of Education
"won't come out flatly and say what you can't do. I don't
feel any kind of control. It just isn't there."[105]

In fiscal year 1971 the Office of Education finally moved to
recover $381,497 of misused funds from Wisconsin, Illinois,
Ohio, Oregon, and Utah. The success of this modest move
encouraged the office to demand repayment of $5.6 million in
misspent funds from seven more states. Maintaining that
government auditors had "found no error in terms of fraud,
dishonesty or bad faith," Commissioner Marland confessed
that states had misused about $30 million of Title I money
since the act's passage. An HEW confidential internal report,
"not to be made available even upon request, to members
of the press and the general public," set the figure above
$7.8 billion.[106] Though Marland was after only a fraction of
the misused funds, this unexpected action met resistance from
three of the seven states. Chief state school officers in California, Washington, and Arizona stood by their own audits.
The comments of one of the Arizona officials were typical.
There was room for discussion, the official claimed, on only
10 percent of the total sum the office wanted Arizona to repay.
"Unless they can produce new evidence, we are convinced
we couldn't owe anymore." He continued, "There are no
provisions in our state laws for repayment of funds to the
Federal Government . . . and we haven't been advised by
the Government of any alternatives."[107] Although the outcome

of the Office of Education's position was unclear, the examples
of past stands did not encourage hope.

For example, the Office of Education has occasionally tried
to influence the administration of the ESEA by issuing guidelines. In most cases the guidelines meet overwhelming local
and state opposition. Faced with stiff resistance, the Office of
Education characteristically backs down. As Dr. Nolan Estes,
associate commissioner for elementary and secondary education, recalled, "We have time and time again attempted
to establish criteria in Title I . . . that would provide a more
significant return and each time we have attempted to do this,
there have been pressures, there have been forces brought to
bear which substantially nullify the impact or the influence
that we have had in this area."[108]

The office's attempts to have Title I concentrated on funding
projects for some disadvantaged children rather than spreading them thin to include a larger number shows the process
of gradual withdrawal under pressure. The early draft of the
1965 guidelines contained a provision that implied concentration of funds. As Congress and interest groups complained, Keppel decided to "slenderize" the requirements.
Later, on 14 April 1967, the office made another attempt by
issuing criteria suggesting that the amount spent on each
Title I child should equal about half the sum that both the
state and local area spent educating the child.[109] This indicated a substantial concentration of Title I funds which became increasingly important as it became clear that appropriations would not increase because of the war. Within
ten days local and state complaints to Congress forced the
office to retreat from this stand. The office now released a
"clarifying" memorandum stating that its discussion guides
were to provide "guidance" and might "not be fully applicable to every project application."[110] Another strong draft
memorandum on the issue never got off Commissioner Howe's
desk on 20 November 1968. Political pressure resulted in
rewriting and emasculation. The final memorandum issued
later the same day merely encouraged state school officers
to plan their programs "so that by 1970 the average Title I
expenditure per child in high priority areas is raised to a

significant level."[111] The states were left to interpret the key terms. Eventually Congress wrote concentration requirement into law but delayed its implementation until 1972. Clearly, the Office of Education guided neither Congress nor the states and local communities.

Even if the Office of Education had had the aggressive drive or the formal powers to impose its interpretation of Title I on the country, its staff was inadequate to carry out an active policy. As of January 1970, there were no more than thirty professionals working on all areas of Title I. Such a small staff could hardly furnish advice to local areas forming their projects or check up on Title I operations even had it wished.[112] Until 1970 the Office had only three area desk officers for the whole country, who had other responsibilities in addition to their Title I work. One area desk officer described his job as one "of trouble-shooting, answering complaints, and providing services." He admitted he had no time to find out what was happening at the state level, and that he thus depended on the good will of state officials for his information.[113]

The states realized that their powers were superior to those the Office of Education wielded. The relationship had always been unequal, and the states approved. In 1968 the Council of Chief State School Officers gave its interpretation of the appropriate federal role in education. "The Federal Government should assist the states financially, but it should not seek to require uniformity . . . through regulation or other techniques affecting eligibility of state or local educational agencies to receive federal funds."[114] The ESEA had essentially confirmed this view.

If HEW theoretically had areas of control, so too did the states. The act had entrusted the states with vital responsibilities. First, they were to see that Title I operated as intended on the local level, and, second, they were to report to HEW on the programs. Authorized to approve or reject local projects and to ensure that money really went to deprived children, the states were also responsible for evaluating projects and concluding how effectively local areas spent Title I money. The state thus seemed to stand in a crucial position to enforce the bill on the local level and to control what information got to Washington.

Studies show that although each state was different, few of them lived up to their administrative or supervisory obligations under the legislation. In 1971 the National Advisory Council reported, "There are few examples of exemplary state administrative techniques."[115] The HEW Audit Agency found evidence of poor management in twenty-five of thirty-eight states audited. In twelve out of fifteen states, the state department of education did not audit local areas effectively.[116] Ohio's local audits, for example, consisted of verifications that it had proof of cash receipts and local expenditures.[117] Moreover, states did not take the critical job of reviewing project applications seriously. The Center for Urban Education's study of New York disclosed that New York approved projects that had no objectives or means of implementation. The board never tried to discover how schools were selected to participate in local projects. Nor did it ever make constructive suggestions on the proposals. In one project, for example, the board's comment was merely that the supplementary reading was out of date and uninteresting. The research staff concluded that the New York board had "never to our knowledge, refused even one approval of a project."[118] Other studies and one HEW audit made the same point.[119]

States also failed to oversee the operation of projects. In 1970 the comptroller general issued a study of Ohio that gave a picture of state indifference to Title I. Cleveland worked out a special arts project for 1,500 educationally deprived children for the summer of 1968. Since the city was apparently planning to open the project to all children, the state board turned down Cleveland's application twice. Finally, on 31 May, the state approved the city's application, which now answered some of the board's criticisms. After that, however, the state never bothered to see whether the project went according to plan. It did not. Only 593 students took part, and of those students an estimated 71 percent were not educationally deprived. Title I monies were in essence misspent.[120]

When the federal government drew such information to a state's attention there was no assurance of change. In a special report to the Office of Education in March 1969, the HEW Audit Agency outlined administrative weaknesses and evidence of misused funds that their audits had uncovered. In each case state and federal officials discussed the audit findings, giving the state the opportunity to justify its actions. Occasionally, states made necessary changes. Some did nothing. In four states a second audit showed the same violations as the first audit had uncovered.[121] Indiana was an extreme example of recalcitrance. There "the state representatives did not avail themselves of the opportunity to discuss the findings and recommendations presented in our report at the exit conference arranged for that purpose. They stated, instead, that they wished to be quoted as neither agreeing or disagreeing with our findings and recommendations."[122]

So, although the state had more power than the federal government had over the ESEA, it did not exercise its authority effectively over local districts. The 1971 National Advisory Council drew attention to this point. "Only in a few states," the report stated, "is there significant interaction between the SEA (state educational agency) and LEA (local educational agencies)."[123] Too often the state neither knew how money was spent nor whether projects were successful.[124] In the absence of information there could be no organized effort to improve projects.

There were several reasons why the states did not live up to their responsibilities. State departments of education, like their federal counterpart, are understaffed. Although Title I set aside 1 percent of the state's Title I grant to pay administrative and evaluation costs, this sum was too small to have real impact on departments of education. In 1968 Massachusetts, for example, received a mere $160,000. The state had only five full-time people working on more than 440 Title I projects.[125] With other duties this staff could not even hope to visit the many projects during the year. It certainly could not do a thorough investigation to see how Title I was working in local communities. The National Advisory Council's 1972 report saw this as a general problem, since its research showed forty states were unable to check yearly on Title I programs in their local districts.[126] But more important than understaffing was the attitude normally pervading state education departments. Although each department saw its own authority as surpassing that of the federal government, it viewed itself as submissive to local and state capital pressures. On the one hand, state education departments have rarely had much power over local districts and the way these districts spend their money. And on the other, state legislators have often controlled the state education department. Discussing charges of laxity against state education departments, the *New York Times* commented in 1969,

> Unfortunately, the charges sound plausible. The educational outlook of too many state departments remains routinely conservative. Dominant political pressures on these education officials, many of whom continue to be elected on political party tickets, come from legislatures whose philosophies are at once antiurban and neglectful of chronic rural poverty areas. With much of the control over the distribution of funds in the hands of these conservative power centers, the interests of the urban and rural poor are often badly served.[127]

In reality, it was the local areas that had the most critical role to play in implementing Title I and that provided a test case of whether local control worked. And the actions of local communities would show how accurately government planners saw the mechanism of reform. Local communities selected eligible areas for Title I projects, identified educationally deprived children, and submitted project applications to the state for its approval. And most important, local communities carried the projects out. Power rested with local leaders. Fewer than 10 percent of local areas were subjected to audit reviews.[128] Under the formula arrangement allocation of money was more or less automatic. A local area had neither to compete for funds nor to match them.[129] Nor did it have to do much to deserve them.

The way in which local areas viewed federal funds was, therefore, an important factor in how Title I money would be spent. In 1966 one statistical survey of local and state officials revealed that 70 percent felt that Title I funds should not be allocated on the basis of poverty.[130] The implication was clear. Local authorities wanted federal money with no

strings attached. Chicago's Superintendent Willis exemplified the underlying attitude of many local leaders. In a 1965
interview Willis commented, "I think that once money is col-
lected by the federal government it should be used to finance
things that are for the benefit of people generally. When these
funds are redistributed, they should be considered as shared
taxes. I don't think they should be. handled as though you
were finding money in the sky and then distributing it to people who didn't have any part in producing it. . . . The actual
control over the expenditure of school funds should be kept
as localized as possible."[131]

Sensing this mood, the National Advisory Council feared
as early as 1966 that Title I funds would be spent on all children rather than just deprived children.[132] In its 1971 report
the council noted that using Title I funds as general aid was
a recurring violation and suggested that there was an "apparent lack of compliance mindedness."[133] Other reports and
congressional hearings substantiated the accusation that local areas often used federal funds in this way.

An investigation of New Jersey carried out by the comptroller general's office focused on Camden in the study because it suspected that the city used a large part of its Title I
allocation as general aid. The study revealed several problems.
First, Title I administrators spent $240,000 for projects in
areas that did not even have the required concentration of
deprived children. Federal officials commented that the "Title
I coordinator informed us that the selection of school attendance areas for participation in the Title I program was based
primarily on his general knowledge of economic deprivation
in the city. The basis for the selection was not documented
although documentation was required by Title I regulations."[134] Second, Camden officials admitted that they thought
it was acceptable to spend 15 percent of Title I funds for
schools outside the project area. They claimed that the state
department of education had informed them this was acceptable practice.[135]

The study reviewed local project applications that the state
had approved from fiscal year 1966 through fiscal year 1969.
Some of these projects definitely were intended to aid all

children. Camden officials disclosed that they had not determined the special educational needs that projects were to
meet. The Title I coordinator noted that, in his opinion, all
Camden children needed services because the system did not
have a multiethnic textbook, enough audiovisual aides or
supplementary research material, or physical education for
elementary children. Thus, Title I funds supported physical
education for all students in the fourth, fifth, and sixth grades
and in six of the nine private schools.[136]

The report concluded, "We believe that, if the New Jersey
SEA (state educational agency) had conducted adequate reviews of the Camden . . . project applications, monitored
project operations, and utilized the . . . evaluation reports
to improve program effectiveness, many of the weaknesses in
the . . . Title I program . . . could have been avoided."[137]

Other studies confirmed the Camden picture. Title I benefits went to children who really did not need them. The HEW
survey of elementary schools for 1967-68, which was the
largest study of the ESEA, pointed out that Title I benefited
a larger number of scholastically able children from economically solid families than disadvantaged children. In
cities of over 500,000, 18 percent of Title I children came
from such backgrounds. In the suburbs over half of the children receiving Title I services were not disadvantaged.[138]

Many community projects showed poor planning and, not
surprisingly, little knowledge of the problem of treating educational deprivation. Local people just did not have the commitment or the know-how to live up to the many responsibilities the ESEA created. Of course, in 1964, the formulators
of the bill themselves had had little idea of how to deal with
educational problems of poverty, and they had provided
little guidance for local communities. Yet, unless local areas
planned carefully and creatively, unless they were flexible
enough to modify their own school systems that had neglected
the poor for so long, any impact the ESEA might have on
poor children would be minimal.

Unfortunately, local areas were not able to meet the challenges the ESEA posed. In the first year of the ESEA this
failure was predictable. Local districts were inexperienced in

the task of formulating and implementing projects aimed at their needy students. Since money came late in the school year, local districts had to think up ways to use their allocations quickly. Of necessity many initiated summer projects and made substantial investments in equipment and construction.[139] In 1966-67, the first full year of ESEA funds, there was less emphasis on equipment and construction. The proportion of Title I money spent on these categories dropped from 21 percent to 12.7 percent. At the same time money going for instruction rose from 51.6 percent of total funds to 65.8 percent.[140]

There were, of course, a great variety of projects established in the course of five years. Some provided instruction in remedial arithmetic; others reduced class size, initiated individual tutoring, or tried to foster positive self-images in their pupils. Remedial reading classes were a favorite. In 1967–68, 47 percent of money spent for Title I instruction in elementary schools went to special reading programs.[141]

Other projects supported services like guidance counseling. Eighty percent of Title I programs included some health care.[142] Helpful as such activities sounded, they often were poorly planned and lacked clear goals. In looking over New York City project proposals, the Center of Urban Education noted that "one is struck by the lack of conformity between statements of objectives located in different sections of the proposals, as well as by the difference in the degree to which they are specified. In addition, the proposals list the objectives without any explicit indication of their relative importance."[143] This kind of poor planning and uncertain direction had predictable results. Many Title I programs offered deprived children little that was new. Evidence from two years of Title I programs in large city schools, for instance, indicated minimal change in traditional teaching practices.[144] A regional laboratory survey of Title I showed that over half of the Title I teachers had no special training in dealing with educationally deprived children.[145] The HEW survey of elementary schools reported that 70 percent of Title I children received less than four hours of academic instruction a week.[146] In 1967 a group within HEW, troubled by lackluster programming, formed the Committee to Form Strategy for Improving Title I. The group commented that "the record shows that the Title I program is fast bogging down to nothing more than an extra teacher or two, a few more trips into town, or a few minutes a day with [a] remedial reading teacher. The Office of Education is in danger of losing its chance to provide leadership in the education of hard-core disadvantaged children as our program settles with fixed general aid."[147] Despite this genuine concern, the National Advisory Council concluded in 1968, "only a small portion [of Title I money] was spent on genuinely new approaches to guiding and stimulating learning."[148]

These miscellaneous, poorly directed, often inadequately funded programs offered little chance of breaking the pattern of failure and educational weakness that poverty children exhibited. HEW Secretary Robert Finch told assembled congressmen in 1969, "As I say, from the massive evidence we have, I do not think we can claim unqualified success. . . . Many curriculum developers are not aware of the best methods of meeting the educational needs of poverty children. Schools and school districts differ greatly in their capacity to provide quality educational programs for disadvantaged children."[149]

Yet, few denied that some ESEA programs were promising in raising achievement levels. In 1969, using careful work by the American Institutes of Research, the National Advisory Council published its conclusions on successful Title I programs. After studying a sample of 1,000 programs, the council decided that only 21, or 2 percent, were successful. Its "highly restricted" definition of success meant that Title I children made measurable gains in language or arithmetical skills when compared with scores of a similar control group.[150] The features that the council isolated as producing these results included careful planning of programs with clearly stated objectives and small groups with intensive instruction and teacher training. The study concluded that mere service without planning would not work and the addition of teachers without training would not result in "real compensatory education."[151] The council's findings also implied that effective compensatory education would be expensive. Since Title I provided only $120 per child in 1969, local areas would have to concentrate their funds for results unless the government increased appropriations dramatically, which was unlikely for the duration of the Vietnam war. Yet, local districts did not concentrate funds. In the 1967–68 school year HEW estimated that about $68 per child was spent on reading skills, $23 on mathematics, and $27 on cultural enrichment.[152] These meager sums hardly added up to strong programs.

The operation of the ESEA was a disappointing commentary on the possibilities of local control. Local control in this case meant careless administration and programming and only a halfhearted commitment to serve the poor whom federal planners sought to help. In 1967 Robert Kennedy summed up his impression of the ESEA. "I will say this from my experiences in travelling around in these communities. I question whether anything is being accomplished in a major way. . . . I also very seriously question whether the people in the ghettos feel that anything is really being done."[153]

The people in the ghettos, however, reacted to the failure of local leaders to respond to poverty problems. Like the Economic Opportunity Act and perhaps because of it, the ESEA proved to be an opportunity for certain groups of the poor to mobilize. This was, from the original planners' point of view, an unexpected result of the bill, since they had visualized reform from within, not as a result of outside pressure.[154] Local authorities were bitter about the confrontation. The assistant superintendent of the Hicksville, New York, public schools expressed the prevailing feeling:

> As I travel about the country, I see a crescendo of bitter disagreements about the whole underlying purpose and concept of ESEA Title I expenditures. . . . Local poverty groups have appointed themselves prosecutor, judge, and jury, and have bitterly blasted many fine schoolmen with wild charges about misappropriation and misuse of ESEA funds. They have tried smear campaigns and terrorist activities in some communities in an attempt to force local school administrators to use ESEA funds only in ways which are acceptable to these local poverty leaders.[155]

The assistant superintendent overstated the organization and power of local poverty groups. But both federal and local government began to feel the uncomfortable new awareness of the poor. In 1967 community groups appearing at House hearings asked for increased community participation in Title I programs. Money was misused locally they claimed; the board of education had "deaf ears." Because the power structure was unresponsive to the poor, the ESEA was failing.[156] A year later, Commissioner Howe invited sixteen poverty representatives to Washington to discuss their complaints. "We spent considerable time discussing the operation of Title I," Howe recalled.[157] Once again, representatives had a clear idea of what their grievances were. The federal government, they said, had to put its foot down. Money for the board of education was money down the drain since the board did not solve poverty problems. In fact, "middle-class people are benefitting just as much from federal funds as the poverty stricken people." "Can we get the power to implement these things ourselves?", they asked.[158]

The NAACP and the Washington Research Project sensed the growing militancy of local community and poverty groups. In 1969 they added fuel to the fire by releasing the McClure Report, a scathing expose of how Title I funds were mismanaged and misused at local, state, and federal levels. The report gave examples of the failure of local officials to involve parents and give them information on Title I.[159] Testimony of the poor before the Senate subcommittee in 1969 confirmed the picture.[160] One Harlem father explained that the poor were coming to view the ESEA as "a first step for community control."[161]

The voices of the poor began to get some results in Washington. The McClure Report jolted the Office of Education into adding twenty more professionals to its staff.[162] Howe's 1968 meeting with the sixteen representatives of the poor "reinforced the Commissioner's decision to provide for involvement of the poor in federal programs through specific regulations and guidelines."[163] The commissioner could not require participation of poor groups since the ESEA only provided for "cooperation" between school boards and com-

munity action groups.[164] But HEW did issue a series of memorandums to encourage parent involvement. On 14 April 1967
the Office of Education had already called for "appropriate"
parent participation. Almost a year later (18 March 1968),
HEW suggested that parents be included "in the early stages
of programs planning and in discussions concerning the
needs of children in eligible attendance areas." But on 2 July
1968 the Office of Education went too far. Its memo stated
that "local Advisory Committees . . . need to be established." Predictably, the office retreated from this bold position
seventeen days later under pressure from local, state, and
congressional groups. The final memo in this series, dated
30 October 1971, merely provided for "system wide" parent
councils. As usual, the Office of Education had succumbed to
the public school lobby. But now the poor, too, had become
a pressure group, and had prevented the Office of Education
from retreating completely from its position on parent participation. As one member of the NEA remarked, the Office
of Education "has been getting pressure from some groups
I've never heard of. I don't know whether they represent a
constituency or not." Moreover, failure to achieve parent
participation through guidelines instigated HEW to push for
changes in the act itself.[165]

Local poverty and community action groups also exerted
pressure. In New York City, for example, the New York
Council Against Poverty and local educational committees
tried to negotiate with the Board of Education so that they
could consult on Title I plans. Although the board agreed to
make a "reasonable" effort to cooperate, community groups
wanted more power than the board was willing to yield.[166]
Decentralization in 1968 aided local groups, but the struggle
was unresolved. As the Urban Research Center observed, "The
great potential for local community participation had not been
realized even in those projects specifically designed for the
purpose."[167]

In other areas, however, local poverty groups were able to
organize effectively and to force some response from local
and state leaders. In Providence, Rhode Island, the persis-
tence of Patricia Overberg, chairman of the Title I Parents

Advisory Committee, led to significant victories over local officials. Local officials initially picked Mrs. Overberg to be chairman of the committee. She later confessed, "I didn't even know what Title I was. . . . They figured . . . I'd be a good parent." But Mrs. Overberg soon dispelled this hope. At the first meeting as a parent advisor, Mrs. Overberg "learned that Title I was for children from five to seventeen. Then at my second meeting all they talked about was spending Title I money on adult education. There was disagreement, but not over spending the money on adults. I hopped up and said if there are only supposed to be children in the Title I program, it seems to me you'd be breaking the law. That stopped the adult-education thing, but not one of those experts and professionals had mentioned the law all day. That started me thinking."[168]

Mrs. Overberg, a natural activist, built up a small group of supporters from among these attending the advisory meetings. By 1969 the group attempted to win veto power over project applications and soon went on to investigate alleged Title I violations in the city. Despite the hostility of much of the board and the school superintendent, the group sued city, state, and local officials in September 1970. The suit enumerated several accusations: that parents, except for 1970, had never been able to examine Title I proposals; that the concentration formula allowed any child to participate in programs if he lived in certain areas; that officials used Title I funds to pay for services that state funds supported in other school districts.[169]

Sensing that Title I was a vehicle that could force a response from local leaders and that might furnish a clothing allowance that it had been unable to get from the welfare department, the National Welfare Rights Organization supported Overberg's efforts.[170] The welfare organization was able to get Title I officials to use $96,000 of their Title I grant for school clothing. Parents agreed with the NWRO that clothes were important to the child's self-image and the teacher's view of the child. Once the grant was won, parents and children cooperated with the Brown University Department of Sociology, which studied the clothing program. The study of parent and student attitudes, then, supported this use of Title I money but held that the $48 allowance per child needed to be increased "so that a greater positive effect on children might be made." One victory had laid the groundwork for another. The superintendent agreed to continue clothing grants for an additional year.[171]

Other local parent groups, sometimes triggered by middle-class activists, also confronted the local educational establishment in court. Using the ESEA as their weapon, they won some significant victories. In October 1970 the Federal District Court in Maine handed down a decision which confirmed that Title I parents did have the right to bring suit to enforce Title I in federal courts.[172] The parents, spurred on by a young lawyer in Calais, claimed that school authorities misused some Title I funds as general aid. A year and a half later, the court settled the case by providing for an elected Parents Advisory Committee for Title I with powers to help develop proposals, receive evaluations of programs, and hear complaints. In San Jose, California, another suit against the school district resulted in a consent decree establishing guidelines for parental participation in Title I projects.[173] Slow as the judicial method is, it provided one tool with which poor people and their advocates could force middle-class power groups to respond to their demands.

Although most Title I parents did not form pressure groups, those who did implicitly questioned the political compromises made to pass the ESEA and the model of reform underlying them. The rigidity of the local educational power structures, their unwillingness to respond to poverty, were exposed. Reform of the educational establishment would be difficult because pressure had to come from the poor themselves. Then, too, the actions of poverty groups suggested that reform of the educational establishment might have unexpected results. As parents tried to win a voice in community decision-making, they sometimes sought ends that were not strictly educational. The decision to use Title I funds for clothing grants was not welcome to educators, who felt that "the funds that are available to them are better spent on items directly related to education, such as books and teachers."[174] Parent groups also occasionally pushed out educators and teachers, not because they were incompetent, but because their color or attitudes were unacceptable.[175] The process of reform and change led in different educational and political directions than the planners of the ESEA had expected and exposed the weakness of the administrative and intellectual framework planners had accepted.

The first five years of the ESEA brought to life problems concerning money, religion, race, and federal-state-local relations just as opponents of federal aid had prophesied. In most cases, however, the problems were the opposite of those conservatives envisioned. Catholics did not get their share of Title I funds, blacks did not push their way into white schools, and the Office of Education did not dominate state and local authorities. Local areas used funds as they wished. In many ways, the ESEA had realized the conservatives' dreams.

But for the liberals, the dream had ended. In 1970 one of the act's developers wrote, "The euphoria of 1965 has now given way to grim soul searching."[176] The original faith that once the public school system received the dollars it craved, it would reform from within and reach out to poor children whom it had neglected for so long, now seemed naïve. The dream faded because policy-makers never questioned whether education could solve poverty, because they never faced up to the nature of the public school system, because they made a series of damaging political compromises under-girded by an inaccurate model of reform. It faded because national priorities shifted, pressure groups splintered, and the political climate changed. Some wondered "if the ESEA has yet had a fair trial."[177] Many would argue because of the war it had not. Others, pointing to the act's internal weaknesses, would argue it had. But fair trial or no, the promises of the legislation left many of the poor "embittered." They had seen "precious little change for the better in the quality of their children's education."[178]

1. *Public Papers of the Presidents of the United States: Lyndon B. Johnson, 1965*, 1:415–17.

2. Stephen K. Bailey and Edith K. Mosher, *ESEA*, pp. 72–97.

3. Ibid., pp. 106–7, 110–13. See also U.S. Dept. of Health, Education, and Welfare, Office of Education, *History of Title I, ESEA*, p. 19.

4. National Advisory Council on the Education of Disadvantaged Children, "Summer Education for the Children of Poverty" (unpublished, 1966), p. 1.

5. *Hearings before the Committee on Education and Labor on the Extension of Elementary and Secondary Education Programs*, 91st Cong., 1st Sess., 1969, House, p. 5.

6. National Advisory Council on the Education of Disadvantaged Children, *Title I—ESEA: A Review and a Forward Look—1969*, p. 22, and *House Hearings*, 1969, p. 2912.

7. Quoted in Jerome T. Murphy, "Title I of ESEA," p. 41.

8. Department of Health, Education, and Welfare, "History of the Office of Education" (unpublished, Lyndon Baines Johnson Library, no date), appendix, p. 8.

9. *Hearings before the General Subcommittee on Education of the Committee on Education and Labor on the Elementary and Secondary Education Amendments of 1966*, 89th Cong., 2d Sess., 1966, House, p. 814.

10. U.S. Department of Health, Education, and Welfare, Office of Education, *Education of the Disadvantaged: An Evaluative Report on Title I Elementary and Secondary Education Act of 1965, Fiscal year 1968*, p. 18.

11. Ibid., p. 15. The document defines as a low-expenditure district one that spends less than $425 per pupil from non-federal sources. A high-expenditure district spends more than $625.

12. Ibid., p. 9.

13. Ibid., p. 85.

14. John A. De Silva, "The First Year of the Elementary and Secondary Education Act, p. 21.

15. *Congressional Record*, 91st Cong., 2d Sess., 1970, p. 8494.

16. *House Hearings*, 1966, p. 77.

17. Ibid., p. 85.

18. John C. Donovan, *The Politics of Poverty*, pp. 117–20.

19. Allan C. Ornstein, *Race and Politics in School/Community Organizations*, p. 76; Nathan Glazer, "The Great Society Was Never a Casualty of the War," p. 51.

20. *Hearings before the Committee on Education and Labor on the Elementary and Secondary Education Act Amendment of 1967*, 90th Cong., 1st Sess., 1967, House, p. 228.

21. Ibid., p. 221.

22. *Hearings before the General Subcommittee on Education of the Committee on Labor and Public Welfare on Education Legislation*, 1967, 90th Cong., 1st Sess., 1967, Senate, pp. 1287–88.

23. *House Hearings*, 1969, pp. 2844, 363.

24. *Hearings before the Subcommittee on Education of the Committee on Labor and Public Welfare on the Elementary and Secondary Education Amendments of 1961*, 91st Cong., 1st Sess., 1969, Senate, p. 173.

25. Eugene Eidenberg and Roy D. Morey, *An Act of Congress*, p. 180; see also pp. 186–202.

26. Robert Lekachman, "The Cost in National Treasure, $400,000,000 Plus," p. 48.

27. Public Law 89-10, Sec. 205.(a)(2).

28. Memorandum to the president, 1964, Executive File, Le/Fa 2, Lyndon Baines Johnson Library.

29. *Hearings before the Subcommittee on Education of the Committee on Labor and Public Welfare on the Elementary and Secondary Education Act of 1966,* 89th Cong., 2d Sess., 1966, Senate, p. 383.

30. National Advisory Council, *Titile I—ESEA: A Review* p. 35.

31. *House Hearings,* 1969, p. 2291.

32. Barbara R. Heller and Richard S. Barrett, *Expand and Improve: A Critical Review of the First Three Years of ESEA Title I in New York City,* p. 146. $21,450,000 was to be used for both private and public children together. See also Jacob Landers, "An Investigation of the Implementation of Title I of the Elementary and Secondary Education Act of 1965 in New York City during the Fiscal Year 1966," pp. 192–94.

33. *House Hearings,* 1969, p. 2182, 2173.

34. National Advisory Council, *Title I—ESEA: A Review* appendix B, pp. 1–3.

35. *House Hearings,* 1969, p. 2176.

36. Ibid., p. 2178.

37. Ibid., p. 2166.

38. Ibid., p. 2165. The National Advisory Council's 1972 report saw the problem as still unresolved. See the National Advisory Council, *Educating the Disadvantaged Child,* p. 15.

39. James W. Guthrie, "A Political Case History," p. 303.

40. Gary Orfield, *The Reconstruction of Southern Education,* pp. 94–95.

41. Bailey and Mosher, *ESEA,* p. 145.

42. Ibid., p. 147.

43. Orfield, *The Reconstruction of Southern Education,* pp. 109–13.

44. *Public Papers: Lyndon B. Johnson, 1965,* 2:957.

45. Orfield, *The Reconstruction of Southern Education,* p. 113.

46. David Seely, "Southern Desegregation," p. 28.

47 *House Hearings,* 1967, p. 335.

48. Ruby Martin and Phyllis McClure, *Title I of the ESEA,* p. 21.

49. *Senate Hearings,* 1967, pp. 2341, 2346.

50. Ibid., p. 2346.

51. Ruby Martin and Phyllis McClure, *Title I of the ESEA,* 2d ed., p. 16.

52. *Senate Hearings,* 1967, p. 2346.

53. Martin and McClure, *Title I,* 1st ed., p. 21.

54. *Senate Hearings,* 1967, p. 2347. See Martin and McClure, *Title I,* 2d ed., pp. 12, 72. Also see *The Status of School Desegregation in the South, 1970.*

55. Orfield *The Reconstruction of Southern Education,* p. 260; *Senate Hearings,* 1967, p. 2347.

56. Orfield, *The Reconstruction of Southern Education,* pp. 113, 115–16.

57. Congressional Quarterly Service, *Congressional Quarterly Almanac, 1966* (Washington, D.C.: Congressional Quarterly Service, 1967), p. 478.

58. U.S. Commission on Civil Rights, *Federal Enforcement of School Desegregation* (Washington, D.C.: Government Printing Office, 1969), p. 9.

59. Ibid., p. 7.

60. *House Hearings*, 1969, p. 2439.

61. *Senate Hearings*, 1969, p. 220.

62. Ibid., p. 348.

63. *House Hearings*, 1969, p. 1623.

64. *Senate Hearings*, 1967, pp. 2360–62.

65. Orfield, *The Reconstruction of Southern Education*, p. 152. See Robert L. Crain, *The Politics of School Desegregation*, pp. 66–67, also pp. 46–47. It should also be noted that towns and small- or medium-sized cities with small black populations did desegregate their schools with some success. See Robert J. Havighurst, "These Integration Approaches Work—Sometimes," p. 73.

66. Ibid., p. 168.

67. Ibid., p. 171.

68. Marilyn Gittell and T. Edward Hollander, *Six Urban School Districts*, pp. 190–91.

69. Orfield, *The Reconstruction of Southern Education*, p. 181.

70. Ibid., pp. 181–85; "The Keppel-Page Letter," p. 35.

71. Orfield, *The Reconstruction of Southern Education*, pp. 193–95; Bailey and Mosher, *ESEA*, pp. 152–53.

72. Orfield, *The Reconstruction of Southern Education*, p. 195.

73. Ibid., p. 153.

74. Congressional Quarterly Service, *Congressional Quarterly Almanac, 1967* (Washington, D.C.: Congressional Quarterly Service, 1968), p. 613. Memorandum from Mike Manotos to the president, 8 December 1967, Executive File Le/Fa 2, Lyndon Baines Johnson Library.

75. HEW, *Education of the Disadvantaged*, p. 36.

76. Lewis M. Killian, *The Impossible Revolution?*, p. 126; Benjamin Muse, *The American Negro Revolution*, p. 64.

77. Muse, *The American Negro Revolution*, p. 66.

78. Ibid., p. 68.

79. Ibid., pp. 112–13.

80. Quoted in Killian, *The Impossible Revolution?*, p. 86.

81. Muse, *The American Negro Revolution*, p. 116.

82. Orfield, *The Reconstruction of Southern Education*, pp. 164–65.

83. Ibid., p. 206.

84. Quoted in Killian, *The Impossible Revolution?*, p. 119.

85. Ibid., pp. 115–20; Muse, *The American Negro Revolution*, p. 258.

86. Muse, *The American Negro Revolution*, p. 124; for a picture of what was happening on the local level, see David Rogers, *110 Livingston Street*, chap. 4.

87. Killian, *The Impossible Revolution?*, pp. 120, 122; Allen J. Matusow, "From Civil Rights to Black Power: The Case of SNCC, 1960–1966," in Barton J. Bernstein and Allen J. Matusow, eds., *Twentieth-Century America*, pp. 533–56.

88. Killian, *The Impossible Revolution?*, p. 112.

89. Muse, *The American Negro Revolution*, p. 241.

90. Ibid., p. 230; Elliot Rudwick and August Meier, "Organizational Structure and Goal Succession: A Comparative Analysis of the NAACP and CORE, 1964–1968," in James A. Geschwender, ed., *The Black Revolt: The Civil Rights Movement, Ghetto Uprisings, and Separatism* (Englewood Cliffs, N.J.: Prentice-Hall, 1971), pp. 64–73.

91. Quoted in Muse, *The American Negro Revolution*, pp. 243–44.

92. Kenneth B. Clark, "Eighteen Years after Brown," p. 10.

93. Murphy, "Title I of ESEA," p. 40.

94. National Advisory Council, *Title I—ESEA: A Review*, p. 13.

95. Murphy, "Title I of ESEA," p. 40.

96. Ibid., pp. 44–45.

97. Martin and McClure, *Title I*, 1st ed., p. 96.

98. Samuel H. Beer and Richard E. Barringer, eds., *The State and the Poor*, pp. 229–30.

99. Murphy, "Title I of ESEA," p. 43.

100. National Advisory Council on the Education of Disadvantaged Children, *Title I, ESEA—The Weakest Link*, p. 2.

101. Ibid.

102. Murphy, "Title I of ESEA," pp. 54–55.

103. National Advisory Council, *Title I, ESEA—The Weakest Link*, p. 8.

104. Martin and McClure, *Title I*, 1st ed., p. 97.

105. Quoted in Murphy, "Title I of ESEA," p. 58.

106. *New York Times*, 6 September 1971; 19 September 1971; 12 September 1972.

107. Ibid., 19 September 1971.

108. HEW, "History of the Office of Education," appendix, p. 18.

109. Murphy, "Title I of ESEA," pp. 48–49.

110. Quoted in ibid., p. 49.

111. Ibid.

112. Howard A. Glickstein, "Federal Educational Programs and Minority Groups," p. 307.

113. Murphy, "Title I of ESEA," p. 42.

114. Quoted in Martin and McClure, *Title I*, 1st ed., p. 85.

115. National Advisory Council, *Title I, ESEA—The Weakest Link*, p. 13.

116. Martin and McClure, *Title I*, 2d ed., p. 50.

117. National Advisory Council, *Title I, ESEA—The Weakest Link*, p. 6. See also Martin and McClure, *Title I*, 1st ed., pp. 185–86.

118. Heller and Barrett, *Expand and Improve*, p. 46.

119. Martin and McClure, *Title I*, 1st ed., pp. 90–91; National Advisory Council, *Title I, ESEA—The Weakest Link*, p. 113.

120. Comptroller General of the United States, *Report to the Congress: Improvement Needed in Administration of the Federal Program of Aid to Educationally Deprived Children in Ohio*, pp. 10–13.

121. National Advisory Council, *Title I, ESEA—The Weakest Link*, p. 43.

122. Quoted in Martin and McClure, *Title I*, 1st ed., pp. 88–89.

123. National Advisory Council, *Title I, ESEA—The Weakest Link*, p. 13.

124. Beer and Barringer, *The State and the Poor*, p. 230.

125. Ibid., pp. 230, 233.

126. Murphy, "Title I of ESEA," p. 53; National Advisory Council, *Educating the Disadvantaged Child*, p. 15.

127. *New York Times*, 1 December 1969. For a picture of good state administration, See Frederick M. Wirt and Michael W. Kirst, *The Political Web of American Schools*, pp. 159–63.

128. National Advisory Council, *Title I—ESEA: A Review*, p. 43.

129. Murphy, "Title I of ESEA," p. 39.

130. Bailey and Mosher, *ESEA*, appendix C, pp. 306–7.

131. "Benjamin C. Willis: An Interview," *U.S. News and World Report*, pp. 38–39.

132. National Advisory Council, "Summer Education," p. 3.

133. National Advisory Council, *Title I, ESEA—The Weakest Link*, p. 2.

134. Comptroller General of the United States, *Report to Congress: Improved Administration Needed in New Jersey for the Federal Program of Aid to Educationally Deprived Children*, p. 11.

135. Ibid., pp. 14–15.

136. Ibid., pp. 19–20.

137. Ibid., p. 30. For similar incidents see Martin and McClure, *Title I*, 1st ed., pp. 12, 13, 30; Mark G. Yudof, "The New Deluder Act: A Title I Primer," p. 6; Heller and Barrett, *Expand and Improve*, p. 24. See also the case study of New York City: Landers, "An Investigation of the Implementation of Title I."

138. HEW, *Education of the Disadvantaged*, p. 97.

139. U.S. Department of Health, Education, and Welfare, Office of Education, *History of Title I, ESEA*, p. 26.

140. Ibid.

141. HEW, *Education of the Disadvantaged*, pp. 86–87.

142. National Advisory Council, *Title I—ESEA: A Review*, p. 7.

143. Heller and Barrett, *Expand and Improve*, p. 36.

144. Robert A. Dentler, "Urban Eyewash," p. 33.

145. National Advisory Council, *Title I, ESEA—The Weakest Link*, p. 1.

146. HEW, *Education of the Disadvantaged*, p. 101.

147. Quoted in Glickstein, "Federal Educational Programs," p. 305.

148. Quoted in ibid., p. 306.

149. *House Hearings*, 1969, p. 2833.

150. National Advisory Council, *Title I—ESEA: A Review*, p. 20; *Hearings before the General Subcommittee on Education of the Committee on Education and Labor on Emergency School Aid*, 91st Cong., 2d Sess., 1970, House, p. 372.

151. Ibid., pp. 23–24; see also Heller and Barrett, *Expand and Improve*, pp. 168–71.

152. HEW, *Education of the Disadvantaged*, p. 89.

153. *Senate Hearings*, 1967, p. 995.

154. Personal communication from Francis Keppel to the author, 5 July 1973.

155. Quoted in Frederick W. Hill, "More Fights Over Title I," *American School and University* 42 (January 1970): 18.

156. *House Hearings*, 1967, pp. 1553–57.

157. U.S. Department of Health, Education and Welfare, Office of Education, *Report of Meeting of 16 Representatives of Poor People with U.S. Commissioner of Education and Members of His Staff: October 22–23, 1968, Washington, D.C.* (Washington, D.C.: Government Printing Office, 1968), p. i.

158. Ibid., pp. 5, 8, 10.

159. Martin and McClure, *Title I*, 1st ed., pp. 68–79.

160. *Senate Hearings*, 1969, pp. 349, 358.

161. Ibid., p. 894.

162. Murphy, "Title I of ESEA," pp. 42–43.

163. HEW, *Report of Poor People,* p. ii.

164. *House Hearings,* 1967, p. 267.

165. Murphy, "Title I of ESEA," pp. 46–48.

166. *Senate Hearings,* 1969, pp. 886–98.

167. Heller and Barrett, *Expand and Improve,* p. 140.

168. Tom Parmenter, "Power to the People through Title I? *Maybe,*" pp. 5–6.

169. "Providence Suit Alleges Typical Range of Urban Title I Violations," p. 30.

170. Parmenter, "Power to the People," pp. 6; 7.

171. Bob Cohen, "Title I Clothing Grants Found to Improve Student Self-Image and School Attendance," p. 35.

172. Parmenter, "Power to the People," pp. 1–8; "Clothing; Comparability; Parents; Standing," *Inequality in Education* 6 (November 1970): 27.

173. Ibid., p. 27; Roger Rice, "Maine Parents Win Broad Control of Title I Program Funds," pp. 35–36.

174. "Modeling in Front of 3-Way Mirror," p. 32.

175. Ornstein, *Race and Politics in School/Community Organizations,* pp. 14–15, 41.

176. *Congressional Record,* 91st Cong., 2d Sess., p. 8492.

177. Ibid., p. 8494.

178. Ibid., p. 8492.

5

Evaluation

On 14 September 1970 President Nixon reviewed
the government's varied educational efforts of the 1960s.
"Congress was extraordinarily generous in its support of
education, particularly in its enthusiasm for trying to compensate through education for the environmental disadvantages of our least fortunate children," he noted. "Much of
this activity was based on the familiar premise that if only
the resources available for education were increased, the
amount youngsters learn would increase, so . . . we thought
we knew what education was all about." But, the president
suggested, it turned out that "the programs and strategies
. . . are . . . based on faulty assumptions and inadequate
knowledge." It was hardly surprising that Nixon wished to
dissociate himself from the efforts of the previous administration. Measures like the ESEA now had a tarnished image
because of their administrative weaknesses and operational
difficulties, and, as Nixon pointed out, "It is time to realize
that every time we invest a billion dollars in a compensatory

program we raise the hopes of millions of our disadvantaged citizens, whose hopes are more than likely to be dashed."[1]

Practical failures, disappointed expectations, and doubts about the intellectual assumptions of the educational components of the poverty program were all evident in 1970, as Nixon said. The most serious challenge to the ESEA and other educational attacks on poverty was probably intellectual. Both the 1966 Coleman Report, *Equality of Educational Opportunity*, and the 1967 Civil Rights Commission Report, *Racial Isolation in the Public Schools*, implicitly suggested that the approach embodied in the ESEA was unlikely to improve the academic achievement of poor children. Yet at the same time other data maintained that compensatory programs, if generously handled and well directed, could and did succeed in raising their achievement level. What was needed, this data implied, was only a greater effort in the education of the poor. With such conflicting evidence it was difficult, if not impossible, to make a definite decision about the significance of the ESEA as a measure of social policy. But some major insights did emerge from the confusion. If poverty was to be banished from the nation, as the first warriors on poverty had so confidently expected, an extraordinary remedy and an extraordinary commitment from the American people would be essential.

The first study undermining the intellectual foundations of the ESEA began before Title I was even in operation. One section of the 1964 Civil Rights Act had directed the Office of Education to document the unequal opportunities that different racial, religious, and ethnic groups faced in the nation's schools and colleges. In early 1965 the Office of Education commissioned the study under the direction of James S. Coleman, professor of social relations at Johns Hopkins. Aided by a staff of experienced behavioral scientists, Coleman gathered and interpreted data for his report, which was released in July 1966.

Equality of Educational Opportunity (popularly known as the Coleman Report) was one of the most extensive surveys ever made of American education. The basic concern of the survey was clear: "Public schools are the principal means in our society for providing opportunity by developing mental skills and imparting knowledge. . . . The question of this report becomes a simple one: How well do the schools of our Nation provide such opportunity for minority group children?"[2] To answer this question, the survey administered achievement tests and questionnaires in late 1965 to more than 570,000 pupils in the first, third, sixth, ninth, and twelfth grades in 4,000 schools. In addition to material provided by students, 60,000 teachers and numerous principals also filled out questionnaires. In all, the survey used forty-five measures to evaluate school facilities, characteristics of student bodies, student backgrounds, and attitudes of both majority and minority groups. The major goals of the research was to relate these factors to student achievement scores. Although achievement test scores were far from the ideal way of judging education, the report argued that using these measures was valid. The test assessed "the skills which are among the most important for getting a good job and moving up to a better one, and for full participation in an increasingly technical world. Consequently, a pupil's test results at the end of public school provide a good measure of the range of opportunities open to him as he finishes school."[3]

Some of the results of the survey were hardly surprising. The study documented the achievement gap between whites and minority groups, with blacks showing the lowest scores.[4] Since blacks were the largest minority group, their performance was, of course, really crucial in an evaluation of the schools.[5] Coleman's report showed that minority children in the first grade were already testing lower than average white children. Over the years the gap in achievement scores widened.[6] By the twelfth grade, 85 percent of black students in public schools had test scores below the average white senior.[7]

Since other studies had produced similar results, the gap between black and white achievement was not unexpected. But other results definitely were. Coleman reported, "As we examined the performance in different kinds of schools, we found a fact which occasioned some surprise on our part and some reassessment."[8] The researchers had fully expected that they would document the traditional explanation for differences in achievement, unequal facilities and curricula offerings. But these findings never surfaced. It appeared that blacks and whites had roughly equal school facilities, services, and curricula.[9] When different schools were compared, there was very little variation in their impact on students. Greater differences lay in the achievement of different pupils within the schools than between them. As the report concluded, "Most of the variation in achievement could not possibly be accounted for by school differences, since most of it lies within the school."[10]

If achievement differences did not result from unequal facilities, what caused them? The answer to this question would have a significant impact on social measures like the ESEA that subsidized school programs to break the cycle of poverty. The survey suggested an insight into the problem of what contributed to student achievement that was familiar to sociologists but not to the public at large. Using information concerning the socioeconomic background of the students' families (urbanism of background, parents' education, structural integrity of family and its size, items in the home) and information on the perceived interest of parents in education, the survey discovered that these factors had a far more important effect on the outcome of education than did the school itself. Background factors explained from 30 to 50 percent of the total variance in achievement for all groups and from 10 to 25 percent of the difference in individual achievement.[11] The results also seemed to indicate that the family's socioeconomic position explained more of the variance in achievement in the early years than in the later years.

The second finding that Coleman and his colleagues uncovered was that the qualities of other students in the school affected minority student achievement more than either the school facilities or the attributes of the staff.[12] The study measured the characteristics of the school student body by determining the educational background of the students, their educational aspirations, the degree of student mobility in the school, school attendance, and the average amount of homework as reported by the student.[13] The study found that children from similarly deprived home situations showed different patterns of achievement in schools with different student body characteristics. Students with high aspirations from solid socioeconomic backgrounds stimulated their poorer classmates. The student who already had a strongly supportive background, however, was less sensitive to the influence of his peers. For white twelfth-grade students the characteristics of the student body explained only 2.01 percent of the variance in verbal achievement, for instance, but for twelfth-grade Negroes the figure was 6.77 percent.[14]

Such findings had obvious racial implications, since the report found that "the great majority of American children attend schools that are largely segregated—that is, where almost all of their fellow students are of the same racial backgrounds as they are. Among minority groups, Negroes are by far the most segregated."[15] Because most minority groups ranked low in social and economic class, this meant most minority students went to schools with children from similarly deprived backgrounds and missed out on the stimulating environment that students from higher social and economic classes could provide. Thus, Negroes in typical integrated middle-class schools would do better than they did in lower-class segregated schools. Coleman concluded, however, that improved performance was not due to racial mixture. "The higher achievement of all racial and ethnic groups in schools with greater proportions of white students is largely, perhaps wholly, related to effects associated with the student body's educational background and aspirations."[16]

Coleman summed up the major conclusions of the Report. "Altogether, *the sources of inequality of educational opportunity appear to be first in the home itself and the cultural influences immediately surrounding the home; then they lie in the schools' ineffectiveness to free achievement from the impact of the home, and in the schools' homogeneity which perpetuated the social influences of the home and its environments.*"[17] The report did not explain why the schools had failed to overcome student deprivation, nor did it suggest how or why the schools could overcome it.[18] As Coleman noted, "The survey results do not lend themselves to the provision of simple answers."[19]

Yet even though the survey itself carefully refrained from

drawing out the implications of the data, the report had significant meaning for education in general and for the War on Poverty's educational components like the ESEA in particular. For the study emphasized that "differences in school facilities and curriculum, which are made to improve schools, are so little related to differences in achievement levels of students that, with few exceptions, their efforts fail to appear in a survey of this magnitude."[20] Thus, the study suggested that money and conventional improvements that programs like the ESEA provided would do little to break the cycle of educational deprivation and implied that massive changes were necessary to solve the problems of poverty. Either there would have to be a direct attack on the student's home environment or a complete transformation of the schools themselves.

Although Coleman observed that "it is hard to believe that we are so inept in educating our young that we can do no more than leave young adults in the same relative competitive positions we found them in as children," he did not feel that changes were impossible.[21] "It is not, I suggest, that schools cannot have a powerful effect in reducing inequality. It is rather that they have not yet learned how to do so."[22] Whether efforts sponsored by the ESEA could teach the schools how to approach this formidable task was, however, questionable in light of the way the legislation was being implemented locally.

When Coleman and his staff finished the report, they sent it on to the Office of Education. There, understandably, the reaction was one of dismay.[23] The House Committee on Education and Labor was finishing its deliberations in executive session on the two-year extension of the ESEA.[24] The conclusions of the report seemed to undermine the bill's approach, and could offer political fuel to those opposing school aid. Officials within HEW decided to draw attention away from the survey by issuing a summary of the report. Coleman noted that this summary appeared " 'flat,' lacking in emphasis and policy implications," and saw this flatness as due partly to "the government agency's uneasiness with survey findings that may have political repercussions."[25] The language of the summary was tentative. What appeared in the actual report as a statement that average minority pupils suffered more in low-quality schools than did average white children, for example, was changed into a conditional statement. "The average minority pupil's achievement *may* suffer more in a school of low quality than *might* the average white pupil's."[26] The major conclusions of the Coleman study were obviously being played down. Thus the summary stated, somewhat misleadingly, that the survey's first finding was "that the schools are remarkably similar in the effect they have on the achievement of their pupils."[27] The report and the summary were released just before the Fourth of July, no doubt in an effort to minimize further the possibility that the report's implications would be discussed in the press and in Congress.[28] Initially, the Office of Education's attempts were successful. Newspapers hardly referred to the surprising findings of the survey, and no staff members of either the Senate or House education committees ever read the entire report.[29] There were no memorandums or reports made on the Coleman survey for legislators involved with educational matters, and there was little Congressional interest.[30] When the ESEA came up for discussion in the next few years, Coleman was hardly ever mentioned.[31]

Interest in the report continued within the HEW, however. Commissioner of Education Howe called on a group of social scientists and educators to help his department understand the complexities of the report and to aid the government in responding to the report's conclusions. The group, which included Daniel Moynihan and Kenneth Clark, gathered on 2 October 1966 with the commissioner. Howe went over the report's conclusions that social-class factors had a larger effect on achievement than racial factors, telling the group that he interpreted the survey to mean that changing school facilities was less useful than attacking the problems of the social environment.[32] Surprisingly, the specialists at the meeting did not appear to understand the report's implications. Howe, who had originally hoped to use the group to advise him on a continuing basis, announced that the group lacked imagination.[33] He decided not to call the group again and moved away from his radical impulses on changing the social environment. Within government, then, the report had minimal initial impact.

In educational circles the reaction to the Coleman Report was "sluggish," which was hardly surprising in view of the report's damaging conclusions about the schools. Silence appeared the best defense.[34] In research circles, however, there was a lively response to Coleman's findings. Although the report received support, it also aroused harsh condemnation and accusations that almost all its findings could be questioned.[35] Criticism on the report focused on several points.[36] A series of researchers claimed the over-all design of the survey was flawed. Some insisted that Coleman had chosen the least important school characteristics to measure, others that the design was weighted against school factors.[37] A second group of criticisms pointed out the inadequacies resulting from the responses to the survey. A significant number of large city school systems had refused to cooperate with the survey. For example, only 59 percent of the high schools participating gave a complete set of answers.[38] Another group of reviews alleged that there were technical limitations in the analysis of data. The linear regression technique that Coleman had used, they claimed, was ill-suited to his material. It had been a mistake to control for social class before weighing the influence of school factors on achievement.[39] Finally, there were obvious weakensses in the survey because all the information was gathered at one point in time. There was no possibility of using this information to determine the initial intelligence of pupils or to judge correctly the impact of the schools over time.[40] These criticisms initiated a lively debate over the methods used and the results of the survey. This meant that the report was in many ways in a state of "perpetual suspension," and that few firm policy judgments were immediately appropriate.[41]

Many of the technical criticisms made of the report were valid. Furthermore, it was true, as Coleman admitted, that the methods used in the report did not prove that different factors like student environment caused the variations in minority achievement. Statistically the report merely showed that the various factors studied were related to differences in achievement. But despite the validity of some of the criticism and the conditional nature of some of the report's conclusions, the major findings of the survey stood up under attack and restudy. A massive reexamination of the Coleman data at Harvard that corrected many of the original study's technical weaknesses reaffirmed Coleman's most important finding that the family had a more significant influence on achievement than did the schools. This part of the restudy, directed by sociologist David Armor, used the individual school as the basic unit of analysis instead of all the schools, as Coleman had. Armor felt that this change offered a more accurate means of evaluating the relative influence of school factors and social background factors.[42] Armor's data on 1,562 schools showed few differences between school facilities for blacks and whites, between teacher quality except for verbal achievement, or between expenditures in black and white schools within major geographical regions.[43] Armor documented differences in black and white achievement scores similar to those found by Coleman and reaffirmed the social class differences between white and black schools.[44] Armor's restudy once again established that variations in family backgrounds best explained variations in achievement, although he did not feel that schools were without influence on their pupils.[45] He also confirmed that the social class and racial mixture within the school did have an important effect on achievement. Blacks performed best in schools in which they composed 1–25 percent of the student body, Armor discovered.[46] But Armor stressed the significant finding that black students in white middle-class schools *still* did not achieve as well as their white classmates even though they out-performed comparable blacks in lower-class schools.

Armor judged that mixing schools by social class and race was not a sufficient remedy for overcoming the damages of a deprived background. "The policy implication here," Armor stated, "is that programs which stress financial aid to disadvantaged black families may be just [as] important, if not more so, than programs aimed at integrating blacks into white neighborhoods and schools."[47] Armor concluded, "There does not seem to be any way for blacks to catch up with whites if family factors are ignored."[48] By 1970 another reevaluation of the data claimed that the data had finally been milked dry. "The overall results should be clear to policy makers and researchers alike. With regard to the differences among schools in resources that we conventionally measure and consider in making policy, there are few that give us great leverage over students' achievement."[49]

The Coleman Report not only had major implications for the educational aspects of the War on Poverty but also brought the racial issue into prominence by documenting the pitiful academic performance of many black children relative to whites. Before the release of the Coleman Report, a more specific discussion of the problems of race and education was already under way. On 17 November 1965 President Johnson had requested the U.S. Civil Rights Commission to investigate racial segregation in the schools and report their findings to him. "As a first and initial step, the Nation needs to know the facts," Johnson said. Then the president was hopeful that "your findings may provide a basis for action not only by the Federal Government but also by the states and local school boards."[50]

In carrying out the study, the commission established an advisory committee made up of educators, sociologists, economists, and psychologists. The head of the advisory committee, Thomas Pettigrew, was an associate professor of social psychology at Harvard and an authority on racial matters. The committee gathered all kinds of information, holding hearings in different cities and commissioning special in-depth studies and papers. Their focus was on cities and metropolitan areas, since two-thirds of American children went to urban schools.[51] The committee also undertook a reanalysis of the Coleman data. This reanalysis involved not just going over the Coleman report's conclusions but examining raw material on the IBM tapes.[52] In reworking the Coleman data, the committee concentrated on information on twelfth-grade Negroes in the metropolitan Northeast and on ninth-grade Negroes in eight regions. Instead of merely examining the racial composition of entire schools, the committee studied the racial divisions in individual classrooms.

The report, entitled *Racial Isolation in the Public Schools*, was released on 20 February 1967, echoing Johnson's hope that it would "serve as a basis for remedial action by local school authorities, the States, and the Federal Government."[53] The study's first finding emphasized that racial segregation in public schools was widespread and increasing. In a survey of seventy-five cities, for example, the report noted that 75 percent of black elementary school children went to schools that were 90 percent or more black. Of elementary school white children, 88 percent were in schools that were essentially white.[54] In the South the proportion of black children in all-black schools had decreased, but the actual numbers had increased.[55] Having established the extent of racial isolation in the public schools, the study went on to discuss the effects of such isolation. In this section the report reached far more emphatic conclusions about the relation of racial integration to achievement than had Coleman, who thought that social-class differences explained the improved achievement scores of blacks in integrated learning situations.[56] Although the Civil Rights Commission study acknowledged that the social-class composition of the student body was the most important school factor affecting achievement, it maintained that race had a separate influence on achievement. "The complexity of the problem of educational disadvantage should not be allowed to obscure the central fact," the report proclaimed. "Racial isolation is the heart of the matter and . . . enduring solutions will not be possible until we deal with it."[57] The difference between Coleman's conclusions and the commission's could be explained either by the statistical techniques Coleman used, which confused race and class, or by the regression analysis, which used the school rather than the classroom as the basic unit of study.[58]

The study provided evidence to support the commission's belief that the racial composition of a classroom had a separate influence on achievement apart from social-class background. No matter what the racial composition of the entire school, the study discovered that Negro achievement scores in individual classrooms rose when a majority of their classmates were white. The amount of the improvement varied with the situation.[59]

Although there was a possibility that such improvements resulted from better education in the white schools rather than the racial mixture in the classroom, an examination of this possibility indicated that most improvement was not due to facilities or curriculum.[60] Nor did the quality of teachers have a significant effect. Disadvantaged Negroes in lower-class white schools with poor teachers still performed better than disadvantaged blacks in black schools with better teachers.[61] Moreover, the longer blacks went to integrated schools, the better their achievement was. A deprived black ninth-grader in a lower-class school in the metropolitan Northeast was 2.6 grades behind white average verbal achievement if he had been in a desegregated situation in his first three years of school. But had he never been in desegregated classes, he was 3.4 grades behind by the ninth grade. For an equally deprived child who had been in desegregated classes in the first three school grades and who also was in a middle-class school, the gap was only 1.8 years.[62] Such information indicated that black students needed not merely integrated schools but integrated classrooms. The major conclusion appeared simple: "The analysis thus suggests that changes in the social class or racial composition of schools would have a greater effect on student achievement and attitudes than changes in school quality."[63]

The commission's emphatic conclusions did not attract the vigorous attacks that the Coleman Report had.[64] Yet, the findings, though suggestive, were hardly conclusive. On 10 May 1967 Coleman wrote to Commissioner Howe about *Racial Isolation in the Schools*. "Our interpretation of the data in the report," he commented, "is that racial integration per se is unrelated to achievement insofar as the data can show a relation."[65] Moreover, Alan Wilson's in-depth longitudinal study of Contra Costa County, California, which was included in the commission's report, did not support the commission's viewpoint. Wilson's survey led him to the conclusion that "racial composition of the school, while tending to favor Negro students in racially integrated schools, does not have a substantial effect—not nearly so strong as the social class composition of the school."[66] Wilson did feel, however, that in the long run social and racial segregation would have harmful effects on achievement, and pointed out that his sample was too small to allow a comprehensive study of blacks in all the possible social and racial classroom situations.[67] In November 1967, when the report was released, Pettigrew suggested other reasons for Wilson's findings. It was possible, for example, that disparities between Wilson's data and the commission's could be explained by Wilson's use of the school rather than the classroom as the unit for analysis.[68] But whether Wilson's study was flawed was almost beside the point. Faced with contradictory evidence, the commission decided to accept the racial explanation as valid. This resulted in an accusation that the commission was trying to work up a case for integration to reinforce its congressional request for a racial imbalance law.[69] Yet, it was not of great importance ultimately if the commission overstressed the racial aspect of achievement. Since only one-quarter of the black population was middle class, lower-class black children could only go to schools with whites if they were to have social-class integration.[70]

The implications of *Racial Isolation in the Public Schools* further undermined the intellectual assumptions of the ESEA. Since it emphasized the role schools could play in overcoming the poor achievement correlated with poverty, the study first appeared to support measures like the ESEA more than the Coleman Report had. But this was largely a matter of presentation. Although the study did acknowledge the influence of family background on achievement, which Coleman had delineated, it had minimized its importance by devoting only a few pages to the subject.[71] The overwhelming amount of discussion concerned integration, and the report thus gave the impression that changes in schools rather than changes in the social environment were of first importance. Moreover, the study never grappled with the fact of the achievement gap between blacks and whites in integrated situations. It was this gap that had led David Armor to maintain that social changes were probably more important than changes in the schools themselves.

Yet even beyond the fact that the report focused on the

less-promising avenue of changing conditions through the schools, its conclusions did not actually lend great support to the ESEA's approach. If the report was correct, integration plans on a scale defying political reality, not ESEA programs, were needed to change achievement patterns. Moreover, the ESEA lacked desegregation requirements and, in many cases, reinforced racial and social-class isolation.[72] Compensatory education could, of course, occur in segregated or integrated settings. But the method of allocating funds had encouraged treating poor children separately, as Thomas Pettigrew pointed out to the House Research Technical Programs Subcommittee in 1967. "Title I of the Elementary and Secondary Education Act of 1965 is a clear example of the wrong way to attack problems of poverty," Pettigrew said.

> Its large extension to over one-and-a-half billion dollars in 1966 by the 89th Congress further exemplifies the total neglect by Congress of even social research directly called for by Congress itself. The basic weakness of Title I is that it encourages (though it does not require) that something special be done educationally for disadvantaged children apart *from advantaged children.* Yet . . . the principal resource public schools can provide for disadvantaged children is close educational contact with advantaged children. By fastening further economic and racial separation in the nation's public schools, Title I is contributing directly with federal money to the educational retardation of America's poorest children.[73]

The Civil Rights report also devoted attention to compensatory education programs implemented by segregated schools. In its survey of thirteen cities between 1965 and 1967, the commission discovered that in a majority of cases, ESEA funds set up compensatory programs in schools whose student bodies were 50 percent or more black.[74] This finding preceded other studies like the 1969 McClure report, which later confirmed that local school districts often used funds to maintain racial separation in the schools.

If it were true that compensatory funds went to segregated schools, it was important to establish whether they worked in all-black environments. In all, the commission investigated twenty-three programs in black schools.[75] Although Title I funds did not necessarily initiate these programs, the programs themselves were well known and often models for Title I efforts. The commission determined that it would judge a program successful only if it resulted in measurable improvement in academic performance. In *Racial Isolation in the Public Schools* the commission included its findings on three programs: the Banneker project in Saint Louis, Higher Horizons, and the All Day Neighborhood School Program in New York City. In Saint Louis the program, which began in 1957-58, sought to increase achievement through raising teachers' expectations and motivating the students and their parents. No extra funding existed for Banneker schools. In New York, Higher Horizons, established in 1959, tried to reach disadvantaged students through teacher training, guidance, cultural environment, and remedial help. In 1962 an average of $50 to $60 was spent on each Higher Horizon child in addition to the base state expenditure. The All Day Neighborhood School Program, held in elementary schools, provided special teachers and after-school programs designed to offset the destructive effects of the environment of poverty. These services came to $60 per child.[76] The results of these three projects and the other city programs that the commission explored showed mixed results. Often the data were incomplete, and there were complaints of inadequate funding. Nevertheless, "in most instances," the commission found, "the data did not show significant gains in achievement."[77] The commission concluded, "Compensatory education programs have been of limited effectiveness because they have attempted to solve problems that stem, in large part, from racial and social class isolation in schools which themselves are isolated by race and social class."[78]

A further section of the commission's study of compensatory education compared the achievement of black students in compensatory programs in Syracuse, Berkeley, Seattle, and Philadelphia with the achievement of similar black pupils in white schools (in the same cities) that had no compensatory programs.[79] In Philadelphia, for example, the commission investigated students participating in the Education Improvement Program, which focused on improving reading scores and encouraging student aspirations, as well as students in slightly higher-class black schools without a special program, and finally students bused to white schools. The commission reported that the Education Improvement Program failed to significantly raise reading scores of students who performed behind both those going to the slightly higher-class schools and behind similarly deprived students sent to white schools.[80]

The commission did not reject the possibility that compensatory education could overcome the effects of poverty; it merely stated that, so far, compensatory education had failed.[81] Accepting the commission's conclusions as tentative, since the programs investigated were so poorly funded, Commissioner Howe kept the old hopes going. More money would mean success.[82] But the commission did not see inadequate funding as the only problem. The weakest link in compensatory education lay in the

> attempt to instill in a child feelings of personal worth and dignity in an environment in which he is surrounded by visible evidence which seems to deny his value as a person. This does not appear to be a problem which will yield easily to additional infusions of money. More funds clearly are required and investments in programs that will improve teaching and permit more attention to the individual needs of students undoubtedly will benefit many children. The evidence suggests, however, that the better services additional funds will provide will not be fully effective in a racially isolated environment, but only in a setting which supports the teacher's effort to help each child to understand that he is a valuable person who can succeed.[83]

Equality of Educational Opportunity and *Racial Isolation in the Public Schools* were two massive studies suggesting that the approach embodied in the ESEA was not the best one to eliminate the academic disadvantages of the children of poverty. The one study indicated the need for either basic social changes or widespread changes in the schools, the other, for massive racial integration. Neither study could offer a methodologically definitive case to support its point of view, but each offered substantial evidence for its stand. The remedies called for were far-reaching and would be politically difficult to enact. Yet, as one authority said of the Coleman Report,

"If the Report's analysis is correct, then most of the money now being spent to improve the public schools is going down the drain."[84]

Money down the drain was perhaps politically more acceptable than the solutions the large studies seemed to indicate. It was not until specific reports of Title I and Headstart failures began to trickle back to Congress that legislators at last began to consider seriously the specific question of whether the compensatory effort supported by the ESEA and its preschool counterpart was successful. A controversy was brewing, and the sides were lining up. In 1969 Chairman Carl Perkins announced that the hearings of the House Committee on Education and Labor had shown that "this is the greatest program which has ever been enacted by the Congress . . . the critics to a great extent have outmoded information."[85] The grass roots support for the legislation, Perkins remarked, was unbelievable.[86] Grass roots support for continuing the ESEA was hardly surprising. Local and state desire for federal funding had facilitated the act's passage, and local authorities did not favor seeing the federal bounty withdrawn, whether or not Title I programs were successful. Failure was easy to explain: inadequate funding due to the war.[87] Robert Finch, Nixon's new secretary of HEW, disagreed with Perkins and his grass roots support. "There is an uneven quality to the performance of these various programs across the country," he noted. "We would like to evaluate these programs."[88] Later in the day Finch was more specific. "From the massive evidence we have," he stated, "I do not think we can claim unqualified success."[89]

The controversy over whether compensatory efforts succeeded raised the issue of what the goals of the ESEA actually were. Much of the rhetoric surrounding the enactment of the bill had stressed the importance of breaking the cycle of poverty and ignorance in which so many of the nation's children were caught. Although Keppel had initially suggested using data like school attendance figures, the delinquency rate, and the proportion of lower-income students going to college to provide some kind of an objective test within three years of whether Title I was effective, it was soon clear that a three-year period was insufficient for the difficult task of measuring a long-term goal like breaking the poverty cycle.[90] Keppel was, however, correct in realizing the need for multiple measures. But local schools did not and could not collect all these disparate statistics. In practical terms, therefore, the ESEA's clearest social objective came to be the elimination of the easily measurable achievement gap that existed between middle-class white children and their deprived black and white classmates. This narrow focus on achievement scores was supported by the belief that raising scores was the essential precondition for ending the cycle of poverty. This, of course, had been one of the initial assumptions of planners in 1965 even though the linkage between low achievement and poverty was not clearly understood. Arguments about the success or failure of compensatory education thus tended to center around improvement or lack of improvement in test scores of Title I children. Few questioned whether these statistics were the crucial ones that related to ultimate objectives.[91]

Yet, many problems stood in the way of even deciding whether Title I had raised test scores of the nation's poor children significantly. As HEW admitted in 1969, evaluation of Title I's impact "often seems to produce results which are more confusing than they are illuminating. At times . . . the results are even conflicting."[92] Inadequate data caused most of the confusion. A major part of the ESEA information came from states and localities that, in 1969, were responsible for reporting on the 20,000 ongoing Title I projects. The act had directed that evaluation must include "objective measurement of educational achievement."[93] But since school districts had successfully resisted using uniform national tests, each district was free to select its own achievement test.[94] The data that districts provided were so varied that it was difficult to see how the program was working out on a national scale.[95] Districts also reported evaluation information in different ways. For example, some areas reported changes in median scores of Title I children, and others used mean scores. No true comparison between the two was possible. Other evaluations gave figures on the proportion of successful projects rather than the numbers of children showing improvement.

Moreover, it was not unusual for states and localities to offer incomplete data. It was both time-consuming and expensive to carry out a careful evaluation, and few areas had the means, talent, or will for such an effort. Massachusetts, for example, took the entire evaluation requirement so lightly that its study yielded little useful information about Title I's impact.[96] One Massachusetts area described a project as successful in which Title I children appeared to improve in reading scores compared to non-Title I children. Actually neither group improved; Title I children merely lost ground more slowly than the others.[97] Often, reports on Title I projects did not have information on control groups or had poorly matched controls. This made it difficult to discover whether target children were improving more than children not receiving special help. Such data did not yield enough material to allow definite generalizations about the impact of Title I.

The inadequacy of data stemmed not only from the freedom that states and localities had in submitting their ESEA evaluations. Even more basic problems were involved in the evaluation process itself. The typical way of determining whether a program was successful was to test the selected children before and after their exposure to the program. Any improvement in scores was attributed to the program. Actually, however, improvement might be due to the natural development of the children or to extraneous influences.[98] Pre- and post-test results did not yield definitive information on the program's success or the reasons for it. Moreover, the method of testing at only two intervals was obviously unable to detect long-range effects of programs; few school districts followed up on Title I target children over the years.[99] It was no surprise that there was not a clear answer to the question of whether Title I was meeting even its limited goals.

A few large-scale studies carried out during the first five years of the ESEA avoided some of these problems. But these studies, too, created a cloudy picture of Title I's impact. In 1965-66 and 1966-67 General Electric investigated selected compensatory education programs in fourteen large cities. The study planned to compare the two years and relate any change in test scores to the compensatory program stimulated by Title I. The study ran into typical problems in data collection. Five cities did not have suitable material to be included in the evaluation. Test-score information provided by the cities varied. More important, different children took the tests in the two years because most school systems test selected grades every year, not the same children. Finally, few of the school systems kept detailed financial records, so that it was impossible to form an over-all picture of how much money was really being spent on compensatory education.[100]

G.E.'s report was, in the words of one congressman, "not entirely one which gave us cause for optimism."[101] G.E. concluded that although the lowest achievers improved slightly, the average performance of the sampled grades declined.[102] When it correlated financial, program, and test-change information, the study found no meaningful relationships beyond the fact that concentrating resources in large amounts was useful.[103] Yet, though these results were disappointing, as one commentator remarked, the G.E. study did not show much of anything at all. "It showed only how hard it is to find out anything about input-output relations in education, especially from a quick, low budget project using existing data."[104]

In 1970 HEW issued its own study of the ESEA. Far larger than any other survey on Title I, HEW's study covered 4,000 elementary schools and the results of some 55,000 reading tests. As usual, the tests were of several different types. But since almost three-quarters of the children participating in Title I programs during the 1967-68 school year took reading, reading scores were regarded as the key to any judgment about Title I activities.[105] Pre- and post-program test scores were reported for 55,335 pupils, but only 11,578 permitted analysis because HEW did not have the necessary comparative data for the other students. HEW did not regard this group as representative of the entire sample; most of the students came from urban areas, and a large portion of them belonged to minority groups.[106] Yet even though the data were not completely satisfactory, the statistics did "offer some indications of the impact of compensatory reading programs upon the pupils"[107]

The results of the survey, as interpreted by HEW, were depressing. "Compensatory reading programs did not seem to overcome the reading differences that stem from poverty."[108] Each grade tested showed a slightly different pattern. Title I pupils in the second grade whose reading scores were below those of children not in the program caught up with these children at the end of the year.[109] But in the fourth grade Title I children did not catch up. The gap between them and the children not in the program remained the same.[110] In grade six the gap between Title I and non-Title I children was larger than in grade four, but the gap itself did not increase over the year.[111] Thus, poverty pupils, the survey suggested, never caught up to other children and, in fact, showed less progress than children from better financial backgrounds who had taken part in the program.[112]

At first glance the findings of the HEW data corroborated the conclusions of the Coleman Report. Increased spending brought few concrete results. The survey pointed out that students attending schools with students from higher socioeconomic backgrounds improved more than those attending school with deprived classmates.[113] But although the survey supported the Coleman Report and although HEW gave a negative interpretation to the data, it still did not conclusively prove that the ESEA had failed. For example, the tests measured growth only over the period of a year. Even HEW concluded, "While there is no indication that compensatory reading programs are eliminating the deprivation of participants within one school year, this is an unreasonable expectation."[114] Furthermore, the survey used test information about different pupils at different grade levels instead of following the same Title I pupils over several years. The survey did not, therefore, provide any evidence of the cumulative effects of the ESEA. Finally, as the report emphasized, compensatory programs spent only about $68 helping each disadvantaged child in special reading programs, a sum far too small to overcome educational deprivation.[115]

Another large study of an educational component of the poverty program did give some cumulative results. The Westinghouse report was important not only because its cumulative data offered information on the impact of compensatory education over time but also because the report studied preschool intervention. Although Title I funded some preschool programs, most of the focus was on the elementary school years. Headstart, however, was exclusively a preschool program until 1968, when Follow Through was established to give additional aid to Headstart children during kindergarten and their first three years of school.[116] It thus had the chance to attack educational deprivation early. And since Headstart was, for the most part, run by community action or other local groups rather than the local school system, its programs promised to be more innovative and flexible and less bureaucratic than Title I programs.[117]

This study cannot treat Headstart or other preschool intervention programs in the detail that they deserve. Another book or perhaps several must trace the development of preschool education, the administrative and political pressures under which the programs operated, and the kinds of curricula and educational strategies they used.[118] But since Headstart, in particular, was a complementary program to the ESEA, some observations about it are important in assessing the overall impact of the educational attack on poverty.

Headstart, in some respects, was an administrative afterthought, but it was a significant one. During hearings on the Economic Opportunity Act, Dr. Urie Bronfenbrenner pointed out that the poverty bill focused too exclusively on the sixteen- to twenty-two-year-old age group. Federal money, Bronfenbrenner argued, would be far better spent on the very young, "striking poverty where it hits first and most damagingly—in early childhood."[119] Bronfenbrenner's testimony, of course, was based on the rich educational literature emphasizing the vital importance of learning in early childhood. During the first years of life, children learned skills and attitudes crucial to their later development. But the child of poverty had so few enriching experiences that he was crippled by the time he reached school and, too often, was maimed for life after school. Early compensatory education, however, offered the possibility of making up for the disabilities of these early home experiences. Children who had good preschool experiences would be able to enter the conventional school system and succeed in it.[120] Thus, preschool education might well be more crucial than help later and might eventually eliminate most of the need for compensatory education during elementary or secondary school.

Shriver was struck by this idea of preschool intervention and so were congressmen. An amendment to set aside community action program funds for some kind of a preschool program was received enthusiastically by the House Committee on Education and Labor. When OEO made it clear that it would willingly sponsor preschool programs, the unnecessary amendment disappeared. Headstart was on its way. In January 1965, as planners puzzled over the ESEA, Johnson announced to the country that funds would be available for Headstart. Shriver, ever eager to get programs started fast and big, decided to begin the effort that summer. Headstart was the perfect program for Shriver. It was appealing, it would use allocated money quickly, and it would be useful in the struggle for new appropriations the following year. Any community action program could adopt it; moreover, Headstart could be a catalyst for the formation of new community action groups. Finally, the program was very popular with the public.[121]

That summer Headstart was launched. For two months 561,000 children in 1,398 communities went to Headstart centers for $94.5 million of enrichment, medical care, and food.[122] At the end of the summer, the administration decided to expand Headstart into a yearlong program.[123] By the time of the Westinghouse evaluation, there were more than 12,000 Headstart centers in operation. Over $440 million had been allocated to the program in FY 1968, but only a portion of poor children had been reached.[124] Still, Headstart was an impressive effort. Unlike many Title I programs, Headstart was not just a learning program. It was concerned with health, nutrition, and adjustment as well. Although diversity marked the projects, most were characterized by a "whole-child-orientation, [a] . . . strategy of watching and waiting, and . . . [a] resultant low degree of structure."[125] The focus on adjustment and the whole child rather than

just learning made Headstart comprehensive but also a difficult program to evaluate.[126]

The Westinghouse study followed up children who had been
at 104 Headstart centers in their first three years of school.
The scores of these Headstart children were compared with
a group of control children who had not been to Headstart
but who were eligible for the program. The study made points
similar to evaluations of Title I. Summer programs had no
discernible effect on achievement. Full year programs showed
some, but not significant, results in the first and second
grades. The third-grade sample was too small to make a positive statement.[127] Still, the children tested below the national
means on most tests.[128] Furthermore, there was little difference in self-concept between Headstart children and the controls. Nor did their teachers rate their classroom behavior in
strikingly different ways than teachers of the control
groups.[129] These results predictably caused an uproar. The
White House and President Nixon, eager to minimize support
for Headstart, accepted the findings although Finch, secretary of HEW, proclaimed that the study "contained insufficient facts and the data was sloppy."[130]

Although the Westinghouse survey confirmed the negative conclusions of other studies of compensatory education,
it, too, was unable to prove the failure of all compensatory
aid. The study itself was, of course, attacked on statistical
grounds and defended as "the most vigorous national assess-
ment of Headstart which has been undertaken since the program's conception."[131] Some explained the findings by arguing that the public schools that Headstart children had entered
had destroyed benefits or that other children entered a period
of rapid growth in their first years that enabled them to
catch up with Headstarters. Others felt that there had been
no "over all, systematic changes" as a result of Headstart.[132]

Later evaluations confirmed the general pattern of the
Westinghouse survey, however. Interventions like Headstart
usually raised the IQ by 5 to 10 points immediately; highly
enrichened programs achieved quick gains of 15-30 points.[133]
But when intervention stopped, gains faded no matter what
kind of intervention had taken place.[134]

The truth was that the Westinghouse survey and other evaluations were not, in the short term at least, able to prove anything conclusively about compensatory education. They proved what did not work, not what might. But the lackluster results from large-scale programs were suggestive. "The spate of negative results across a whole gamut of programs betokens a series of important shortcomings," wrote one observer.[135] Compensatory education, as most often organized, did not appear able to overcome the effects of poverty with any predictability. As Daniel Moynihan pointed out, "Compensatory education as we now have it, doesn't seem to do much. It doesn't follow that compensatory education and the way you *could* have it wouldn't do much; it's just saying that the *present* system doesn't have many effects."[136] Much more careful testing and experimentation were evidently in order to learn whether compensatory education could become an effective part of a national policy against poverty.

The National Advisory Council pursued the problem in its 1969 report, which showed that Title I projects could succeed in certain situations. The American Institutes of Research studied 21 programs, selected from a total of 400, that showed pupils making significant gains in language or arithmetic. The National Advisory Council carefully pointed out that "significant" gains did not merely mean improvement. Gains "*had to exceed*" those made by a control group over a similar period.[137] Project R-3 in San Jose, California, was an example of such a program. Mexican-American children in the eighth grade whose test scores in math and English were between one and two years behind their grade level participated in a special learning program designed by the school district and Lockheed Missiles and Space Company. The program began in February 1967, with thirty-seven children who received a second year of help in the ninth grade.[138] Tests compared reading and arithmetic gains of project children with the program of a random sample of forty students serving as a control group. In the 1967–68 program boys gained 1.7 years in reading and 1.2 years in math against the controls' gain of 1.3 and 0.5 years. Usually, deprived children progressed only seven months (0.7 percent) in a ten-month school year. Yet, although progress of the Title I children was impressive, they still did not test at grade level. Moreover, students chosen to be part of the experimental group were already performing above disadvantaged norms and would be expected to show progress. Still, a few other programs with less-selective standards also duplicated favorable results. The cost for such a program was substantial, coming to approximately $300 per child per year in addition to the normal per-pupil expenditure.[139]

The National Advisory Council tried to isolate the factors that made the twenty-one programs so successful. Admitting that it was offering *"analytical judgments rather than inevitable demonstrations,"* the council concluded that success relied on careful planning and good management.[140] Teacher-training and small-group sessions also appeared to be important factors in teaching poor children.[141] Careful evaluations of preschool programs came to similar conclusions. These conclusions, which suggested compensatory education as a possible way to attack educational deprivation, did not contradict the implications of the Coleman Report. Successful programs were quite different from normal compensatory school programs or kindergartens and concentrated attention and resources on a scale unusual in most public schools. The most successful preschool programs were highly structured and thus unlike Headstart. Moreover, the programs *did not* bring the deprived achievement up to national norms, and preschool gains faded away.[142] To change these results, more fundamental changes in school, in the process of education, and in society might well be necessary.

The council's description of fruitful compensatory programs implicitly raised several issues. Out of 400 programs the council had characterized only twenty-one. These appeared to be atypical Title I efforts. Was, then, successful compensatory education likely under the present legislation? Careful planning and management demanded firm commitment and energetic leadership from local communities. As the first five years of the ESEA had amply documented, the act gave excessive freedom to those controlling local education, who all too rarely responded with any real commit-

ment to the poor. Moreover, successful compensatory education apparently would demand either focusing the available
money on only a few children, a difficult political task for
school districts, or increasing federal funds substantially.
David Cohen, professor at the Joint Center for Urban Studies
at MIT and Harvard, estimated that the federal government
would have to spend between $100 and $160 billion in the
first ten years in order to have an effective Title I program.[143]
The figure suggested the necessity for a new estimate of
national priorities. Such a reordering was highly unlikely,
if not impossible, in a government obsessed with the Vietnam conflict and presented with lackluster evaluations of
educational programs.

The council's report on successful compensatory programs raised other questions too. By accepting improved
scores as the sign of success, the council seemed to retreat
not only from the program's rhetorical goal of ending the
poverty cycle but also the goal of breaking the achievement
gap. Was this merely a short-term adjustment, or a lowering
of sights for the whole program? Probably no one ever considered this issue. Nowhere did the council broach the central problem of why the achievement gap still remained and
how it related to lifelong poverty. Was it because changes
were not massive enough, or was it because students were
receiving help too late? Or was it because the program was
still in its beginning stages? Would the gains the Council
hailed be lasting, or would they disappear as the Headstart
gains had done? One authority speculating on some of these
questions did reach a conclusion. "A poor child receiving a
good educational experience at an early age has many
chances to dissipate the value of the experience before he
reaches an age when it can directly benefit his earnings;
that is the nature of the poverty environment, and it does
not lead to putting weight on educational programs."[144]

Altogether, even though the council showed that compensatory education could achieve limited success despite its
over-all lackluster record, it was apparent that no one could
decide, without more information, whether compensatory education represented an effective long-term approach to de-

privation. What was needed was not just more funds, as David Cohen had indicated, but more funds plus an ambitious plan of systematic experimentation.[145] Different programs had to be carefully compared and the same programs tested under different conditions so that promising approaches could be isolated.[146] Reliable estimates of costs were necessary. Target children should be followed into the job market to make the real test: whether compensatory education's focus on raising scores made any difference in the long run. As one social planner noted, "The federal government should undertake the design and evaluation of social experiments as a major task in the 1970's."[147]

By 1970 the lack of clear results for compensatory education strengthened the voices of those who felt an alternative approach to educational deprivation was needed. Dr. Neil Sullivan's testimony in 1970 Senate hearings exemplified this pragmatic shift away from typical Title I efforts. Sullivan described the Berkeley schools' experiences with ESEA funds. Initially, the school system spent up to $1,200 on compensatory services for each deprived child with disappointing results. "After two-and-a-half or three years [results] clearly indicated that not only did the child in the inner city not improve, he had retrogressed."[148] Berkeley decided to enlarge its integration program and bus its students. Although the results of integration were not final because of incomplete or flawed evaluation studies, Berkeley's experience was the same as other communities, such as Hartford, Connecticut.[149] Students in integrated schools performed better than those in schools with compensatory programs.[150] The HEW survey itself had noted deprived students in high-socioeconomic-level schools made greater gains than those in majority lower-class schools.[151]

In 1970 a newly appointed National Advisory Council issued a report concentrating on "what is best for the children."[152] Reviewing the contributions of the ESEA, the council pointed out, "A summary of the benefits of Title I ESEA would include the national commitment to upgrading the education of the poor, identification of the educationally deprived, and some excellent attempts to conquer the problem."[153] These were hardly impressive results. The council then turned to the issue: "to integrate or to compensate?"[154] Still maintaining that compensatory education could result in higher achievement for segregated black pupils, the council, nevertheless, came out in favor of integration with special compensatory help for black pupils. This approach, the council argued, was less expensive than compensatory education in racially isolated settings.[155]

Other experts agreed that integration was necessary but contended that compensatory education in deprived schools had little potential. Coleman, for example, testified in 1970, "Although the results of our survey do not say it is impossible to provide equality of opportunity in all-black schools, the results of other research do not show promising methods for doing so."[156] So far, Coleman remarked, educators had not found the way of setting up compensatory programs that substantially improved blacks' school performance. Thomas Pettigrew was equally unenthusiastic about compensatory education. "I don't think it is completely wasted," he said. "I think it is better than complete neglect or something; but we do know that compensatory programs do work in interracial and interclass situations."[157]

The failure of segregated compensatory programs to prove themselves clearly and the consistent, if not conclusive, evidence in support of integration undermined the basic approach of the ESEA, which treated disadvantaged children separately.[158] In reality, as the large HEW survey documented, 83 percent of Title I students sampled attended classrooms where 90 percent or more of the students belonged to the same race.[159] The combined approach of integration with compensation supported by the National Advisory Council appeared the most promising, least expensive, and most democratic solution to deprivation. There was, of course, nothing to prevent using available ESEA funds to encourage and support social and racial integration. But this kind of integration was becoming more and more difficult as the nation's central cities turned increasingly into lower-class black ghettos. Local white communities were often intransigent and refused to use ESEA funds for integration. Busing for racial purposes aroused hostility and occasionally violence in sub-urban areas. Congress was unwilling to encourage outright integration in the North or the South by modifying the leg-islation. Yet, if poverty were to be dealt with effectively, some revisions and reinterpretation of the ESEA were necessary.

Unsatisfactory and inconclusive as much of the evidence was on the relative merits of the ESEA versus integration, neither approach appeared able to overcome the educational effects of poverty. The indications that no school program could wipe out the achievement gap led back to Coleman. "In effect, what educators have found, to their dismay," Coleman noted in 1970, "is that school is not as effective a means of increasing opportunity as it has been expected to be."[160] Educators were searching for new ways to improve the school's effects on poor children, but so far it appeared that they had been too cautious. By 1970 several facts were becoming clear. Typical compensatory education programs were usually next to useless, although inadequate evaluations did not give enough information to show why. Carefully planned projects had some initial effect on target children, but the elements of success were not identified. Integration also had a continuing effect on achievement. No program lived up to the original expectations of the War on Poverty or the intent to eliminate the achievement gap. Goals perhaps had to be reduced or bolder measures taken. "If improved student achievement is one goal," wrote one authority, "the Coleman Report's implication is obvious: we must alter the whole social system rather than just tinker with the schools."[161]

Some rejected the continuing controversy over whether education could overcome the effects of poverty as meaning-less. Test scores, so often cited as proof of success or failure, measured only limited areas of knowledge and intelligence. Schools were more than the sum of their reading scores. Thus, the argument went, the ESEA could not be evaluated merely by its ability to change scores. And as the National Advisory Council itself remarked in 1969, no one even knew whether improvement in reading and arithmetic would really break the cycle of poverty.[162] Early sociological studies suggested that it did not. Nevertheless, more detailed evidence relating test scores to jobs and economic success were necessary.[163] But even if reading scores did improve, HEW noted, it was impossible to tell what part of the improvement resulted from the Title I program.[164]

Nixon's 1971 Urban Education Task Force brought up another important consideration: the ESEA was not a traditional attempt to bring about educational change. The aims of the bill were vague and vast.[165] They ranged from breaking the cycle of poverty and reducing unemployment to passing legislation for federal aid to education and reforming the school system from within. Headstart had an equal range of objectives. Thus, no single evaluation measure could ascertain whether school legislation had attained the planners' mixed goals. But despite the difficulties of evaluation and the limited usefulness of objective evaluation measures, there had to be some attempts to measure how well a program was achieving its goals. Without such attempts there would be little progress in dealing with the social problems that policy-makers sought to improve. There would be no abandonment of ineffective programs or certainty about promising programs. Some beginning at evaluation, however inadequate, was imperative despite the controversy over its necessity and value. What was called for was strong government leadership in the whole complicated area of measuring social policy and its results.

It was obvious that Title I had not lived up to the rhetorical claims made for education in the early days of the War on Poverty. Nor had its companion, Headstart. Gains were modest, but it was hard to argue that they were of no value. The real question was whether there were better ways to get results. Policy-planners were now faced with the issues they had evaded in 1963 and 1964. If education could not help poor people break out of their poverty, if the liberal belief in education as a panacea was false, a new approach to poverty was necessary. The question was, however, whether policy-makers still wanted to deal with poverty in the 1970s and whether intellectuals could provide them with any direction.

1. Quoted in John Beckler, "Title I Assessed: How Important Is Money?", *School Management* 14 (November 1970): 4.

2. James S. Coleman et al., *Equality of Educational Opportunity*, p. 36 (hereafter cited as Coleman Report).

3. Ibid., p. 20.

4. Ibid., p. 219.

5. U.S. Commission on Civil Rights, *Racial Isolation in the Public Schools*, 1:3 n. 12.

6. Coleman Report, p. 21.

7. Ibid., p. 219.

8. James S. Coleman, "Equality of Educational Opportunity," p. 20.

9. Coleman Report, pp. 66–183.

10. Ibid., p. 296.

11. Ibid., p. 299.

12. Ibid., p. 302.

13. Ibid., p. 305.

14. Ibid., pp. 303–4.

15. Ibid., p. 3.

16. Ibid., pp. 31, 307.

17. James S. Coleman, "Equal Schools or Equal Students?", pp. 73–74.

18. Frederick Mosteller and Daniel P. Moynihan, eds., *On Equality of Educational Opportunity*, p. 239.

19. Coleman, "Equal Schools," p. 71.

20. Coleman Report, p. 316.

21. Coleman, "Equal Schools," p. 74.

22. Coleman, "Equality of Educational Opportunity," p. 21.

23. Daniel P. Moynihan, "Sources of Resistance to the Coleman Report," p. 24.

24. Gerald Paul Grant, "The Coleman Report," p. 4.

25. Coleman, "Equal Schools," p. 71.

26. James S. Coleman et al., *Equality of Educational Opportunity: Summary Report*, p. 21.

27. Ibid.

28. Harold Howe later denied, however, that the 3 July release date was part of an effort to play down the report. See *Hearings before the Select Committee on Equal Educational Opportunity of the U.S. Senate*, 92nd Cong., 1st Sess., 1971, Senate, 5652.

29. Moynihan, "Sources of Resistance," p. 25.

30. Grant, "The Coleman Report," p. 5.

31. Exceptional references to the Coleman Report appear in *Hearings before the Committee on Education and Labor on the Elementary and Secondary Education Act Amendments of 1967*, 90th Cong., 1st Sess., 1967, House, pp. 252, 552, 561; and in *Hearings before the Committee on Education and Labor on the Extension of Elementary and Secondary Education Programs*, 91st Cong., 1st Sess., 1969, House, p. 2918.

32. Grant, "The Coleman Report," pp. 12–13.

33. Quoted in ibid., p. 13.

34. Moynihan, "Sources of Resistance," p. 25.

35. For a positive reaction see William H. Sewell, Leonard A. Marascuilo, and

Harold W. Pfautz, "Review Symposium," p. 479. Quoted in Grant, "The Coleman Report," p. 24.

36. *Equal Educational Opportunity*, p. 4.

37. See Meyer Weinberg, *Desegregation Research*, p. 192; Edmund Gordon, "Introduction," p. 10; Samuel Bowles and Henry M. Levin, "The Determinants of Scholastic Achievement," p. 8.

38. Bowles and Levin, "Scholastic Achievement," pp. 6–7.

39. For further references see *Equal Educational Opportunity*, p. 4, n. 5.

40. Ralph Gabor Lewis, "Academic Achievement and the Effects of School Racial Composition," p. 33.

41. Grant, "The Coleman Report," p. 21.

42. Mosteller and Moynihan, *On Equality of Educational Opportunity*, pp. 174–76.

43. Ibid., pp. 185, 188, 195.

44. Ibid., pp. 196–97, 206–9.

45. Ibid., pp. 215–17, 225.

46. Ibid., p. 197.

47. Ibid., p. 226.

48. Ibid., p. 225.

49. Ibid., p. 315. Of course, as Gerald Grant points out in "Essay Reviews," p. 113, the survey did not measure teacher attitudes or the allocation of resources and policies within the school. These may well affect how well children learn.

50. *Racial Isolation*, 1:iv.

51. Ibid., p. v.

52. Meyer Weinberg, *Desegregation Research: An Appraisal*, 2d ed. (Bloomington, Ind.: Phi Delta Kappan, 1970), p. 293.

53. *Racial Isolation*, 1:iii.

54. Ibid., p. 3.

55. Ibid., p. 10.

56. Coleman Report, p. 307.

57. *Racial Isolation*, 1:195.

58. Ibid., 2:42.

59. Ibid., 1:91; 2:50. The study does not use the term *middle-class* but refers to the educational levels of parents. I use the term to mean the possession of a high school diploma.

60. Ibid., 1:95.

61. Ibid., p. 99.

62. Ibid., 2:50.

63. Ibid., 1:100.

64. See, however, Meg Greenfield, "What Is Racial Balance in the Schools?", p. 26.

65. Quoted in Grant, "The Coleman Report," p. 43.

66. *Racial Isolation*, 2:186.

67. Ibid., pp. 190, 184.

68. Weinberg, *Desegregation Research*, 2d ed., p. 295.

69. Grant, "The Coleman Report," p. 45; Greenfield, "What Is Racial Balance," p. 20.

70. Thomas F. Pettigrew, "Race and Equal Educational Opportunity," p. 70.

71. *Racial Isolation*, 1:81.

72. Thomas F. Pettigrew, "Racial Implications of Title III, ESEA," p. 42.

73. *The Use of Social Research in Federal Domestic Programs*, 2, Committee on Government Operations, Research and Technical Programs Subcommittee, 90th Cong., 1st Sess., 1967, House, pp. 265–66.

74. *Racial Isolation*, 2:119.

75. Ibid., 1:120.

76. Ibid., pp. 120–21, 123–26.

77. Ibid., p. 127.

78. Ibid., p. 205.

79. Ibid., pp. 128–33.

80. Ibid., 2:245–46.

81. Ibid., 1:138.

82. *House Hearings*, 1967, p. 542.

83. *Racial Isolation*, 1:194.

84. Christopher Jencks, "Education," p. 21.

85. *House Hearings*, 1969, p. 2554.

86. Ibid., p. 2353.

87. Ibid., p. 2356.

88. Ibid., p. 2796.

89. Ibid., p. 2833.

90. *Hearings before the General Subcommittee on Education of the Committee on Education and Labor on Aid to Elementary and Secondary Education*, 89th Cong., 1st Sess., 1965, House, p. 141.

91. See Amitai Etzioni and Edward W. Lehman, "Some Dangers in 'Valid' Social Measurement," *Annals* of the American Academy of Political and Social Science, vol. 373 (September 1967), pp. 1–15, for a discussion of problems in measurement.

92. *House Hearings*, 1969, p. 33.

93. Public Law 89–10, Sec. 205.(a)(5).

94. Alice M. Rivlin, *Systematic Thinking for Social Action*, p. 82.

95. Edward L. McDill, Mary S. McDill, and J. Timothy Sprehe, *Strategies for Success in Compensatory Education*, p. 43.

96. Samuel H. Beer and Richard E. Barringer, eds., *The State and the Poor*, p. 231.

97. Jerome T. Murphy, "Title I of ESEA," p. 56 n. 62.

98. McDill, McDill, and Sprehe, *Strategies for Success*, pp. 7, 10.

99. Ibid., p. 9.

100. Rivlin, *Systematic Thinking*, p. 82.

101. *House Hearings*, 1969, p. 30.

102. Ibid., p. 31.

103. Rivlin, *Systematic Thinking*, pp. 82–83.

104. Ibid., p. 83.

105. *House Hearings*, 1969, p. 2901.

106. U.S. Department of Health, Education, and Welfare, Office of Education, *Education of the Disadvantaged*, p. 127.

107. Ibid., p. 125.

108. Ibid., p. 127.

109.   *House Hearings*, 1969, p. 2904.

110.   Ibid., p. 2906.

111.   Ibid., p. 2909.

112.   HEW, *Education of the Disadvantaged*, p. 127.

113.   Ibid.

114.   *House Hearings*, 1969, p. 2911.

115.   HEW, *Education of the Disadvantaged*, p. 125.

116.   Harvey A. Averch et al., *How Effective Is Schooling?*, p. 101.

117.   *New York Times*, 8 June 1975.

118.   For a discussion of some small-scale successful preschool programs, see Julian C. Stanley, *Preschool Programs for the Disadvantaged*. For a discussion of some of the political and administrative aspects of Headstart, see Robert A. Levine, *The Poor Ye Need Not Have with You*, chap. 4; for a discussion of various evaluations, see Sheldon H. White et al., *Federal Programs for Young Children: Review and Recommendations* (Washington, D.C.: Government Printing Office, 1973).

119.   Quoted in Levine, *The Poor Ye Need Not Have*, p. 135.

120.   David K. Cohen and Michael S. Garet, "Reforming Educational Policy with Applied Social Research," p. 22.

121.   Levine, *The Poor Ye Need Not Have*, pp. 136–37.

122.   John C. Donovan, *The Politics of Poverty*.

123.   Levine, *The Poor Ye Need Not Have*, p. 37.

124.   Ibid., pp. 140–41.

125.   Quoted in Averch et al., *How Effective Is Schooling?*, p. 101.

126.   Jerome Hellmuth, ed., *Disadvantaged Child, Compensatory Education*, p. 168.

127.   Ibid., p. 175.

128.   Marshall S. Smith and Joan S. Bissell, "Report Analysis," p. 52.

129.   Averch et al., *How Effective Is Schooling?*, p. 104.

130.   Smith and Bissell, "Report Analysis," pp. 52–53.

131.   Ibid., pp. 51–104; McDill, McDill, and Sprehe, *Strategies for Success*, p. 27.

132.   McDill, McDill, and Sprehe, *Strategies for Success*, p. 23.

133.   White, *Federal Programs*, 2:188.

134.   Averch et al., *How Effective Is Schooling?*, p. 125. For a recent discussion of results, see Urie Bronfenbrenner, "Is Early Intervention Effective?", p. 289.

135.   Carol H. Weiss, "The Politicization of Evaluation Research," p. 65.

136.   "Moynihan Believes Class Is the Issue," p. 10.

137.   National Advisory Council on the Education of Disadvantaged Children, *Title I—ESEA: A Review and a Forward Look—1969*, p. 20.

138.   U.S. Department of Health, Education, and Welfare, Office of Education, *Secondary Program in Compensatory Education 4*, p. 1.

139.   Ibid., pp. 12–14.

140.   National Advisory Council, *Title I—ESEA: A Review*, p. 22.

141   Ibid., pp. 23–24.

142.   White, *Federal Programs*, 2:88–89, 125, 129.

143.   David K. Cohen, "Policy for the Public Schools," p. 135.

144.   Levine, *The Poor Ye Need Not Have*, p. 142.

145.   Rivlin, *Systematic Thinking*, p. 90.

146. Ibid., p. vii.

147. Ibid., p. 108; Thomas Ribich, *Education and Poverty*, p. 77.

148. *Hearings before the Select Committee on Equal Educational Opportunity*, 91st Cong., 2d Sess., 1970, Senate, p. 856.

149. U.S. Department of Health, Education, and Welfare, Office of Education, *Elementary Program in Compensatory Education 2*, pp. 8–9.

150. *Senate Hearings on Equal Educational Opportunity*, 1970, p. 859.

151. HEW, *Education of the Disadvantaged*, p. 127.

152. National Advisory Council on the Education of Disadvantaged Children, *Title I, ESEA—The Weakest Link*, p. iii.

153. Ibid., p. 2.

154. Ibid., p. 15.

155. Ibid., pp. 15–18. The council felt that compensatory education was still a possibility because of the results of a Rochester, New York, study that showed students performing as well in compensatory but segregated classes as those students in integrated classes. Recent testimony by Rochester's superintendent, who was the director of the compensatory program, corrects this picture. Dr. Franco says that the integration program was more successful in improving skills than the compensatory program. *Hearings before the Select Committee on Equal Educational Opportunity*, 92d Cong., 2d Sess., 1971, Senate, pp. 625–27.

156. *Senate Hearings on Equal Educational Opportunity*, 1970, p. 93.

157. Ibid., p. 759.

158. Nancy H. St. John, "Desegregation and Minority Group Performance," pp. 111–33.

159. HEW, *Education of the Disadvantaged*, pp. 35–36.

160. *Senate Hearings on Equal Educational Opportunity*, 1970, p. 99.

161. Christopher Jencks, "A Reappraisal of the Most Controversial Educational Document of Our Time," p. 42.

162. National Advisory Council, *Title I—ESEA: A Review*, p. 25.

163. Ribich, *Education and Poverty*, p. 72.

164. *Hearings before the Subcommittee on Education of the Committee on Labor and Public Welfare on the Elementary and Secondary Education Amendments of 1969*, 91st Cong., 1st Sess., 1969, Senate, p. 1277.

165. Wilson C. Riles, *The Urban Education Task Force Report*, p. 207.

6

Intellectual Fragmentation

The fragile foundations supporting the educational components of the War on Poverty were now exposed. Studies suggeted that schools, as they were, did little to overcome poverty. Actual programs hardly appeared to affect children. The detachment shown by school boards and others in charge of educating poor children indicated how unrealistic it was to expect the school system to reform itself. The model of change held by planners in 1964 and 1965 appeared naïve and unworkable. Not surprisingly, faced with the results of the War on Poverty, intellectuals concerned with social problems and their solutions were uncertain and often discouraged. Contributing to a mood of disillusionment was the difficulty of establishing clearly why poverty programs had failed. The ESEA, for example, had a weak intellectual basis, poor implementation, and inadequate funding. Was one factor more important than others in producing lackluster results? There was no way to determine. Moreover, despite the wealth of statistical data available, surveys like the Coleman Report showed primarily what did not work and could not give the final answers to what were still gripping intellectual questions: How could the nation provide its poor children with equal educational opportunity?[1] What were the best ways to overcome poverty?

In this atmosphere of uncertainty, no new consensus emerged to replace the easy liberal confidence of the early 1960s that social problems were soluble. Although compensatory education had failed to break the poverty cycle, intellectuals still argued over whether education had any chance of providing poor blacks and whites with social and economic opportunity.[2] Some went so far as to picture the whole effort of the previous years as a consciously cynical gesture to the poor. Others disagreed. Maintaining that the ESEA was a well-meaning but misguided, inadequate effort, they concluded that if education were reshaped or radically reformed, it still could have a definite part to play in eliminating poverty. Another group of intellectuals came to contrary conclusions during this period of reassessment, however. The experience of the 1960s had proved one thing: education did not and could not alleviate poverty. The traditional liberal solution for social problems did not work. If Americans were serious about solving problems like poverty, they would have to support sweeping and perhaps expensive measures like income transfers and work programs. But neither the climate of the country nor the temper of the new administration gave indications that such vigorous conclusions were acceptable. With this atmosphere, so unfriendly to social reform, it would hardly be surprising if the 1970s saw "the waning of reformist zeal."[3]

Among those who clung to the traditional faith, Charles Silberman represented the conservative viewpoint. His popular book of 1970, *Crisis in the Classroom*, acknowledged what was inescapable: there had been a serious breakdown in the nation's schools. "I am indignant at the failure of the public schools," Silberman proclaimed. "What grim, joyless places most American schools are," how sterile in atmosphere, how contemptuous of children.[4] Though all American schools were inadequate, Silberman stated, "the slum schools are failing in a way that middle class schools are not." For slum schools did not serve as equalizers of men but helped prolong

social differences. This failure was not the result of evil intentions but stemmed from the mindlessness of educators who
refused "to think seriously about educational purpose," who
were reluctant "to question" established procedures.[5] In
practice, mindlessness resulted in ordered, silent schools
emphasizing rules and traditional standards of performance,
and led to eventual failure for poor students.[6] Grim though
this reality was, however, Silberman still believed the public
school system could be reshaped to make it more responsive
to, and successful with, its lower-class students.

If the schools were to "reverse the reign of error that leads
to failure," they would have to become flexible, warm, humane and purposeful.[7] To illustrate the difference warmth
could make in school and to prove the validity of his solution, Silberman sketched several of the "open schools" he had
visited in England. There the lack of traditional classroom
structure seemed to produce a real enthusiasm for learning.[8]
Silberman described schools in the United States that were
experimenting with the open school concept and even some
ghetto schools where a humane atmosphere, he claimed,
produced high achievement without extra expenditures or extraordinary equipment.[9] Silberman's problem came when he
tried to analyze how schools could create the necessary new
personality. Introducing an open school format, he acknowledged, was not adequate because the format itself was
actually "less an approach or method than a set of shared
attitudes and convictions about the nature of childhood, learning, and schooling."[10] A different method for training teachers and a new relationship between public schools and universities were, of course, vital underpinnings for a new
spirit in the public school system.[11] But his solution, which
involved infusing "the various educating institutions with
purpose . . . with thought about purpose, and about the ways
in which techniques, content, and organization fulfill or alter
purpose," was, in fact vague. Lacking a definite mechanism
for achieving educational change within the system, Silberman
could only offer an optimistic but blurred blueprint for those
who still believed a better education for the poor was meaningful.

A more radical group of educators rejected Silberman's

approach of working through the existing public school system, although they agreed that education still might prove a useful social tool. The reforms of the sixties reinforced their perception of the school system as hopelessly rigid and resistant to any real innovation or concern for children. The first step in reform, then, would be to restructure the public school system and the second, to redistribute political power to parents and the community. After accomplishing these goals, education might have a different effect on children. The rationale for this structural approach grew out of experience, the Coleman Report, which had emphasized the detrimental effects powerlessness had on black students, and the widespread belief that free competition produced both diversity and quality. Reformers could not agree on any one method of reorganization but developed several different proposals for reshaping the school system. In some cases implementation even began on an experimental basis.

Kenneth Clark sounded the call for a system of competition and free choice in an article published in 1968. In the early days of the War on Poverty, David Hackett, of the President's Committee on Juvenile Delinquency, had talked of the necessity of challenging established institutions like the school system that he saw blocking opportunity. This suggestion had faded as Keppel and others decided to reform through the system. Now, Clark resumed this line of thought. "The rigidity of present patterns of public school organization and the concomitant stagnation in quality of education and academic performance of children," he wrote, "may not be amenable to any attempts at change working through and within the present system. Alternatives—realistic, aggressive, and viable competitors—to the present public school system must be found."[12] The alternatives Clark visualized were new schools, financed by universities, labor unions, industry, and even the army. These schools could bring dynamism and variety back into education, Clark suspected, and their example would instigate the public system into reforming itself.[13] As Clark pointed out, "Truly effective competition strengthens rather than weakens that which deserves to survive."[14] Although Clark did not deal with the question of choice, his scheme implicitly offered parents the opportunity to select a school for their children and to influence school policy.

Clark did not discuss the central problem of how schools would actually educate deprived children better than traditional schools. In an article written a year earlier, James Coleman had considered methods for stimulating innovation in teaching. Viewing the public school as "trapped by its own organizational weight," Coleman proposed "the transformation of schools from closed institutions to open ones."[15] The open school Coleman visualized would be a home base to provide teaching and to coordinate each student's outside activities. Teachers in the school would teach basic reading and arithmetical skills but so too would outside contractors. Since contractors would only be paid if students' test scores improved, Coleman thought they would be eager and likely to discover innovative teaching methods. Every time a contractor succeeded, the school would learn an effective teaching method that would act as a challenge to the way in which the school was handling its programs.[16]

The open school plan had several other advantages. Its flexibility could encourage racial and social mixing in outside programs.[17] The plan also gave the parents some control over education, since parents would decide whether their children would learn in school or with contractors. As Coleman pointed out, "The parent could, for the first time in education, have the full privileges of consumer's choice."[18]

Harvard Associate Professor of Education Christopher Jencks and his colleagues developed the most complete scheme for competitive education under a 1969 grant from the Office of Education. Working along the lines of Coleman and Clark, Jencks suggested improving the public school system by freeing it "from the restrictions which inevitably accompany . . . present monopolistic privileges." Legislators, school boards, and educators controlled education, Jencks maintained; parents needed some way to make those in power more responsive to their demands.[19] Educational vouchers would do this. In Jencks' plan all local, state, and federal education funds were to go to a special agency that would then distribute vouchers worth the area's average per-pupil expenditure to every parent. Armed with vouchers, parents could use them to pay tuition for their children at any voucher public school that satisfied their requirements. "One of the most important advantages of a voucher system" Jencks remarked, "is that it would encourage diversity and choice *within the public system*."[20] Parents would have a real opportunity to select schools for their children and considerable financial power over schools, for unless schools could provide programs parents liked, they would attract neither students nor money.

But although this plan had good points, Jencks did not think it could reverse the trend of educational failure he perceived in the public school system. The voucher system must include both private and parochial schools as well as the public schools. "Only if private initiative is possible," Jencks observed, will the public sector feel real pressure to make room for kinds of education that are politically awkward but have a substantial constituency."[21]

Variety, innovation, free choice, all were to play a part in the voucher plan. But Jencks was also specifically concerned with providing disadvantaged white and black children with the student environment that Coleman had felt was important for achievement. Realizing that a voucher system could easily encourage economic and racial segregation, Jencks emphasized that a system without safeguards "would be worse than no voucher system at all. Indeed, an unregulated voucher system could be the most serious setback for the education of disadvantaged children in the history of the United States."[22] A control on tuition and a rule that all applicants must be admitted to schools while openings existed sought to ensure that minority students attended middle-class schools. If a school had more interested students than places, Jencks suggested that half the vacancies be assigned by lot with the remainder being filled in some other non-discriminatory way. Beyond these control mechanisms, Jencks established an incentive for private schools to accept deprived students by making poor students worth extra money for the schools.

Jencks's proposals led to a lively debate over the practical possibilities of the system. Critics pointed out, for example, that the voucher plan would involve new educational expenditures of $5 billion a year, would not necessarily bring special opportunities for the deprived, and might well create a new bureaucracy to run voucher schools.[23] Others argued that the idea of vouchers was unrealistic because it demanded "a political commitment to values which are weak and vulnerable in America today: a commitment to equality of wealth, power, and race."[24] These writers saw the United States as a racist country, basically uninterested in either desegregation or improved education for the poor.[25] In answer to these criticisms, Jencks could reply that, radical as his proposal seemed, communities in California, Washington, and Missouri were eager to try it. Not all Americans were racists, not all legislators "such a bad lot."[26] True, vouchers would hardly be the panacea for all the ills of education, but Jencks concluded that new ground rules might produce real changes. "A properly regulated system," he observed, "could inaugurate a new era of innovation and reform in American schools."[27]

The educational voucher system and the proposals of Clark and Coleman stressed three elements important in restructuring education. Parents must have the significant power to make choices for their children. Schools must be accountable for the performance of their students. Schools must assume a primary responsibility for meeting the needs of their black and white poor pupils. Although proponents of community control offered quite different solutions for educating the disadvantaged their schemes saw the same concerns as basic to educational reform.

In suburbia some form of local control over schools was a reality, but within the central cities bureaucrats had regulated education since the late nineteenth century. In the late 1960s the bureaucracy was challenged by those who insisted that it was their right to control city schools. Many impulses fed into this often disruptive challenge. By suggesting community participation, the Economic Opportunity Act fostered activism and political awareness.[28] The black power movement contributed to the black desire to run community af-

fairs and to the new sense of black identity. Rejecting the
ideal of assimilation into white society, the new goal was
black control, even confrontation.[29]

Many of those who now demanded community control
of schools had led the struggle for integration.[30] Now integration seemed an insubstantial dream held out by white liberals but rejected by the rest of white society who moved to
suburbia and resisted busing. Compensatory education, once
seen as a major alternative to integration, had failed. Now
the black community was impatient. As one writer noted, "The
poor and the black are now searching out ways for the lower
classes to circumvent the poverty of inner city schools as more
prosperous groups have been able to do."[31]

The demands of those favoring community control differed. Stokely Carmichael epitomized the spirit, however.
"Black people have a right to run their own schools,"
Carmichael claimed.[32] "White decision-makers have been
running . . . schools with injustice, indifference, and inadequacy for too long."[33] Some advocates of community control
only thought of making parents advisers to the schools.[34]
Radicals, however, fought to give the community the power
to elect its own school board, which in turn would select
teachers, work out the school budget, allocate funds, and
decide on programs.[35] The school, radicals suggested,
must respond to the community's wishes and be responsible
to the community.[36] For its part the community had to reach
out to involve itself in school matters and give the school
active support. The schools would have an essential and creative part in forming a total black community.[37]

Some critics viewed these demands as a political ma-
neuver with little intellectual coherence.[38] It was true that
community control envisioned a basic redistribution of political power, but there was also evidence of a real concern
with educational as well as political goals. Community control seemed a way to give the black child, at long last,
quality education.[39] As Floyd McKissick, director of CORE,
noted, "If the school is organized and run differently, and if
the school is more involved with the forces which it now treats
as outside its concern, student achievement would rise."[40]

It was insulting to believe in the necessity of integration. McKissick noted that integration really meant saying, "Mix Negroes with Negroes and you get stupidity."[41]

The belief that, as McKissick put it, "educational excellence without integration is possible" rested on a selective interpretation of the Coleman Report.[42] Coleman had discovered that Negro pupils felt less in control of their environment than whites and that this attitude was strongly correlated to educational achievement.[43] Supporters of community control claimed this finding called for schools under community (black) supervision. Such schools, they reasoned, would create a sense of control in black children and would, therefore, trigger achievement. But these conclusions ignored the more significant evidence Coleman had also presented on the importance of having a mixed socioeconomic student body. Unlike Jencks and others who still believed integration was necessary and possible, many blacks could not accept the idea that middle-class students represented a key factor in black achievement. And they were warmly supported by both disillusioned white liberals who despaired over the possibilities of integration and white conservatives who wished to perpetuate *de facto* segregation.

Although conservatives and radicals of the late 1960s did not agree on how to redistribute power and restructure the school system, they continued to believe education might help deal with some aspects of poverty. But to some observers the experience of the sixties led to the inescapable conclusion that education had little to do with poverty. Those seeking to reform education were involved in a futile task. As one educator pointed out, "There is . . . no evidence that changing the framework of choice in education will. have much effect. It may be that the school's 'failure' to affect the transmission of status from generation to generation will only serve to focus attention on the political arrangements governing education, rather than on the more important need to directly attack the underlying social and economic inequalities."[44] It was with these underlying social and economic inequalities that some intellectuals were concerned.

Education, for example, did little to overcome one central

problem of poverty: inadequate income. Thomas Ribich's 1968 study, *Education and Poverty*, focused on this issue. Using techniques of benefit cost analysis developed by economists, Ribich explored whether education really did increase the income of the poor. Information on the educational aspects of the War on Poverty was incomplete, and Ribich's method of translating test score gains and future income was far from satisfactory. Yet Ribich argued that without a short-term measurement of gain, "the economic evaluation of educational innovations will have to be postponed for intolerably long periods."[45]

Ribich's tentative conclusions were "not particularly encouraging." For example, the cost of special compensatory education programs exceeded predicted monetary benefits for those participating in them.[46] Increasing pupil expenditures over the entire school career also yielded few rewards.[47] Gains resulting from such programs were probably insufficient to help children move out of the cycle of poverty.[48] Vocational programs, Ribich concluded, yielded "a higher rate of payoff" than general education.[49] Moreover, he noted that although there were many benefits from education aside from financial ones, other solutions for poverty like income transfers or better housing could also create some of these same benefits.[50]

An approach complementing the very tentative findings of Ribich's work showed that outside factors prevented education from paying off financially. In *Poverty and Discrimination* Lester Thurow used econometric methods to study causes of poverty and the value of poverty programs. Thurow concluded that discrimination prevented education from raising black incomes in the same way as white incomes. "Discrimination and poverty are as intertwined as Siamese twins," he wrote. "They need two policies, one to fight the causes of poverty and another to reduce discrimination."[51] S. M. Miller and Pamela Roby agreed with these findings in *The Future of Inequality*. "The roots of black poverty lie in the discriminatory practices of the larger society as well as their own lack of education. As long as discrimination exists, education alone will not solve the problems of redistributing incomes and occupations between whites and minority members."[52] Any program that sought to eliminate poverty, therefore, had to "operate on racial discrimination" itself.[53] Such studies insisted that the solution to the poverty problem involved the whole society.

In 1969 a new and bitter factor entered into the discussion over the failure of education. Starting on a relatively noncontroversial note, Arthur Jensen's article in the *Harvard Educational Review* stated, "Compensatory education has been tried and it apparently has failed."[54] For proof Jensen pointed to familiar evidence showing that programs like the ESEA and Headstart had not closed the achievement gap between blacks and whites. So far the article was unexceptional. But then Jensen went on to attack some of the basic arguments of compensatory educators: that all children were inherently equal in basic intelligence and that environmental deficiencies and the cultural bias of tests explained the achievement gap.[55] These were ideas that were still generally accepted despite the results of compensatory programs and that provided a necessary underpinning for many other social reform measures. After examining the explanations for differences in mental ability, Jensen concluded that the evidence suggested that genetic factors were more important in explaining ability differences than environmental factors were.[56] Writing later, he claimed, "The major races are simply breeding populations that have a relatively high degree of inbreeding and differ from one another in the relative frequencies of many genes. They differ in so many known gene frequencies in fact, that it seems highly improbable that they would not also differ in the frequencies of genes related to behavioral traits such as intelligence."[57]

Reduced to the simplest level, Jensen was saying that the average black had less native intelligence than whites. This lack of intelligence explained the failure of compensatory education, "a misguided hope," as well as the failure of other schemes that tried to achieve equal academic results.[58] Jensen's conclusions also implicitly questioned other kinds of social measures predicated on the innate equality of all Americans. Yet Jensen, though negative about compensatory

education, still saw some role for schools. Special school programs could improve habits, motivation, and values of disadvantaged students.[59] Moreover, Jensen perceived a significant difference between the learning patterns of advantaged
white and disadvantaged black children. Whites could think
abstractly, whereas black children were skilled at learning by
association.[60] Since schools catered exclusively to abstract
thinkers, they frustrated blacks. Schools had to develop new
approaches to tap associative abilities.[61] Schools thus had a
conservative, not a radical, function in society. "Equality of
performance is a misguided hope," Jensen concluded. "The
important things for the welfare of children and society in
general would seem to be to try and create conditions that
will maximize the proportion of the population that can learn
and work successfully."[62]

Jensen's article, which attacked such basic liberal beliefs,
triggered controversy and debate.[63] Critics admonished Jensen for making claims unwarranted by the evidence. Social
scientists pointed to studies which indicated that environment had a large effect on I.Q. scores. Others rejected the
implications of Jensen's work that rendered social measures
impotent and unnecessary. The furor caused Jensen to retort,
"The only sensible conclusion one can draw from a perusal
of this evidence is that the key question in everyone's mind
about racial differences in ability—are they genetic?—has, in effect, been ruled out as a serious alternative hypothesis in the
search for the causal factors involved in inequalities of educational performance."[64]

After several years of social experimentation in education,
there was a good deal of disagreement, uncertainty, and
murkiness in thinking about the future course of education
and social reform. In 1972, with what was both a research
document and a proposal, Christopher Jencks and his colleagues again joined the discussion about the relationship
between education and poverty. Pulling together a wide
variety of studies like the Coleman Report, the Plowden
study of English primary schools, and data compiled by many
other scholars, Jencks's book *Inequality: A Reassessment of
the Effect of Family and Schooling in America* was clearly the

most significant study of education since the 1966 Coleman survey.[65] But Jencks's work, which supported both those who said that education did not matter and those who said that it did, which advocated socialism but acknowledged that it was unlikely, could not bring peace or consensus to intellectual circles or provide an underpinning for new social reform measures.

As Jencks reviewed the reforms of the 1960s, he argued that these efforts had tried to help the poor move into better jobs and make more money. Poverty, reformers had assumed, was an absolute condition that would end once the poor person earned a certain amount of money and crossed the "poverty line."[66] The goal, then, was a good job. Since the reformers all shared the belief that economic success resulted from academic success, their efforts to improve the schooling of poor children were logical.[67]

Jencks felt, however, that policy-makers had been concerned with the wrong problems and had used the wrong approach. Poverty was not an absolute state ending once the worker had earned a certain number of dollars but a relative state. The real problem was not whether the worker crossed the poverty line but adult inequality. Social and economic mobility existed but not equality.[68] "Only a handful of radicals," Jencks pointed out, "talked about eliminating inequality per se."[69] And since policy-makers had not clearly faced what Jencks saw as the real problem, their reform efforts failed. "Equalizing opportunity is almost impossible without greatly reducing the absolute level of inequality, and the same is true of eliminating deprivation," Jencks reasoned.[70]

Furthermore, Jencks argued, the educational approach was misguided. There was no evidence that educational reforms affected academic skills.[71] Title I, for example, had channeled money to poor children, but their test scores did not rise consistently. "In fact," Jencks commented, "the results of evaluation appear to be virtually random. Students in Title I programs do worse than comparison groups as often as they do better."[72] Recapitulating and refining what was already known, Jencks showed that school differences affected students only slightly in the long run, that money spent on schools did not explain the differences in how much children learned, and that there were greater differences between the scores of students within a school than between students in different schools.[73] Jencks explained once again the determinants of what children learned. "Variations in what children learn in school depend largely on variations in what they bring to school."[74] What children brought to school not only included family background but, as Jensen had argued, genetic makeup. Realizing that his findings might "make many people angry," Jencks concluded, as others also had, that 45 percent of the difference in test scores could be explained by genes (not 80 percent as Jensen had claimed), 35 percent by family environment, and 20 percent by the interaction between genes and family background.[75] Even if the quality of all elementary schools were uniform, then, Jencks suggested, academic inequality would be reduced by 3 percent or less; if all high schools were similar, cognitive inequality would shrink by only 1 percent.[76]

Yet despite these findings that schools did not affect achievement, Jencks did not deny them an important role. Disagreeing with Coleman, Jencks felt that school achievement had little relation to job success.[77] But schools were "certification agencies" that legitimized inequality. Arguing that a diploma signified primarily the number of years spent in school and not what had been learned, Jencks asked who won diplomas and why.[78] Obviously, middle-class children went to school longer than poor children and earned diplomas. There were many reasons why more middle-class children received academic credentials. Coming from a family situation that encouraged the development of school-oriented skills, middle-class children were also more likely to have genes that favored academic success and the money to pay for years of education.[79] More important than these factors were those of motivation and value. The typical middle-class child expected to stay in school, and might even enjoy it.[80] But schools did not have to reward students for remaining there. It was certainly possible to award degrees by national examinations and avoid making the schools certification agencies.[81] But if the present system remained, Jencks pointed out, and "if we want to equalize the educational attainment of children from different economic backgrounds, we will probably have to change not only their test scores and financial resources but also their attitudes and values."[82]

Jencks's work raised the crucial question of whether credentials awarded by schools directly affected occupation and income later in life. There was a link, Jencks found, between the kind of job held after school and the amount of education an individual had. On the other hand, Jencks qualified this finding with the reminder that although job and academic credentials were linked more closely than any other variables, there were "still enormous status differences among people with the same amount of education."[83]

Did credentials, explain why some people earned more money than others? This was the central concern of *Inequality* and one that set the book apart from many of the earlier studies. On the basis of a wide variety of evidence, Jencks judged that family background, cognitive skills, credentials, and occupation all failed to account for financial success.[84] Jencks believed, although he did not claim he could prove, that personality factors and a variety of nonacademic skills had some bearing on income. Some of these skills might come from schools, but they could not be measured.[85] Then, too, chance probably played a role in producing financial success: acquaintances who gave good job advice, "a hundred other unpredictable accidents."[86] These nonrational factors standing behind social and economic mobility made the educational approach irrelevant. If an attack on inequality was to be made, Jencks counseled adopting a number of different strategies to redistribute income.[87] Realizing that Americans were a long way from feeling that income inequality was a social evil, however, Jencks saw his job as one of arousing political and moral consciousness.[88]

Despite the reinforcement *Inequality* lent to intellectuals and to politicians, who could claim that the study proved once again that education did not matter, Jencks and his colleagues favored both spending money for education and equalizing spending between the rich and the poor. Schools must, of course, teach basic skills; for without the ability to read and write, a person was vocationally crippled.[89] Furthermore, for the lower-class student coming from a non-supportive family background, elementary school was vital.[90] And, as Jencks was aware, his study had focused on the average school spending funds in average ways. A different use of money might bring very different results.[91] As Jencks said, his data meant that "we cannot say much about the theoretical limits of what can be done in . . . a school."[92] Experimentation was in order, although Jencks was cautious about the potential of educational innovations.

Then, too, the quality of life within the school was important. The child spends between one-sixth and one-fourth of his life in school, and this time should be enjoyable. Both teachers and students felt that there was a connection between spending and the quality of school life, and this justified school expenditures. Although none of the reasons supporting increased or equalized spending had a long-term "hard" effect, Jencks felt that demands of social justice reinforced the plea for equal spending.[93] These were arguments, however, that might not be politically compelling.

Jencks took up the whole issue of racial and social integration. No study had been able to offer conclusive results on integration, but what evidence there was suggested that the social composition of a school did affect achievement.[94] Desegregation, too, also improved scores: "Our best guess is that desegregation raises black scores by 2-3 points."[95] The reasons for this small effect were unclear.[96] Once more for reasons of social justice, racial segregation had to end. But blacks and whites would do well to recognize that "economic success depends largely on other factors. We could then try to tackle economic inequality between blacks and whites directly."[97]

The attacks on Jencks's book were not long in coming. By 1972 the type of criticism was predictable in its emphasis on statistical errors, the amount of guesswork involved in combining different kinds of data, and the policy conclusions. The inescapable significance of the book, which brought together so many studies, no doubt motivated some of the responses. So too did Jencks's acknowledgment that the reasons for success were, to a large extent, unknowable. Jencks was, in fact, stripping away various liberal illusions about the nature of the American system and the nature of reform. The real purpose of education was not social change. If liberals actually believed what they said, then they would have to adopt new assumptions and different kinds of measures than they had in the 1960s. "Until we change the political and moral premises on which most Americans now operate, poverty and inequality of opportunity will persist at pretty much their present level," Jencks wrote.[98] He was posing a choice and offering a challenge. But even as he did so, he realized the practical difficulties of what he suggested. "The crucial problem today, is that relatively few people view income inequality as a serious problem."

Indeed, Jencks saw the concern with any method for equalizing incomes as "an interesting but politically irrelevant exercise."[99] To establish any form of socialism was a tremendous task.[100] Jencks's awareness of the virtual impossibility of true reform and his knowledge that he was one of a minority seemed fitting in a period of intellectual fragmentation and discouragement. It appeared that neither the contradictory nor the bold suggestions of intellectuals were likely to persuade government planners to formulate bold new social programs.

1.   Walter Williams, *Social Policy Research and Analysis*, p. 58.

2.   Jerome Hellmuth, ed., *Disadvantaged Child, Compensatory Education*, p. 6; David K. Cohen, "Public Schools," p. 165.

3.   Michael B. Katz, "The Present Moment in Educational Reform," p. 343.

4.   Charles E. Silberman, *Crisis in the Classroom*, p. 10.

5.   Ibid., pp. 62, 53, 11.

6.   Ibid., pp. 122–42.

7.   Ibid., pp. 98, 94, 279.

8.   Ibid., pp. 208–37.

9.   Ibid., pp. 98–105, 443.

10.   Ibid., p. 208.

11.   Ibid., pp. 320, 473.

12.   Kenneth B. Clark, "Alternative Public School Systems," pp. 108, 111.

13.   Ibid., pp. 112–13.

14. Ibid., p. 111.

15. James S. Coleman, *Toward Open Schools*, pp. 25, 24.

16. Ibid., pp. 24–26.

17. Ibid., p. 26.

18. Ibid., p. 25.

19. Judith Areen and Christopher Jencks, "Education Vouchers," p. 329; Christopher Jencks et al., *Education Vouchers*, p. 1.

20. Areen and Jencks, "Education Vouchers," p. 329.

21. Ibid.

22. Ibid., p. 332.

23. Eli Genzberg, "The Economics of the Voucher System," pp. 377–79; Robert Lekachman, "*Education Report*: Vouchers and Public Education," p. 13.

24. Stephen Arons, "Equity, Option, and Vouchers," p. 361.

25. Ginzberg, "Economics," p. 381.

26. Areen and Jencks, "Education Vouchers," p. 8.

27. Ibid.,; Jencks et al., *Education Vouchers*, p. 17.

28. Mario Fantini, Marilyn Gittell, and Richard Magat, *Community Control and the Urban School*, p. 10.

29. Cohen, "Public Schools," p. 162.

30. Fantini, Gittell, and Magat, *Community Control*, p. x.

31. Colin Greer, *Cobweb Attitudes*, pp. 18–19.

32. Quoted in Gerald Grant, "Developing Power in the Ghetto," p. 76.

33. Stokely Carmichael and Charles Hamilton, "Dynamite," p. 101.

34. Fantini, Gittell, and Magat, *Community Control*, pp. 81–82.

35. James K. Kent, "The Community School Concept," p. 46.

36. Fantini, Gittell, and Magat, *Community Control*, p. x.

37. Kent, "Community School Concept," p. 2; Cohen, "Public Schools," p. 162.

38. Annette T. Rubinstein, *Schools against Children*, p. 284.

39. Fantini, Gittell, and Magat, *Community Control*, p. 90.

40. Floyd McKissick, "A Communication," p. 35.

41. Henry M. Levin, ed., *Community Control of Schools* (Washington, D.C.: Brookings Institution, 1970), p. 102.

42. Ibid., p. 35; Maurice R. Berube, "Community Control," p. 42.

43. Coleman Report, pp. 319–25.

44. Cohen, "Public Schools," p. 170.

45. Thomas I. Ribich, *Education and Poverty*, p. 77.

46. Ibid., pp. 76–77.

47. Ibid., p. 95.

48. Ibid., p. 102.

49. Ibid., p. 97.

50. Ibid., pp. 124–25.

51. Lester C. Thurow, *Poverty and Discrimination*, pp. 136, 77–84, 154–55, 1.

52. S. M. Miller and Pamela A. Roby, *The Future of Inequality*, p. 128.

53. Thurow, *Poverty and Discrimination*, p. 160.

54. Arthur R. Jensen, "How Much Can We Boost I.Q. and Scholastic Achievement?", p. 2.

55. Ibid., pp. 4–5.

56. Ibid., pp. 5–116; Hellmuth, *Disadvantaged Child*, p. 103.

57. Arthur R. Jensen, "Can We and Should We Study Racial Differences," in Hellmuth, *Disadvantaged Child*, p. 137.

58. Arthur R. Jensen, "Reducing the Heredity-Environment Uncertainty," p. 467.

59. Jensen, "How Much Can We Boost I.Q.?", p. 59.

60. Ibid., p. 112.

61. Arthur R. Jensen, "Another Look at Culture-Fair Testing," in Hellmuth, *Disadvantaged Child*, p. 96.

62. Jensen, "Reducing the Heredity-Environment Uncertainty," p. 467.

63. See *Harvard Educational Review* 39 (Summer 1969).

64. Hellmuth, *Disadvantaged Child*, p. 104; Jensen, "Can We and Should We Study Racial Differences," in ibid., p. 145.

65. Christopher Jencks et al., *Inequality*, pp. vii, 15 n. 4, 359–82.

66. Ibid., pp. 3–4.

67. Ibid., p. 52.

68. Ibid., p. 179.

69. Ibid., p. 3.

70. Ibid., p. 4.

71. Such as the ability to manipulate words and numbers, assimilate information, etc. (ibid., pp. 8–53).

72. Ibid., p. 94.

73. Ibid., pp. 16, 29, 106–7.

74. Ibid., p. 53.

75. Ibid., pp. 64–65, 77. See p. 14 for his explanation of the accuracy of his figures.

76. Ibid., p. 109.

77. See Coleman Report, p. 218.

78. Jencks, *Inequality*, p. 135.

79. Ibid., pp. 138–41, 158–59.

80. Ibid., p. 141.

81. Ibid., p. 135.

82. Ibid., p. 141.

83. Ibid., p. 191.

84. Ibid., p. 226.

85. Ibid., p. 134.

86. Ibid., pp. 131. 227.

87. Ibid., pp. 260–63.

88. Ibid., p. 264.

89. Ibid., p. 6.

90. Ibid., p. 89.

91. Ibid., p. 97.

92. Ibid., p. 13.

93. Ibid., p. 29.

94. Ibid., p. 30.

95. Ibid., p. 106.

96. Ibid., p. 102.

97. Ibid., p. 84.
98. Ibid., p. 9.
99. Ibid., p. 263.
100. Ibid., p. 265.

7

The Political Response

Just as Lyndon Johnson had exuberantly expressed the liberal faith of the early 1960s, Richard Nixon now soberly reflected the new skepticism in his rejection of the faith. The goals of the Great Society programs were unattainable and its methods undesirable, the president implied. "In the maze of antipoverty efforts," he remarked, "precedents are weak and knowledge uncertain. These past years of increasing Federal involvement have begun to make clear how vast is the range of what we do not yet know, and how fragile are projections based on partial understanding."[1] One thing seemed obvious to the president: the educational route had been a failure. "One of the mistakes of past policy has been to demand too much of our schools," he said. "They have been expected not only to educate, but also to accomplish a social transformation." All too often these efforts to transform society were "tragically futile," the president observed, and ended up by using rather than serving the children.[2]

The hesitancy about social reform that Nixon expressed had not emerged with his administration. It was already germinating in the last years of Johnson's presidency as the negative evaluations of the new social programs proliferated. Two HEW planning deputies for education and income maintenance pinpointed "the flaw in the domestic policy of the Johnson Administration . . . it depended on the assumption that spending money in education, job creation, training would lead to effective results." Successful programs, the two concluded, depended on "very careful structuring of governmental efforts, inaugurating large programs only after experiments have indicated success is likely." Evaluation chiefs in the Office of Economic Opportunity also reflected that the faith in action had led social experimenters to "push aside the fact that we had neither the benefit of experience nor much of a realization of the difficulties involved in developing effective techniques."[3]

The realization that Great Society programs lacked the intellectual basis and technical know-how needed for successful social policy suggested a slowing down of the old kind of action programs. But it gradually became evident that the rhetoric about ignorance also masked a disinclination on the part of the new administration to deal with the disadvantaged Americans who had been LBJ's concern. This tendency was especially apparent in the uses that the administration made of social science research. The movement toward research at the expense of large-scale programs was usually explained by the administration in terms of social science findings highlighting what was still unknown and approaches that did not work. Further educational research obviously was necessary, as the administration claimed. But it was also clear that social science surveys, despite methodological uncertainties and gaps, often lent major support to certain policies. Yet, at the same time, the methodological uncertainties could be exploited to justify contradictory policies.[4] Thus, the Coleman Report seemed to suggest that significant changes in the environment of poverty and integration were two possible alternatives for social policy. The Nixon administration favored neither. The Coleman Report could also be used either to hold back on conventional school expenditures or to fund bold educational experiments designed to reduce the achievement gap. The administration preferred the first along with modest research. The selective use made of research indicated administration values rather than science; it raised questions of social justice when programs serving the poor were abruptly cut back. It also suggested that the relationship between research and policy was full of problems. In 1964 and 1965 there had been little consideration of research. In the seventies there was, but the methodological uncertainties of research left room for manipulation rather than guidance.

Once in office, Nixon responded to the current tide of skepticism in intellectual and government circles and started his slow retreat from the world of the Great Society. This retreat accorded with the prevailing climate of opinion, Nixon's own lack of sympathy with the poor, his conservative philosophy on the proper role of the federal government, and his radical view of the power of the executive. It also fit in with his determination to control what he saw as excessive government spending. It was, of course, impossible for the new president to abandon social programs at once. Verbally, Nixon reasserted their importance. On 19 February 1969 Nixon affirmed a commitment to wipe out poverty. "The blight of poverty," the president said, "requireš priority attention." In what soon became a standard part of Nixon's rhetoric, he stressed the need for "full debate and discussion" in dealing with inherited programs.[5] "There still is a great deal to be learned about what works and what does not," Nixon pointed out.[6] Having made the ritualistic gestures to the poverty program, however, the president began to dismantle its organizational features, claiming it was inefficiently run.[7]

Nixon's own antipoverty program focused on payment rather than service: welfare reform, food programs, tax exemption for lower-income groups, and help for minority businessmen. Although these programs represented a new and fruitful approach, in many cases the administration supported them insufficiently and erratically. Nixon's original welfare proposal, for example, only sought $1,600 allowance for a family of four, far below the $3,600 allowance in New York

State in the early seventies. It also contained work requirements. Eventually, when the program ran into trouble in
Congress, the administration abandoned it, leaving scholars
and politicians arguing over who was to blame for its demise.
Philip Pruitt reflected a growing feeling about the administration when he left the Small Business Administration in
July 1969. "There's been lots of rhetoric in Government . . .
but no money has been forthcoming."[8]

After Nixon forced his resignation in 1970, James E. Allen,
his first commissioner of education, analyzed the president's
approach to social policy. "In my opinion," Allen said, "the
principal strategy of this Administration is one of accommodation, that is, of going only so far as is necessary to keep
as many people as possible placated. In and of themselves,
many of the proposals and many actions of the Administration such as the Family Assistance Program, the desegregation efforts . . . are good, but they are not good enough as
solutions for problems which threaten the existence of our
country."[9]

What was conspicuously absent in Nixon's apparent concern with poverty was any belief that education had a central role to play in overcoming it. Indeed, so far was education from Nixon's thinking that he seldom even referred to it
during his first year in office. Former Commissioner Allen
suggested that the president just was not very interested in
education. Nixon's heated insistence that education was a
local, not a federal, matter eventually substantiated Allen's
point of view; so too did his failure to assign any of his
aides to educational matters as Lyndon Johnson had done.[10]
There were still other clues that education was not a presidential priority. During his first meeting with Nixon, for
example, Allen brought along his suggestions for a new federal role in education, but he apparently never had the opportunity to discuss them. After listening to the president
talk about law and order for thirty minutes, Allen finally
asked what the president's understanding of the commissioner's duties was. The president told the amazed Allen,
"I hope, Dr. Allen, that you can do something to improve discipline in the schools."[11] As Allen later recalled, he finally

concluded that "what was lacking was a sense of urgency with respect to education, and that in the absence of this sense of urgency educational policies were shaped more in terms of fiscal constraints than in terms of the nation's educational needs. The vast influence of those persons in the White House and in the Bureau of the Budget who were dealing with education was exerted primarily in terms of economic goals."[12]

One of the first attempts to clarify the slowly emerging administration policy on education came in March 1969 when Secretary of HEW Robert Finch outlined the president's first legislative proposal. The adminstration, Finch told the House Committee on Education and Labor, wanted $25 million to establish new experimental schools to isolate and develop "successful approaches and promising ideas in education." Finch envisioned developing totally new educational approaches in these special schools, but when he was unable to stimulate enthusiastic congressional support, he modified the plans to fund existing schemes in existing schools.[13] This suggestion, too, failed to spark political interest. As the head of the NEA testified before a Senate subcommittee, "It is beyond belief that anyone can imagine that such a project will in any way cure the ills brought on by . . . frustrated neglected pupils in our rural as well as urban schools."[14] Not surprisingly, Congress refused to fund these requests.

This unpromising legislative beginning was, in fact, prophetic of what would become a hostile stalemate between Congress and the White House. Unlike his predecessor, Nixon had little real understanding or sympathy with Congress. Nor did his aides, Bob Haldeman, John Erlichman, and Peter Flanigan, compensate for Nixon's insensitivity. Consequently, administration proposals were often developed with little attempt to involve key congressional figures or lobbies and were viewed by Congess as either irrelevant or politically threatening.[15] As the deadlock with Congress emerged and persisted, Nixon turned to extra legislative means of developing and implementing policy. In the end, the educational thrusts of the administration would contribute to the constitutional case being made against it as the revelations of Watergate united the president's opponents.[16]

These constitutional struggles, however, lay in the future. In three major addresses during the spring of 1970, the president finally presented a clearly defined educational policy to the nation that offered reform, economy, and revenue-sharing as the basis for action. Reform, economy, and revenue-sharing proposals would, in fact, shape the next four years of administration initiative.

As he had with the poverty program, Nixon made a ritual bow to the past. The learning lag of poor children was "the most glaring shortcoming in American education today," the president declared.[17] But the keynote of the first address on 3 March was reform. "American education is in urgent need of reform" and "thoughtful redirection," Nixon asserted.[18] Americans must stop deceiving themselves. The present disjointed programs did not constitute a comprehensive educational policy. Moreover, it was wishful thinking to believe compensatory programs like the ESEA had succeeded. These programs were "ambitious, idealistic, and costly . . . based on the assumption that extra resources would equalize learning opportunity and eventually help eliminate poverty." But they had not worked. Nixon warned, "We must recognize that our present knowledge about how to overcome poor background, is so limited that major expansion of such programs could not be confidently based on their results." "We are not getting as much as we should out of the dollars we spend," the president observed.[19]

Nixon's message contained two specific proposals: the appointment of a Commission of School Finance and the creation of a National Institute of Education. Suggesting that "the first step toward reform" necessitated "a coherent approach to research and experimentation," Nixon offered the NIE as this crucial first step. Staffed by a group of scholars, the institute would conduct some basic research itself and contract out other research projects. Pressing concerns of the institute, Nixon asserted, would be to develop evaluation techniques to assess the success of education programs, to investigate compensatory education, and to study the role of television in learning. The institute would, thus, begin the "systematic search for new knowledge needed to make educational opportunity truly equal."[20] Nixon envisioned that the Institute would have a $25 million budget, a modest beginning indeed. Former Commissioner of Education Harold Howe later gave his opinion that the NIE "ideally . . . should be launched with an appropriation of approximately $400 to $500 million . . . to meet its needs for a period of three years."[21] When the NIE eventually got going in 1972, its starting budget stood at $90 million.[22] Howe's sums were out of the question.

If Nixon's 1970 message suggested a moderate commitment to research, it also indicated the administration's strong determination to control spending on ongoing education programs. As *Newsweek* commented, "If there are any lingering doubts that the education boom of the 1960's is indeed over, President Nixon's message . . . should finally dispel them."[23] Nixon's intention to curb spending under the ESEA had already become evident in Congress, and would sour relations with that body for the rest of his time in office. As one member of the House General Subcommittee on Education reflected bitterly in 1970, "The President has not asked for one nickel since he has been in office to increase Title I funding. We have had to fight him every step of the way to keep the program going."[24] In January 1970, Nixon had appeared before television cameras to veto the HEW appropriations bill (for fiscal year 1970), which had added $300 million to the ESEA beyond his budget request. Although Congress upheld the veto, later in the spring it passed an appropriations bill for fiscal year 1971 once more providing the ESEA with substantially more money than the president thought necessary. On 11 August, Nixon vetoed this bill only to see both houses override his decision within a week. In justifying the veto, Nixon claimed a large education budget was inflationary and reiterated that Title I had many weaknesses.[25] The desire to label Democrats in Congress as politically irresponsible in a year of congressional elections may well have motivated the president as much as fear of inflation and recognition of Title I weaknesses.[26] But no matter what the complex sources of Nixon's actions were, no matter what validity they might have had, his arguments angered congressmen, who might have agreed that Title I was unsuccessful but whose districts now expected ESEA funds. The president was not going to be able to eliminate ongoing educational programs easily, but he was prepared to battle Congress to keep them at starvation level if he could.

As time wore on, battles over funding the ESEA and other educational programs took on added dimensions and eventually fused with the battle between Congress and president over the extent of executive power. In the election year of 1972 Nixon once more vetoed two HEW appropriations bills. This time Congress was unable to override the vetoes. As the president cogently explained to inflation-conscious voters during the campaign, "It is very easy for politicians to call for new millions of dollars to be allocated for every new educational spending proposal that spins out of an ivory tower. . . . But . . . there are times when . . . [the President] must have the strength to say 'no' for the sake of the American Taxpayer." Echoed Caspar Weinberger, now secretary of HEW, "This Administration is a prisoner of programs we did not devise, of problems we did not cause."[27] The American Taxpayer gave Nixon his vote, but the monetary stalemate was not resolved. Lacking regularly appropriated operating funds, HEW and the Office of Education maintained day-by-day operations under a continuing resolution from Congress. The impasse dragged on until December 1973.[28]

As congressional tempers rose, another administration strategy for economy in education became clear: impoundment. Between 1969 and 1973 the administration either impounded or otherwise prevented an estimated $1 billion of education funds from reaching their congressionally approved destinations.[29] This use of executive power, which suggested that the president had an "item veto" that allowed him to pick and choose programs to be funded, was hotly contested by many congressmen, who argued that Nixon's actions undercut the legislative powers of Congress. Court suits initiated by congressmen, states, and school districts who found themselves without expected funds resulted. Although the president clearly could veto bills that he did not like, plaintiffs argued, he had the responsibility of seeing that Congress's intent was realized if he signed them.[30] During the summer of 1973 the administration's inflated position was flagging in court, and the furor over presidential use of power merged with Watergate revelations. The president finally began to make a strategic retreat from economy. Stating his wish to end the "climate of uncertainty" that existed as court suits continued, in late December 1973, Nixon released $1.1 billion of health and education funds impounded in 1973. Of this sum, $225 million was Title I money.[31]

The administration's growing preference for government based on an expansive view of executive power, which the policy of economy illustrated, also characterized the program of "Educational Renewal" that the Office of Education developed and that the administration adopted as its kind of program.[32] Faced with the loss of experimental and research programs to the NIE and the disappearance of categorical programs if revenue-sharing became a reality, staff members of the Office of Education developed a proposal for renewal in April 1971.[33] The plans involved consolidating the Office of Education's discretionary funds, which were theoretically the commissioner's responsibility to spend as he thought best, and using them to foster innovation in local school districts.[34] In line with the administration's style of operating, interest groups and congressional staff were not consulted in working out the proposals. Indeed, instead of bringing the idea to Congress for its approval, action on the program went ahead and reorganization of staff began.[35] By the fall, Congress was alarmed that its policy-making function was being undermined. Senator Pell, chairman of the Subcommittee on Education, asked the Office of Education to explain Education Renewal and to clarify what authority the Office of Education had for what essentially seemed to mark a new policy move. Administration officials complied, but failed to convince Congress that the executive branch had the power to begin its program without legislative examination and approval. By February 1972 Congress made its view of its own power quite explicit. As an amendment to the Higher Education act, Congress forbade any consolidation of existing programs or "commingling" of funds without the prior approval of Congress.[36]

The tone and intent of Nixon's educational policies differed sharply from those of LBJ. Nixon was just not interested in 1960-style social programs; he never implemented the final report of his Urban Task Force for Education, for example, which proclaimed urban education as a major national priority needing vast increases in federal funding.[37] The report, appearing in 1970, reasserted the traditional liberal faith of the mid-sixties that "the poverty child does not have to repeat the poverty pattern of his parents if he receives a valid and saleable education."[38] Nixon received the report coolly. Allen, who supported the report's recommendations, sadly concluded "that hopes for a major attack on [the weaknesses of] urban education and for substantial increases in funds for other purposes would have to be brought into accommodation with both the need and the Administration's emphasis on building into the educational system better capacity for reform and renewal."[39]

The initial keynote of reform and reexamination justified the cautious stance the administration adopted and reflected the uncertainties among educational reformers. As Allen admitted, "We were at a point in history that called for some reappraisal. . . . At the end of the sixties starts had been made in many directions, but there was a growing recognition of the need for evidence of their effectiveness."[40] But one vital factor about reform that attracted Nixon was that "it did not require, at least immediately, large sums of money."[41] Nixon's educational recommendations were, from the beginning, thrifty.

On 5 April 1971 Nixon revealed the third aspect of his educational program: a plan to increase local control over education through a system of special revenue-sharing. Nixon's recommendations rested on the experience of the previous decade with aid to education. Piecemeal federal aid made genuine reform difficult and meaningful evaluations of what programs helped children learn almost impossible. Nixon proposed consolidating the funds of thirty Office of Education programs and redistributing the $3 billion on an automatic

formula basis to the states. Implicit in the plan was a substantial decrease in the Office of Education's power. Broadly
defined purposes like providing equal educational opportunity and care for handicapped children would indicate
where local areas should focus the funds. But states and local
areas did not need to submit plans for review or approval.
As Nixon noted, "The Federal Government can help provide
resources to meet rising needs, but state and local education
authorities must make the hard decisions about how to apply
these resources in ways that best serve the educational needs
of our children."[42] The good intentions of the federal government, Nixon felt, were no substitute for local undstanding and
local energy.[43]

Critical as Nixon had been about Title I efforts under the
ESEA, he chose to ignore the part localism played in its
failure. The act had given wide leeway to communities to
make their own decisions; ample evidence existed to show
that middle-class leaders decided to use money for other purposes than the ESEA established. Nixon did not acknowledge
the fact that local areas lacked commitment to many noble
purposes like equal educational opportunity, or he did not
care. His overriding determination to "see to it that the flow
of power in education goes toward, and not away from the
local community" made him ignore the clear signs that local
control was not a panacea or even a partial solution to social
problems.[44]

The presidential interest in revenue-sharing was not
matched by Congress, however. The 1971 bill provided almost no new money to stimulate congressional support.[45]
And revenue-sharing would clearly limit congressional power
to determine how funds would be spent.[46] And the president
of the NEA pointed out, revenue-sharing "would weaken federal responsibility and authority for ensuring that minority
group students, poor students and handicapped children, receive a fair share of federal aid."[47] Undeterred by congressional
apathy and stimulated by his massive vote of confidence in
1972, Nixon reintroduced his plan in 1973. But the 1973 ver-
sion that would replace the ESEA had little more money than
the 1971 program, and no more political appeal.[48]

Lengthy hearings merely reinforced congressional reluctance to respond to the administration's argument. "It is time that the federal government ceased acting like a national school board, telling states and communities in great detail what they should spend and how," said Caspar Weinberger, to no effect.[49] By June the administration admitted what it thought would be only a temporary defeat and gave up its attempts to pass educational revenue-sharing for the following fiscal year.[50] The administration would never have the opportunity to present revenue-sharing again.

Although rejected by Congress, Nixon's proposals for cutting back on the ESEA, supporting research, and consolidating program funds certainly incorporated the results of experience and theoretically had some merit. It was obviously useless to pour money into programs that were ineffective for unknown reasons. Money alone was no answer; accountability was essential. Apart from such pragmatic concerns, Nixon was also sensitive to the Coleman Report finding that conventional school expenditures yielded few academic results. As Nixon pointed out in his 3 March 1970 message, "We do know that the social and economic environment which surrounds a child at home and outside of school probably has more effect on what he learns than the quality of the school he now attends."[51] Daniel Moynihan admitted to the *New York Times* that the president had drawn heavily from the Coleman Report. Coleman himself remarked, "The President's message says a lot of things I might have said myself."[52]

But as much as Nixon's conclusions fit the findings of the Coleman Report, many in and out of Congress found fault with his over-all tone. The president appeared to be using social sciences to justify a reduced commitment to education, which still needed reform. Loath to increase educational funds significantly, he awaited the slow process of feedback from modestly financed research even as urban school systems were lurching into bankruptcy.[53] Nixon's attitude so worried Commissioner Allen that he wrote Nixon on 5 May 1970. "I am writing you . . . to express my very deep concern over the critical needs of education and our Administration's current posture towards them. . . . Reform cannot be achieved in a vacuum. The system of education must be sustained and nourished at the same time change and innovation are sought. The children and youth in school today . . . cannot be placed in deep freeze . . . while the institutions are being expected to undergo fundamental reform."[54] Allen proposed increasing educational expenditures by $1 billion in fiscal year 1972. Ignoring this unwelcome advice, Nixon never answered his commissioner's letter. A month later Allen was forced to resign because of his disagreement with the administration over the Cambodian issue and because of his frankly expressed educational viewpoint.

Nixon's education program was actually indifferent to the problems of the achievement gap and educational inequality and the need to reform the schools. Even though the public schools could not eliminate poverty, they should be able to teach all students, not just middle-class white students, basic skills that were needed in later life. But if the schools were to learn how to teach effectively, more funds would have to be devoted to research and experimentation than Nixon was prepared to spend. Nixon's interests lay with appealing to the majority of Americans—now little concerned about the education of the poor—not to minority groups.[55]

As Nixon's term advanced, it became clear that the one aspect of education that really concerned the president and the electorate was the race issue. Although Nixon may have originally hoped to avoid this explosive subject, court decisions, political strategy, an evaluation of the temper of the country, all fused to make race a major concern of government. By March 1970 Nixon himself acknowledged, "Now the focus is on race."[56] Gradually the administration clarified its intention to retreat from supporting racial integration as it reaffirmed a belief in the neighborhood school concept and condemned busing for racial purposes.

Various pressures forced the administration to adopt a position. First of all, a series of court rulings indicated a radical change in the pace of southern desegregation would be required. In March 1967 the Fifth Circuit Court ruled in the case of *U.S. vs. Jefferson Board of Education* that "the only school desegregation plan that meets constitutional standards is one that works." In essence the court was rejecting freedom-of-choice plans that preserved "the essentials of the dual school system while giving paper compliance with the duty to desegregate."[57] The *Green vs. County School Board of New Kent Co.* decision of May 1968 lent the weight of the Supreme Court to desegregation. "The burden of the school board today is to come forward with a plan that promises realistically to work *now*," the Court ruled. Freedom of choice was unacceptable if other methods promised "speedier and more effective conversion to a unitary, nonracial school system."[58] In October 1969 the Supreme Court ruled again in *Alexander vs. Holmes County.* "Under the explicit holdings of this Court," the unanimous Court declared, "the obligation of every school district is to terminate dual school systems at once and to operate now and hereafter only unitary schools."[59]

As court pressure on southern school districts multiplied, racial discrimination in education increasingly became a vocal concern in Congress. Because compensatory education had apparently failed to provide equal opportunity for poor and minority groups, liberals searched for another solution. In the Senate, hearings on equal educational opportunity beginning in 1970 stressed the importance of school integration. Issues of desegregation and integration came to occupy a major part of all other educational hearings from 1969 on. Coleman now became a familiar witness at government hearings, and was joined on some occasions by other race experts like Thomas Pettigrew and Arthur Jensen. In both 1969 and 1970 liberals presented bills on the floor of Congress to improve education in urban ghettos and to end *de facto* school segregation.[60] Meanwhile, conservatives and southerners tried to amend both appropriation and education bills to prevent busing.[61] A conflict over the direction of education for blacks was taking shape that called out for administration leadership.

The race issue was hotter than poverty, and the administration could hardly ignore it. But it could and did delay for some time giving forceful direction to those attempting to deal with racial and educational problems. As one observer of southern education noted, Nixon seemed "locked in a pathetic drifting paralysis on the great issue of ending separation in our public schools."[62]

Nixon's failure to confront the race issue directly had already been evident in his 1968 campaign. Assuring the country that he supported the Brown decision overturning *de jure* segregation, Nixon equivocated on how far his administration would go in fostering desegregation. In a television broadcast on 12 September 1968, Nixon remarked, "When you go beyond that [the Brown decision] and say that it is the responsibility of the Federal Government and the Federal courts to, in effect, act as local school districts in determining how we carry that out, and then to use the power of the Federal treasury to withhold funds or give funds in order to carry it out then I think we are going too far."[63] On numerous occasions Nixon also spoke against busing to achieve racial balance. What all these statements actually meant about the support Nixon was willing to give to desegregation efforts was still unclear, but very early in Nixon's administration it appeared that the president would be neither vigorous nor enthusiastic in his support.

Political strategy reinforced the administration's basic proclivities. Guided by Attorney General John Mitchell, the administration was already planning how to capture the Wallace vote for the Republicans in 1972. With the Green decision, Nixon's ability to dramatize his racial views was limited.[64] But delay and compromise in the South and inaction in the North would convey the right message. Pressures from the White House could and did force HEW to withdraw from an unyielding stand on final desegregation plans and prevented HEW from using fund cutoffs as a weapon against recalcitrant districts.[65] A clear example of the administration's intentions and methods of operation occurred in the summer of 1969 in Mississippi. There, with the help of HEW, thirty districts had developed new desegregation plans to replace inadequate freedom-of-choice plans. Desegregation was to begin at the opening of school that year.[66] Probably responding to pressure from Mississippi's John Stennis, chairman of the Senate Armed Services Committee, who threatened to refuse to act as floor leader for the A.B.M.

authorization bill, the administration sent Justice Department attorneys to argue in the U.S. Fifth Circuit Court of Appeals for a delay in implementing the plans. Since there was only a short time remaining before school opened, the administration argued that the new plans would cause "chaos, confusion and a catastrophic educational setback." The Supreme Court upheld the original deadline, and stated that it was "the obligation of every school district . . . to terminate dual school systems at once and to operate now and hereafter unitary schools." Nixon announced to the press, "I believe in carrying out the law even though I may have disagreed as I did in this instance with the Supreme Court," and apparently felt "he had won a longer war . . . he had ended nearly a year of ambiguity on the desegregation question in a posture that was clearly conciliatory to the South. He had improved his political credentials in the South, and . . . had slowly begun to develop the machinery to bring the H.E.W. bureaucracy under control."[67]

Nixon was determined to bend HEW to his policy. A few months after the Mississippi incident, in February 1970, Leon Panetta, the activist director of HEW's Office of Civil Rights was forced to resign. Commissioner Allen, a firm supporter of integration, soon followed in June.[68] Acquaintances of Allen's mentioned that, while commissioner, Allen had said "privately that he could make no headway with this administration but stayed on in an attempt to try."[69] The attempt had obviously failed. In September 1970 the U.S. Commission for Civil Rights judged that Nixon's approach was a "major retreat in the struggle to achieve meaningful school desegregation."[70] In the future, the burden of desegregation would rest with the courts.[71]

Nixon had unsuccessfully tried to quiet some of the controversy by explaining his policy on the desegregation issue on 24 March 1970. Reasserting his support for the Brown decision, Nixon pointed out that the law left many vital points unclear. "Lawyers and judges have honest disagreements about what the law requires."[72] When issues were in doubt, Nixon remarked, "my responsibilities as Chief Executive make it necessary that I determine, on the basis of my best judgment, what must be done."[73] Nixon's best judgment led him to support the neighborhood school and to resist busing.[74] These stands suggested that the president did not mean integration, or racial mixing, when he spoke of desegregation. Indeed, Nixon found recent progress toward desegregation encouraging. It was important, the president went on, to keep in mind the over-all objectives of increasing educational opportunities for all children and of ending racial barriers.[75] Nixon then brought up what was becoming a familiar theme. Not too much could be expected from schools, since the home environment was the most important factor in educational achievement. As Nixon put it, "It is not really because they serve black children that most of these schools are inferior, but rather because they serve poor children who often lack the environment that encourages learning."[76] Other institutions had to take some of the pressure off the schools, the president said.

Nixon suggested the need for innovative shared-time programs where children of both races would gather for special events and expressed his recurrent plea for more data. Present knowledge supported this cautious plan. But was this so? Actually, Nixon only stressed part of the information available. Coleman, for instance, had written and testified in favor of an active integration policy. Appearing before the Senate Committee on Equal Educational Opportunity, Coleman remarked, "Turning back to the question of effective quality of educational opportunity, matters look much different than before. Children are subject to inequality of opportunity by virtue of the very economic and racial homogeneity of the schools they attend."[77]

Despite his marked lack of enthusiasm for the cause of desegregation, court-induced pressures on the South impelled Nixon to aid the desegregation process. On 21 May 1970 Nixon sent the Emergency School Aid Bill to Congress. The bill diverted $1.5 billion from existing programs to help school systems desegregate. Three kinds of districts were eligible for funds: districts in the process of desegregating that were under court orders or had HEW plans, districts voluntarily trying to reduce *de facto* segregation, and districts unable to desegregate that needed programs to overcome the effects of racial isolation. In the Senate, Jacob Javits, leading Republican member of the Labor and Public Welfare Committee, initially refused to introduce the bill because of provisions forbidding the use of federal funds for busing.[78] The administration agreed to drop the provisions for the time being. To many congressional committee members Nixon's bill seemed hesitant about racial desegregation even though they greeted the bill as a step in the right direction.

One feature that immediately drew criticism was the emergency aspect of the measure. HEW Secretary Finch justified the two-year appropriation by claiming, "We are here trying to deal with an immediate, short term crisis."[79] Claiborne Pell, chairman of the Senate subcommittee considering the bill, disagreed with Finch. "I think we are going to have the problems of segregation in schools going on for a long time," he said.[80] Another aspect of the bill that created suspicion was the fact that it offered aid primarily to the South. The administration pointed out that the South had no choice but to desegregate and needed help; yet many liberals could only see money flowing to the very areas that had for so long resisted desegregation.[81] Too little aid was going to go to *de facto* segregated districts outside the South that also faced massive racial and educational problems.[82] As Pettigrew mentioned in his testimony on the bill, more children were in racially isolated schools in 1970 than in 1954 when the Brown decision was handed down; the problem was most acute in the cities.[83] Nixon's hesitancy in dealing with *de facto* situations had been apparent in his March 1970 message. There he stressed that the government had no constitutional mandate to deal with *de facto* segregation, and it was hardly surprising that his bill concentrated on the South, where he hoped for so much political support.[84]

Critics also claimed that the bill lacked vital controls. The ESEA gave many examples showing that local areas used federal money as they wished. Already indications existed that desegregated southern schools had actually resegregated. Blacks and whites were in the same school building but attended different classes, changed rooms at different times, and ate lunch separately. The 1970 NEA task force reports on conditions in Mississippi and Louisiana turned up numerous examples of such practices. Moreover, southern states even diverted education funds to private all-white schools.[85] Since the bill provided funds for schools that were not actually desegregated but were in desegregated districts, and because there were few strict controls over how money would be spent, the fear of misused funds was quite reasonable.

The kinds of projects that the bill suggested as worthy of support turned out to be the old familiar ESEA programs. As Carl Perkins said, "My fear is that we are not going to accomplish the goals that we really want to accomplish by reiterating things that we can presently do."[86] Perkins felt it was necessary to strike out in a drastically new direction. The administration denied that the bill proposed warmed-over solutions by maintaining that, unlike the ESEA, this bill pinpointed aid at desegregation districts.[87] Few were convinced by administration arguments. One suspicious fact was that compensatory education, once rejected by Nixon as a failure, had reappeared. In large cities and other areas where integration seemed impossible, federal funds would support compensatory programs. Coleman himself suggested that this provision be deemphasized, since he thought the legislation should be "an incentive to school systems to carry out school desegregation," not a way of maintaining separation.[88] Nixon had already clarified his own point of view when it came to a choice between racial balance and compensation. "Considering the always heavy demand for more school operating funds," he noted on 24 March 1970, "I believe it is preferable, when we have to make the choice, to use limited financial resources for the improvement of education . . . rather than buying buses, tires and gasoline to transport children miles away from their neighborhood schools."[89]

The administration's ultimate goal became clear during 1972. No longer did the Justice Department file suits on behalf of black students nor did HEW proffer substantial technical assistance to those school districts involved in making desegregation plans. Title VI became a weapon never used, leading one lower-court district judge to rule in February

1973 that HEW had "not properly fulfilled its obligation" to cut off funds from segregated schools.[90] Having removed the executive from activities that fostered desegregation, Nixon was now free to lead the antibusing campaign, as he announced to the nation in a television broadcast in March 1972.[91] He would, he informed the country, ask Congress to call a moratorium on all court-ordered busing for racial balance in the schools and seek a bill imposing permanent controls on future busing. These actions symbolized an end to further integration efforts, which in many areas depended on busing, and suggested that the president thought Congress could rightfully limit federal court jurisdiction.[92] Claiming that these requests were, in fact, in the interests of quality education, Nixon argued, "What I am proposing is that at the same time that we stop more busing, we move forward to guarantee that the children currently attending the poorest schools in our cities and in rural districts be provided with education equal to that of the good schools in their communities."[93] To promote this quality education, Nixon suggested passage of an Equal Educational Opportunities Act with $2.5 million for the education of black and other minority children in racially and socially isolated settings.

If Nixon's educational policies seemed to "shift with the political winds," the fundamental lack of interest in the educational problems of poor minority groups was obvious.[94] Although the Coleman Report and other social studies pointed out that socioeconomic integration did not wipe out the achievement gap, it did seem to reduce it. But Nixon rejected these studies and the solution of more integration. Instead, he revived the very compensatory approach that he himself had condemned earlier as unsuccessful and unworthy of support. "What does now seem clear," said the president, "is that while many Title I experiments have failed, many others had succeeded." The misuse of funds had "thwarted the act's effectiveness," as had the failure to concentrate funds. But where properly implemented, the president argued, "the results have been frequently encouraging and sometimes dramatic."[95] A few days later, Elliot Richardson testified in hearings that compensatory education "has never had an even chance of success," but that now it would.[96] Bolstering the new administration position, HEW released within a month a document entitled "The Effectiveness of Compensatory Education." In this document the problems of educating the poor were seen as "too great to wait for completely certain knowledge."[97]

If it was too late to wait for new knowledge, it was too early for substantial new funds for compensatory education. Nixon's plan diverted $2.5 million from the ESEA and the Emergency School Aid bill for the new priority. As Senator Ted Kennedy pointed out, the president had "misled the American people. I think most particularly in the areas of resources that are supposedly to be devoted to improving quality education . . . it was misleading. Anyone who viewed that presentation would have had to conclude that there were going to be . . . additional funds; yet we find that the money the president referred to is already in ESEA Title No. I or in the emergency school bill."[98]

The Nixon proposals highlighted the nature of educational policies in the seventies. Although policy-planners in 1963 and 1964 had used education in place of more radical solutions for social problems, they had done so unconsciously. For Nixon this was not the case. Nixon was well acquainted with what education could and could not do. He refused to fund research on a scale that was necessary if the schools were merely to learn how to educate poor children. He turned his back on integration. He proposed more compensatory education as a solution for the schools' failures with the poor. He offered pretense for action. On 16 March 1974 Nixon had indeed completed the classic pattern of educational reform movements.

Unlike the Johnson administration, then, the Nixon administration turned away from leading the nation forward in matters of race, education, and poverty. Of course, the failures of the Johnsonian measures had destroyed the necessary consensus; there was neither overwhelming pressure nor powerful support for bold political departures. Congress and the nation were hesitant. One survey of middle-class attitudes toward poverty discovered that "the vast majority of those interviewed showed little or no concern or insight."[99] Some respondents refused to acknowledge that any problem existed. Some congressional liberals still believed in the possibility of social change through the schools. Yet when votes came up, liberals divided.[100] As Senator Mondale recognized, "We now face the task of rearguing issues we thought were settled."[101] The mood of conservatives was clearly hostile to social change through integration, especially when it involved busing. Even liberals wavered.

Indecision in Congress merely reflected indecision in the nation. Ideals of social justice, hopes of ending poverty, no longer seemed as easy to support as in former years. No simple solutions existed for social problems. As Yale law professor Alexander Bickel pointed out, goals competed and conflicted.[102] Hard choices had to be made as to whether Americans wished to grapple with the problems of poverty, inadequate education, and racial discrimination. Walter Mondale reflected, "This goal of equal education is one which I am sure most Americans would agree with me. But the approaches to this goal can be as elusive and controversial as the attempts to define and answer the problems of poverty and other forms of discrimination."[103]

Mondale was actually summing up the experience of the 1960s. Approaches to social goals were elusive and controversial. In 1965 the ESEA had offered hopes of overcoming the patterns of poverty by diverting special funds for educating the poor. Now it was clear that the goal had not been achieved; the approach had failed. Yet, although it was a failure, educational reform did have several valuable lessons. The over-all history of the ESEA indicated the necessity for careful planning and a realistic model of implementation. Reform usually did not just happen; it had to be methodically plotted in ways that gave some indications for success. The ESEA had not had this kind of planning and had not succeeded. Education, despite popular beliefs, had not and could not solve major social problems. The experience with education suggested that more sweeping and perhaps unconventional solutions to ameliorate social conditions were necessary. Still, the limited success of some Title I programs indicated that schools could succeed in teaching minority and poor students basic skills. This was, as Nixon acknowledged, the appropriate function for schools. Yet, more money had to be devoted to research; schools might have to be restructured and integration supported if deprived students were to perform in ways similar to middle-class students. The irony of the ESEA was, however, that few within government were really interested in these lessons. Instead, when political events demanded, they revived the solution of more education for the poor just as it was discredited.

1. *Public Papers of the Presidents of the United States: Richard M. Nixon, 1969*, p. 112.

2. *Congressional Quarterly Weekly Report* 28 (1970): 864.

3. Quoted in P. Michael Timpane, "Educational Experimentation in National Social Policy," pp. 559–60.

4. Walter Williams, *Social Policy Research and Analysis*, p. 104.

5. *Public Papers: Richard M. Nixon, 1969*, p. 112.

6. Ibid., p. 425.

7. Ibid., pp. 115, 425.

8. *Congressional Quarterly Weekly Report* 28 (1970): 2854; Eugene Keller, "Social Priorities, Economic Policy, and the State," p. 619. See the latter, pp. 627–29, for a discussion of priorities in the Nixon administration. See also Charles Schultze, Edward K. Hamilton, and Allen Schick, *Setting National Priorities*, p. 74.

9. James E. Allen, Jr., "An Interview with James Allen," *Harvard Educational Review* 40 (November 1970): p. 539. Copyright © 1970 by President and Fellows of Harvard College. Reprinted with permission.

10. Harry L. Summerfield, *Power and Process*, pp. 128, 116.

11. Ibid., p. 128; Rowland Evans, Jr., and Robert D. Novak, *Nixon in the White House*, p. 60.

12. Allen, "An Interview," p. 538.

13. Timpane, "Educational Experimentation," pp. 561–62.

14. Quoted in "With Education in Washington," p. 56.

15. Evans and Novak, *Nixon in the White House*, pp. 106–12; Summerfield, *Power and Process*, pp. 135–37.

16. Richard P. Nathan, *The Plot That Failed*, p. 7.

17. *Congressional Quarterly Weekly Report* 28 (1970): 715.

18. Ibid., p. 714.

19. Ibid., pp. 715, 714.

20. Ibid., p. 715.

21. *Hearings before the Select Committee on Equal Educational Opportunity of the U.S. Senate*, 92d Cong., 1st Sess., 1971, Senate, p. 5818.

22. "With Education in Washington," p. 66.

23. 16 March 1970, p. 113.

24. *Hearings before the General Subcommittee on Education of the Committee on Education and Labor on Emergency School Aid*, 91st Cong., 2d Sess., 1970, House, p. 65.

25. *Congressional Quarterly Weekly Report* 28 (1970): 297–98, 1935.

26. Evans and Novak, *Nixon in the White House*, p. 122.

27. Quoted in "Education in Washington," *Education Digest* 39 (January 1973): 63.

28. *Congressional Quarterly Almanac* 29 (1973): 156.

29. Summerfield, *Power and Process*, p. 281.

30. Ibid., pp. 280–81.

31. *Congressional Quarterly Almanac* 29 (1973): 156; "With Education in Washington," p. 66.

32. Nathan, *The Plot That Failed*, p. 7; Stephen S. Kaagan, "Executive Initiative Yields to Congressional Dictate," p. 2.

33. John Merrow, "The Use and Abuse of Discretionary Authority in the U.S. Office of Education," p. 158.

34. Kaagan, "Executive Initiative," p. 2.

35. Merrow, "Use and Abuse of Discretionary Authority," p. 163; Kaagan, "Executive Initiative," pp. 33, 63.

36. Kagan, "Executive Initiative," pp. 64–65.

37. *Hearings before the Select Committee on Equal Education Opportunity of the U.S. Senate*, 91st Cong., 2d Sess., 1970, Senate, p. 3215.

38. Ibid., p. 3216.

39. Allen, "An Interview," p. 536.

40. Ibid., p. 536.

41. Ibid.

42. *Congressional Quarterly Weekly Report* 29 (1971): 826.

43. Ibid., p. 828.

44. Ibid., 28 (1970): p. 715.

45. Kaagan, "Executive Initiative," pp. 27–28.

46. Schultze et al., *Setting National Priorities*, p. 171.

47. Quoted in *Congressional Quarterly Almanac* 27 (1971): 619.

48. *Congressional Quarterly Almanac* 29 (1973): 619.

49. Quoted in ibid., p. 527.

50. Ibid., p. 525.

51. *Congressional Quarterly Weekly Report* 28 (1970): 715.

52. *New York Times*, 6 March 1970.

53. John F. Hughes and Anne O. Hughes, *Equal Education*, p. 197.

54. Allen, "An Interview," p. 540.

55. "With Education in Washington," p. 56; Allen Schick, "From Analysis to Evaluation," pp. 61–64.

56. *Congressional Quarterly Weekly Report* 28 (1970): 899.

57. Leon E. Panetta and Peter Gall, *Bring Us Together*, p. 47.

58. Ibid., p. 52.

59. Ibid., p. 300.

60. *Congressional Quarterly Guide to Current American Government*, p. 143.

61. Ibid., p. 141.

62. *Senate Hearings on Equal Educational Opportunity*, 1970, p. 2292.

63. Henry Leifermann, "Southern Desegregation," pp. 12, 14.

64. Evans and Novak, *Nixon in the White House*, pp. 137–47.

65. Panetta and Gall, *Bring Us Together*, pp. 249–71.

66. Ibid., pp. 249–50.

67. Ibid., p. 255; quoted in Evans and Novak, *Nixon in the White House*, pp. 155–56; *New York Times*, 19 March 1972.

68. Panetta and Gall, *Bring Us Together*, pp. 350–67.

69. *Senate Hearings on Equal Educational Opportunity*, 1970, p. 1155.

70. *Congressional Quarterly Weekly Report* 28 (1970): 2855.

71. Donna E. Shalala and James A. Kelly, "Politics, the Courts, and Educational Policy," p. 226.

72. *Congressional Quarterly Weekly Report* 28 (1970): 895.

73. Ibid., p. 894.

74. Ibid., p. 898.

75. Ibid., p. 896.

76. Ibid., p. 897.

77. *Senate Hearings on Equal Educational Opportunity*, 1970, p. 92.

78. *Congressional Quarterly Weekly Report* 28 (1970): 1585.

79. *Hearings before the Subcommittee on Education of the Committee on Labor and Public Welfare on Emergency School Aid*, 91st Cong., 2d Sess., 1970, Senate, p. 23.

80. Ibid., p. 34.

81. *House Hearings on Emergency School Aid*, 1970, p. 175.

82. *Senate Hearings on Emergency School Aid*, 1970, p. 122.

83. *Senate Hearings on Equal Educational Opportunity*, 1970, p. 744.

84. *Congressional Quarterly Weekly Report* 28 (1970): 895.

85. *House Hearings on Emergency School Aid*, 1970, pp. 180–94; *Senate Hearings on Equal Educational Opportunity*, 1970, p. 1156.

86. *House Hearings on Emergency School Aid*, 1970, p. 55.

87. Ibid., p. 65.

88. Ibid., p. 103.

89. *Congressional Quarterly Weekly Report* 28 (1970): 895.

90. Quoted in *Congressional Quarterly Almanac* 29 (1973): 523–24.

91. Shalala and Kelly, "Politics," pp. 225–26.

92. *Congressional Quarterly Almanac* 28 (1972): 120.

93. *New York Times*, 17 March 1972.

94. *Hearings before the Subcommittee on Education of the Committee on Labor and Public Welfare on the Equal Educational Opportunities Act of 1972*, 92d Cong., 2d Sess., 1972, Senate, p. 544.

95. *Congressional Quarterly Almanac* 28 (1972): 54–55A.

96. *Senate Hearings on Equal Educational Opportunities Act*, 1972, p. 29.

97. Quoted in *Congressional Quarterly Almanac* 28 (1972): 674.

98. *Senate Hearings on Equal Educational Opportunities Act*, 1972, p. 20.

99. Robert H. Lauer, "The Middle Class Looks at Poverty," p. 8.

100. *Congressional Quarterly Guide to Current American Government*, p. 143.

101. *New York Times*, 22 March 1970.
102. *Senate Hearings on Equal Educational Opportunity*, 1970, p. 2214.
103. Ibid., p. 1722.

Conclusion

In 1971 one observer speculated that Johnson's War on Poverty "may have heralded only a transitory period in American public policy."[1] The interests of the Nixon administration lay elsewhere, and, in any case, most aspects of the War on Poverty had been colossal failures. The critical question that this study has asked is why the educational components of the War on Poverty did not produce the significant social or educational changes implicit in their objectives. The answer to this basic question is not a simple one. From one perspective it is clear that both intellectual and political factors interacted to produce in the ESEA a social measure that had little chance of realizing planners' dreams.

First, since planners shared a common ideological framework that supported an educational solution to poverty and agreed that it was vital to strive for a bill that would be acceptable to Congress, they neither examined the assumptions of their program nor looked at relevant but scattered evidence on educational mobility. Second, for both pragmatic and ideological reasons, they accepted existing institutional arrangements giving vital power over the proposed program to local schools, who would have no stake in assuming new functions. Third, the political process interfered with the planning process. The need to come up with politically attractive compromises shaped much of the thinking about educational legislation. Because the president decided to press for speedy passage of the bill, troubling issues were raised but never resolved in Congress. But, whether the period of congressional scrutiny is long or short, congressmen themselves are subject to pressure from constituents and lobby groups and rarely see it as their role to examine social policy from an impartial viewpoint.

Such an analysis suggests that planning for social change is a hazardous process in modern government. Although carefully thought out proposals do not guarantee successful programs, policy-making rarely results in carefully considered proposals. Bureaucratic arrangements hinder planning efforts. The necessity of winning congressional approval means a focus on political issues at the expense of fundamental planning issues. When the bill reaches Congress, it is often too late to remedy fundamental defects in the legislation.

It is hardly surprising that the implementation of the ESEA has dramatized numerous problems with this haphazard method of developing social policy. Local areas have been able to use funds as they wished, and their priorities have often departed radically from the intentions of the bill's planners. Money proves to be an ineffective incentive for reform. Without either substantial powers or a strong drive to upset the status quo, the federal government has been unable to change the way the ESEA operates locally. The federal government's inability to follow through on legislation is not only the result of political compromise and ideological stance, however. It also illuminates a significant problem: those who plan legislation do not administer it. This split between planning and administration creates serious difficulties in implementing social legislation.

The failure of the ESEA can also be explained from another perspective. New forces, unanticipated by planners, contributed to the collapse of the liberal consensus. The civil rights coalition, traditionally a strong supporter of integrated education, split over tactics and ultimate goals. Division weakened black political clout to press either for continued integration or for more compensatory education. The disappearance of a united black pressure group changed the political climate drastically. So, too, did the Vietnam war. As the war obsessed the president and much of the nation, funds and attention were naturally diverted from the domestic sector, and many Great Society programs suffered. Finally, unexpected results of some poverty programs that politically mobilized the poor and numerous race riots made further efforts on behalf of the poor increasingly unpopular. A new political climate encouraged a new president in his efforts to dismantle Great Society programs.

The history of the ESEA has contributed to the recognition of a new problem facing those who would plan for social change: the relationship between research and policy. Before the passage of the ESEA, spending for educational evaluation stood at a few hundred thousand dollars a year. By 1970, however, the government was spending about $5 million yearly for this purpose. Yet, evaluation and educational research have all too often illustrated what does not work and only hinted at what might. Small experiments, for example, have affected student achievement, but similar attempts have often failed. As the RAND Corporation's study on the effectiveness of schooling concluded, "We have no clear idea of why this discrepancy exists. In short, research has not discovered *any educational practice* (or set of practices) that offers a *high probability* of success over time and place."[3]

Research, then, appears to have provided few clear directions for educational policy-makers. And as the debate over education's effects grew in intensity in the late sixties and early seventies, increasing methodological sophistication added to the difficulties of drawing conclusions from research. It may be, as the RAND study suggested, that modern statistical techniques are just inadequate to deal with such a complex question as the effect of education on different social groups.[4] In any case, as one observer has noted, "It seems plain that applied research on the effects of schooling is more complex and difficult to interpret now than it was a decade ago. Improving applied research has produced paradoxical results: knowledge which is better by any scientific standard, no more authoritative by any political standard and often more mystifying by any reasonable public standard."[5]

In the reevaluation of education that has been triggered by evaluation and research of the late sixties and early seventies, intellectuals, educators, and some members of the political sector have turned their attention to three related issues. Some, by examining successful programs, still seek to discover whether education, if reorganized, reformed, or refashioned in some way, can overcome the debilitating academic effects of poverty. Others attempt to discover how different factors like heredity and socioeconomic status explain educational deprivation. Still others have focused on social mobility, with a careful consideration of factors that seem to explain mobility and social status and those that do not. A brief survey of these areas of research will put the analysis of the ESEA into a wider perspective and will call to mind the basic issues about children from poverty groups: To what extent does the child's family and neighborhood prevent him from learning as much in school as his middle-class counterpart? What family and neighborhood factors interfere? What kind of school interventions can compensate for these factors?

It is clear that large-scale evaluations of Title I and Headstart have consistently failed to show much academic improvement among children enrolled in the programs. Yet, both on the elementary level and at the preschool level, where most interventions occur, there have been some successes, at least in the short run.[6] The question is why. There is some evidence to suggest that the match between teacher, method, classroom organization, and student may be significant. Certain teachers, using certain methods and organizing their classrooms in certain ways, may generate student achievement with some groups of students but not with others. The interaction between all the elements of the teaching situation is, perhaps, crucial in explaining success.[7] Other evidence is more concrete and is derived from the characteristics that good programs seem to exhibit. A recent study on federal programs for young children pointed to seven factors that are frequently associated with success in raising scores: explicit program objectives and careful planning, individual or small-group instruction, involvement of parents, teacher-training in methods to be used in the project, instruction directly related to goals, intensive instruction, and a good school atmosphere with high expectations for the performance of the children.[8] But these factors may not be the cause of the program's success even though they are clearly associated with it. As the study pointed out, "Because these variables are typically found together, we do not know whether all, some particular subset, or some critical proportion of them are responsible for producing cognitive gains. The variables, however, are all related to the notions of structure and good management."[9] Structure and good management do seem to make a difference both on the elementary and preschool levels, leading the authors of the study to isolate these factors as consistently related to better achievement. Others disagree, however.[10] Yet, all parties do discover some programs that they deem successful.

In structured preschool and school programs, for example, I.Q. gains are significant. With these findings a number of educators have concluded that disadvantaged children find it difficult to direct their own work and "require constant supervision and guidance much more than relatively more advantaged children."[11] The more disadvantaged a child is, the more the structure seems to help.[12]

Despite these positive results, there is good reason to fear they are not permanent. I.Q. gains growing out of structured preschool programs, for example, are no more lasting than gains in less-structured Headstart programs. Within two or three years they disappear as children progress through public elementary schools.[13] The fade-out effect is, ironically, sharpest for those students who have been in highly organized early programs, perhaps because they are less like a regular public school than Headstart.[14] Though the I.Q. and other test improvements made during preschool programs are encouraging, then, the fade-out suggests that early intervention by itself will not solve the learning problems of disadvantaged children.[15] Some argue that with *"sweeping changes in the organization, structure, and conduct of education experiences,"* the picture will change; others question the importance of preschool education altogether. Whether compensatory education is more lasting at higher levels is doubtful.[16]

With studies that discover both effective programs as well as failures, many educators and intellectuals have adopted the position that "the most profitable line of attack on educational problems may not, after all, be through the schools."[17] Sharing this point of view, Jencks attempted to weigh those outside factors that seemed to account for educational attainment—occupation and income—in his study *Inequality*. He concluded that the correlation between a white child's educational attainment and his father's occupation and income was about 0.55. Some of the family's impact on educational achievement was due to inherited genes (less than 10 percent); about one-quarter of the family's influence could be traced to the home environment that fostered activities useful to school and perhaps 10 to 15 percent to money. The rest of the difference, Jencks speculated, resulted from "cultural attitudes, values and taste for schooling."[18] Apart from the importance of family background, academic achievement seemed most affected by cognitive skills, in itself partly a factor of family experience.[19] Jencks found race to be significant mostly in its effect on test scores and aspiration.[20]

Although Jencks's percentages can be criticized, his attempt to weigh the relative importance of factors that contribute to school achievement is clearly significant. A series of experiments aimed at getting at the roots of educational deprivation have recently lent support to some of his conclusions.

For a number of years there have been several attempts to avoid educational failure by intervening not in the school but in the home during the child's early years. One ongoing experiment that began in 1964 attempted to work with the child through the mother. Over a two-year period mothers attended weekly meetings, where they learned how to use an educational program and toys designed to encourage their child's cognitive and verbal development. Mothers were encouraged to teach their children using positive rather than negative reinforcement and were urged to discuss their own problems and goals. Staff members made monthly visits to check on the mothers' teaching progress. None of the children in the program went to a preschool. Though there were problems in finding adequate controls, the I.Q. mean of the experimental children was sixteen points above children outside the program. Using mothers as agents for change is an attempt to attack the problem at one of the places it starts, with parents and their children at home.[21] A report from a similar project, which used professional home visitors to teach the mothers, concluded that results pointed to

> the efficacy of a powerful process in the homes, presumably mediated by the parent, which may serve to improve the educability of young children. . . . We would like to point out that our procedure was clearly parent education with a difference. It was conducted in the homes; it was done by skilled preschool teachers with some experience in working in the homes; it was highly concrete and specific to a given mother's life situation; it was continuous over a long period of time. Indeed, parent education probably is the answer, but in the low-income homes a very different kind of parent education from that usually provided may be needed.[22]

Such experiments suggest that deprived children, like more-advantaged children, learn partly through their personal interaction with their mothers, an interaction that involves both intellectual and emotional factors. Although the mother-child relationship appears crucial, it is possible to substitute for it, however, as a project in Milwaukee indicated. There, soon after birth, infants whose mothers were mentally retarded and poor were picked up and brought to a center where they spent most of the day with their own teacher. This one-to-one relationship continued until the child was two. At that point the child joined five other children; with three specially trained teachers, the youngsters entered a routine structured to stimulate their intellectual development. By creating this substitute relationship, children of retarded mothers showed surprising progress, "far exceed[ing] the expectations of the investigators."[23] Even more interesting than the achievement gains the programs show is the fact that the gains do not entirely disappear as time passes.[24] Although the studies suggest that intervention with two-year-olds seems most successful, another project focusing on the parent-child relationship using older children discovered that, "once again the family emerges as the system which sustains and facilitates development, spurred by educational experience outside the home."[25] Indeed, one survey concluded that some mother-child interactions correlate more highly with I.Q. than class, income, or physical living conditions.[26]

Mother-child interactions are vital but not the only family factor that affects academic achievement. Others that correlate with academic success are the parents' educational level, family size, overcrowding, and such.[27] It is quite possible, then, that various strategies aimed at the family rather than at the children may increase the academic standing of the children at the same time. This view has led one group to conclude that integration and the redistribution of income and political power would be more influential in changing the family and its children than home-based programs.[28]

These efforts highlight the difficulties of legislation like the ESEA or Headstart that have tried to change achievement patterns through school programs. Achievement seems to be related to background and family, and it may be that the schools may not be able to find techniques that can overcome the influence of environment completely. But reform through the schools has been an approach to social problems that traditionally has had some acceptability. The financial, social, and political implications of dealing with poverty through the family raise doubts about feasibility. Various home-based programs seem to have expensive yearly price tags ranging from $255 to $600 a child.[29] They need large numbers of trained or paraprofessional visitors; they are time-consuming. Not every poverty mother is likely to want to participate; the Milwaukee solution of taking children out of their homes for most of their waking hours would be, no doubt, socially and politically unacceptable on a large scale. Other family strategies like redistribution of income and political power seem equally unpalatable to many Americans. Though some hints about coping with educational deprivation have emerged, then, it seems hard to imagine they will become the basis for social policy in the near future.

One result of the educational strategies of the 1960s has been renewed interest in the components of social mobility. The link between formal education and social mobility seems frail. As Jencks concluded, occupational status seemed to be related to I.Q., educational credentials, influence of home environment on cognitive skill, and a number of undetermined sources. Moreover, he argued, "neither family background, cognitive skill, educational attainment, nor occupational status explains much of the variation in men's incomes."[30] This analysis, though heatedly criticized, makes it difficult to propose "equalized environments" as a sure solution to income problems and social inequality.[31] Jencks himself warns that it is difficult to create strategies to facilitate social mobility because the strategies may end up by creating a new system less mobile than the original.[32]

The investigation into factors that contribute to social mobility or retard it implicitly raises the question of how much mobility is either likely or tolerable in the United States and what strategies, if any, are politically viable. The pattern of American social mobility resembles that of other industrialized societies and is related in a major way to economic development. It has been stable over time. Small changes in the pattern do occur, of course. For the last few decades, for example, blacks "have begun to edge their way up the occupational ladder" (although the income gap has not closed for that group).[33] But without substantial economic growth and development or drastic changes in the fertility of the middle and upper class, substantial changes in the pattern of mobility might be both socially and politically disruptive.[34] It seems reasonable to speculate that one reason for the ESEA's political survival and that of its preschool counterpart is precisely because neither has made significant changes in the pattern. Both were originally aimed at providing mobility for children from poor families. Neither came near to realizing this ambitious goal for all the reasons this study has suggested. Yet, as one of the original planners of the ESEA optimistically noted, "Today, renewal of the act is never in doubt."[35] Set within this kind of a context, the ESEA of 1965 provides a somewhat frustrating comment on the process of reform and social change in the United States.

Equally frustrating are indications about what the public has learned from the recent period of educational reform. Some of the uncertainty about achieving social change through education has filtered down. In a 1973 poll, for example, a majority of respondents were lukewarm to integration in the schools and were almost equally divided on the issue of whether money made any difference in education or not. But, at the same time, 79 percent of those polled replied that class size made a considerable difference in explaining achievement, and 76 percent still thought that school was very important to future success.[36] Some of the traditional, tenacious, belief in the powers of education remained, although it was hard to find among intellectuals or policymakers. The remnants of this popular faith in education was another ironic comment on the history of the ESEA: a social policy born in faith, failed in action, yet its promises still believed by those who had always agreed with Lyndon Johnson, "The answer for all our national problems comes down to one single word: education."[37]

1. *Hearings before the Select Committee on Equal Educational Opportunity*, 92d Cong., 1st Sess., 1971, Senate, p. 8653.

2. David K. Cohen and Michael S. Garet, "Reforming Educational Policy with Applied Social Research," p. 18.

3. Harvey A. Averch et al., *How Effective Is Schooling?*, pp. x, xi (italics added); but see Sheldon H. White et al., *Federal Programs for Young Children*, 2:191, where the authors argue that structure and good management are techniques that promise success.

4. Averch et al., *How Effective Is Schooling?*, p. 47.

5. Cohen and Garet, "Reforming Educational Policy," p. 33.

6. Averch et al., *How Effective Is Schooling?*, p. 101. White et al., *Federal Programs*, 2:91, point out that only 64% of projects that provided usable data and that were successful were also successful the year after initial identification; only 50% of the elementary schools were successful for two years running.

7. Averch et al., *How Effective Is Schooling?*, pp. xii, 77.

8. White et al., *Federal Programs*, 2:107.

9. Ibid., p. 191.

10. Ibid., 3:66; Averch et al., *How Effective Is Schooling?*, p. 154.

11. Quoted in Averch et al., *How Effective Is Schooling?*, p. 121.

12. Ibid., p. 123.

13. The evidence of their progress in special Follow Through programs is too indefinite to warrant discussion: White et al., *Federal Programs*, 2:85; but see Urie Bronfenbrenner, "Is Early Intervention Effective?", p. 289, where hopeful results are noted but where the author warns that the findings "must be viewed with caution."

14. Averch et al., *How Effective Is Schooling?*, p. 125.

15. Bronfenbrenner, "Is Early Intervention Effective?", p. 288.

16. Averch et al., *How Effective Is Schooling?*, p. 158; White et al., *Federal Programs*, 3:15.

17. Averch et al., *How Effective Is Schooling?*, p. xii.

18. Christopher Jencks et al., *Inequality*, pp. 138–41.

19. Ibid., pp. 146, 159.

20. Ibid.

21. Merle B. Karnes et al., "Educational Intervention at Home by Mothers of Disadvantaged Infants," pp. 925–34.

22. Susan W. Gray and Rupert A. Klaus, "The Early Training Project," p. 922.

23. White et al., *Federal Programs*, 2:227, 226.

24. Ibid., p. 260.

25. Bronfenbrenner, "Is Early Intervention Effective?", p. 296; see the whole article for a summary of recent work.

26. White et al., *Federal Programs*, 3:94.

27. Ibid., p. 88.

28. Ibid., p. 89.

29. Averch et al., *How Effective Is Schooling?*, pp. 122–24.

30. Jencks et al., *Inequality*, pp. 179–80, 226.

31. "Editor's Introduction: Perspectives on *Inequality*," *Harvard Educational Review* 43 (February 1973): 48.

32. Jencks et al., *Inequality*, pp. 198–99.

33. Stephan Thernstrom, *The Other Bostonians*, p. 255. See all of chapter 9 as well.

34. Ibid., p. 260; Peter M. Blau and Otis Dudley Duncan, *The American Occupational Structure*, p. 435.

35. Samuel Halperin, "Federal Aid to Education: A Retrospective Look at 'The Great Education Act,'" *Christian Science Monitor*, 9 June 1975.

36. George H. Gallup, "Fifth Annual Gallup Poll of Public Attitudes toward Education," p. 39, 41, 43, 44.

37. Quoted in Henry J. Perkinson, *The Imperfect Panacea*, frontispiece.

Bibliography

Books

Addams, Jane. *Twenty Years at Hull House*. New York: Macmillan Co., 1945.

Altshuler, Alan A. *Community Control: The Black Demand for Participation in Large American Cities*. New York: Bobbs-Merrill Co., Pegasus Books, 1970.

Averch, Harvey A., Stephen J. Carroll, Theodore S. Donaldson, Herbert J. Kiesling, and John Pincus. *How Effective Is Schooling? A Critical Review and Synthesis of Research Findings*. Santa Monica: RAND Corp., 1971.

Bailey, Stephen K., and Edith K. Mosher. *ESEA: The Office of Education Administers a Law*. Syracuse: Syracuse University Press, 1968.

Barlow, Melvin L., ed. *Vocational Education: The Sixty-Fourth Yearbook of the National Society for the Study of Education*. Chicago: University of Chicago Press, 1965.

Beggs, David W., III, and R. Bruce McQuigg, eds. *America's Schools and Churches: Partners in Conflict*. Bloomington: Indiana University Press, 1965.

Beer, Samuel H., and Richard E. Barringer, eds. *The State and the Poor*. Cambridge, Mass.: Winthrop Publishers, 1970.

Benton, William. *This Is the Challenge: The Benton Reports of 1956-1958 on the Nature of the Soviet Threat*. New York: Associated College Press, 1958.

Berg, Ivar. *Education and Jobs: The Great Training Robbery*. Boston: Beacon Press, 1971.

Berman, Daniel M. *A Bill Becomes a Law: Congress Enacts Civil Rights Legislation*. New York: Macmillan Co., 1966.

Bernstein, Abraham. *The Education of Urban Populations*. New York: Random House, 1967.

Bernstein, Barton J., and Allen J. Matusow, eds. *Twentieth-Century America: Recent Interpretations.* New York: Harcourt, Brace & World, 1969.

Bibby, John, and Roger Davidson. *On Capitol Hill: Studies in the Legislative Process.* New York: Holt, Rinehart & Winston, 1967.

Blau, Peter M., and Otis Dudley Duncan. *The American Occupational Structure.* New York: John Wiley & Sons, 1967.

Bloom, Benjamin S., Allison Davis, and Robert Hess. *Compensatory Education for Cultural Deprivation.* New York: Holt, Rinehart & Winston, 1965.

Bloomberg, Warner, Jr., and Henry J. Schmandt, eds. *Urban Poverty: Its Social and Political Dimensions.* Beverly Hills: Sage Publications, 1970.

Braeman, John, Robert H. Bremner, and Everett Walters, eds. *Change and Continuity in Twentieth-Century America.* Columbus: Ohio State University Press, 1964; reprint, New York: Harper & Row, Colophon Books, 1966.

Budgeting for National Objectives: Executive and Congressional Roles in Program Planning and Performance. New York: Committee for Economic Development, 1966.

Burkhead, Jesse, Thomas G. Fox, and John W. Holland. *Input and Output in Large-City High Schools.* Syracuse: Syracuse University Press, 1967.

Campbell, Roald F., Luvern L. Cunningham, and Roderick F. McPhee. *The Organization and Control of American Schools.* Columbus, Ohio: Charles E. Merrill Books, 1965.

Caudill, Harry M. *Night Comes to the Cumberlands: A Biography of a Depressed Area.* Boston: Little, Brown & Company, 1962.

Clark, Donald H., ed. *The Psychology of Education: Current Issues and Research.* New York: Free Press, 1967.

Clark, Kenneth, and Jeanette Hopkins. *A Relevant War against Poverty: A Study of Community Action Programs and Observable Social Change.* New York: Harper & Row, Torchbooks, 1970.

Cloward, Richard A., and Lloyd E. Ohlin. *Delinquency and Opportunity: A Theory of Delinquent Gangs.* Glencoe, Ill.: Free Press of Glencoe, 1960.

Coleman, James S. *Adolescents and the Schools.* New York: Basic Books, 1965.

———. *Incentives in American Education.* Baltimore: Johns Hopkins University, Center for the Study of Social Organization of Schools, 1969.

Coleman, James S., and Nancy Karweit. *Measures of School Performance.* Santa Monica: RAND Corp., 1970.

Conant, James Bryant. *Shaping Educational Policy.* New York: McGraw-Hill, 1964.

———. *Slums and Suburbs.* New York: McGraw-Hill, 1961. *Congress and the Nation, 1945–1964: A Review of Government and Politics in the Postwar Years.* Washington, D.C.: Congressional Quarterly Service, 1965.

Congressional Quarterly Guide to Current American Government. Washington, D.C.: Congressional Quarterly Service, 1971.

Congressional Quarterly Weekly Report, vol. 28. Washington, D.C.: Congressional Quarterly Service, 1970.

Congressional Quarterly Weekly Report, vol. 29. Washington, D.C.: Congressional Quarterly Service, 1971.

Crain, Robert L. *The Politics of School Desegregation: Comparative Case Studies of Community Structure and Policy-Making.* Chicago: Aldine Publishing Co., 1968.

Cremin, Lawrence A. *The American Common School: An Historic Conception.* New York: Teachers College, Columbia University, 1951.

―――. *The Transformation of the School: Progressivism in American Education, 1876-1957.* New York: Alfred A. Knopf, 1961.

Cronin, Thomas E., and Sanford D. Greenberg, eds. *The Presidential Advisory System.* New York: Harper & Row, 1969.

Daly, Charles U., ed. *The Quality of Inequality: Urban and Suburban Public Schools.* Chicago: University of Chicago Center for Policy Study, 1968.

Davis, Allen F. *Spearheads for Reform: The Social Settlements and the Progressive Movement, 1890-1914.* New York: Oxford University Press, 1967.

Davis, James W., ed. *Politics, Programs, and Budgets: A Reader in Government Budgeting.* Englewood Cliffs, N.J.: Prentice-Hall, 1969.

DeWitt, Nicholas. *Soviet Professional Manpower: Its Education, Training, and Supply.* Washington, D.C.: National Science Foundation, 1955.

Donovan, John C. *The Policy Makers.* New York: Bobbs-Merrill Co., Pegasus Books, 1970.

―――. *The Politics of Poverty.* New York: Bobbs-Merrill Co., Pegasus Books, 1967.

Downs, Anthony. *Urban Problems and Prospects.* Chicago: Markham Publishing Co., 1970.

―――. *Who Are the Urban Poor?* New York: Committee for Economic Development, 1968.

Dropkin, Stan, Harold Full, and Ernest Schwarcz, eds. *Contemporary American Education: An Anthology of Issues, Problems, Challenges.* New York: Macmillan Co., 1965.

Editorial Research Reports on Education in America. Washington, D.C.: Congressional Quarterly Service, 1968.

Education and the Disadvantaged American. Washington, D.C.: Educational Policies Commission of the National Education Association, 1962.

Education and National Security. Washington, D.C.: Educational Policies Commission of the National Education Association and the American Council on Education, 1951.

Eidenberg, Eugene, and Roy D. Morey. *An Act of Congress: The Legislative Process and the Making of Education Policy.* New York: W. W. Norton & Co., 1969.

Elam, Stanley and William P. McClure, eds. *Educational Requirements for the 1970's: An Interdisciplinary Approach.* New York: Frederick A. Praeger, 1967.

The Emergency School Assistance Program: An Evaluation. American Friends Service Committee et al., 1970.

Equal Educational Opportunity. Cambridge: Harvard University Press, 1969.

Evans, Rowland, and Robert Novak. *Lyndon B. Johnson: The Exercise of Power.* New York: New American Library, 1966.

―――. *Nixon in the White House: The Frustration of Power.* New York: Random House, 1971.

Everett, Robinson O., ed. *Anti-Poverty Program.* Dobbs Ferry, N.Y.: Oceana Publishing, 1966.

Fantini, Mario, Marilyn Gittell, and Richard Magat. *Community Control and the Urban School.* New York: Praeger Publishers, 1970.

Federal Role in Education. Washington, D.C.: Congressional Quarterly Service, 1967.

Ferman, Louis A., Joyce L. Kornbluh, and Alan Haber, eds. *Poverty in America: A Book of Readings.* Ann Arbor: University of Michigan Press, 1965.

Flash, Edward S., Jr. *Economic Advice and Presidential Leadership: The Council of Economic Advisors.* New York: Columbia University Press, 1965.

Frost, Joe L., and G. Thomas Rowland. *Compensatory Programming: The Acid Test of American Education.* Dubuque, Iowa: William C. Brown Co., 1971.

Frost, Joe L., and Glenn R. Hawkes, eds. *The Disadvantaged Child: Issues and Innovations.* Boston: Houghton Mifflin Co., 1966.

Gallup, George H. *The Gallup Poll: Public Opinion 1935-1971.* New York: Random House, 1972, vol. 3.

Gardner, John W. *Excellence: Can We Be Equal and Excellent Too?* New York: Harper & Bros., 1961.

————. *No Easy Victories.* New York: Harper & Row, 1968.

————. *The Recovery of Confidence.* New York: W. W. Norton & Co., 1970.

Gettleman, Marvin E., and David Mermelstein, eds. *The Great Society Reader: The Failure of American Liberalism.* New York: Random House, Vintage Books, 1967.

Gittell, Marilyn. *Participants and Participation: A Study of School Policy in New York City.* New York: Frederick A. Praeger, 1967.

Gittell, Marilyn and T. Edward Hollander. *Six Urban School Districts: A Comparative Study of Institutional Response.* New York: Frederick A. Praeger, 1968.

Goldhammer, Keith, *The School Board.* New York: Center for Applied Research in Education, 1964.

Goldman, Eric F. *The Tragedy of Lyndon Johnson.* New York: Alfred A. Knopf, 1969.

Goodman, Leonard H., ed. *Economic Progress and Social Welfare.* New York: Columbia University Press, 1966.

Gordon, Edmund W., and Doxey A. Wilkerson. *Compensatory Education for the Disadvantaged, Programs and Practices: Preschool through College.* New York: College Entrance Examination Board, 1966.

Gordon, Kermit, ed. *Agenda for the Nation.* Washington, D.C.: Brookings Institution, 1968.

Gordon, Margaret S., ed. *Poverty in America.* San Francisco: Chandler Publishing Co., 1965.

Greer, Colin. *Cobweb Attitudes: Essays on Educational and Cultural Mythology.* New York: Teachers College Press, 1970.

————. *The Great School Legend: A Revisionist Interpretation of American Public Education.* New York: Basic Books, 1972.

Griffiths, Daniel E. *The School Superintendent.* New York: Center for Applied Research in Education, 1966.

Gross, Bertram M., ed. *Social Intelligence for America's Future: Explorations in Societal Problems.* Boston: Allyn & Bacon, 1969.

Halsey, A. H., Jean Floud, and C. Arnold Anderson, eds. *Education, Economy, and Society: A Reader in the Sociology of Education.* Glencoe, Ill.: Free Press of Glencoe, 1961.

Hanna, Paul R., ed. *Education: An Instrument of National Goals.* New York: McGraw-Hill, 1962.

Hansen, Donald A., and Joel E. Gerstl, eds. *On Education: Sociological Perspectives.* New York: John Wiley & Sons, 1967.

Harrington, Michael. *The Other America: Poverty in the United States.* New York: Macmillan Co., 1962.

Harris, Fred R., ed. *Social Science and National Policy.* Chicago: Aldine Publishing Co., 1970.

Harris, Seymour E. *Economics of the Kennedy Years and a Look Ahead.* New York: Harper & Row, 1964.

Harris, Seymour E., and Alan Levensohn, eds. *Education and Public Policy.* Berkeley: McCutchan Publishing Corp., 1965.

Havighurst, Robert J., Bernice L. Neugarten, and Jacqueline Falk, eds. *Society and Education: A Book of Readings.* Boston: Allyn & Bacon, 1967.

Heller, Barbara R., and Richard S. Barrett. *Expand and Improve: A Critical Review of the First Three Years of ESEA Title I in New York City.* New York: Center for Urban Education, 1970.

Heller, Walter W. *New Dimensions of Political Economy.* Cambridge, Mass.: Harvard University Press, 1966.

———, ed. *Perspectives on Economic Growth.* New York: Random House, 1968.

Hellmuth, Jerome, ed. *Disadvantaged Child, Compensatory Education: A National Debate.* New York: Brunner/Mazel, 1970.

Hentoff, Nat. *The New Equality.* New York: Viking Press, 1964.

Hughes, John F., and Anne O. Hughes. *Equal Education: A New National Strategy.* Bloomington: Indiana University Press, 1972.

Jencks, Christopher, et al. *Education Vouchers: A Report on Financing Elementary Education by Grants to Parents.* Cambridge, Mass.: Center for the Study of Public Policy, 1970.

Jencks, Christopher, Marshall Smith, Henry Acland, Mary Jo Bane, David Cohen, Herbert Gintis, Barbara Heyns, and Stephan Michelson. *Inequality: A Reassessment of the Effect of Family and Schooling in America.* New York: Basic Books, 1972.

Johnson, Lyndon Baines. *The Vantage Point: Perspectives of the Presidency 1963–1969.* New York: Holt, Rinehart & Winston, 1971.

Kahn, Alfred J. *Studies in Social Policy and Planning.* New York: Russell Sage Foundation, 1969.

Katz, Irwin, and Patricia Gurin, eds. *Race and the Social Sciences.* New York: Basic Books, 1969.

Katz, Michael B. *Class, Bureaucracy, and Schools: The Illusion of Educational Change in America.* New York: Praeger Publishers, 1971.

———. *The Irony of Early School Reform: Educational Innovation in Mid-Nineteenth Century Massachusetts.* Cambridge, Mass.: Harvard University Press, 1968.

Keach, Everett T., Jr., Robert Fulton, and William E. Gardner, eds. *Education and Social Crisis: Perspectives on Teaching Disadvantaged Youth.* New York: John Wiley & Sons, 1967.

Keppel, Francis. *The Necessary Revolution in American Education.* New York: Harper & Row, 1966.

Kershaw, Joseph A., and Paul N. Courant. *Government against Poverty.* Washington, D.C.: Brookings Institution, 1970.

Keyserling, Leon H. *Progress or Poverty: The U.S. at the Crossroads.* Washington, D.C.: Conference on Economic Progress, 1964.

Killian, Lewis M. *The Impossible Revolution? Black Power and the American Dream.* New York: Random House, 1968.

Knapp, Daniel, and Kenneth Polk. *Scouting the War on Poverty: Social Reform Politics in the Kennedy Administration.* Lexington, Mass.: Heath Lexington Books, 1971.

Koerner, James D. *Who Controls American Education? A Guide for Laymen.* Boston: Beacon Press, 1968.

Kolko, Gabriel. *Wealth and Power in America: An Analysis of Social Class and Income Distribution.* New York: Frederick A. Praeger, 1962.

Labovitz, I. M., *Aid for Federally Affected Public Schools.* Syracuse: Syracuse University Press, 1963.

Larner, Jeremy, and Irving Howe, eds. *Poverty: Views From the Left.* New York: William Morrow & Co., 1968.

Lawlessness and Disorder: Fourteen Years of Failure in Southern School Desegregation. Southern Regional Council, n.d.

Lazeron, Marvin. *Origins of the Urban School: Public Education in Massachusetts, 1870–1915.* Cambridge, Mass.: Harvard University Press, 1971.

Levine, Robert A. *The Poor Ye Need Not Have with You: Lessons from the War on Poverty.* Cambridge, Mass.: M.I.T. Press, 1970.

———. *Public Planning: Failure and Redirection.* New York: Basic Books, 1972.

Levitan, Sar A. *The Great Society's Poor Law: A New Approach to Poverty.* Baltimore: Johns Hopkins Press, 1969.

Levitan, Sar A., and Garth L. Magnum. *Federal Training and Work Programs in the Sixties.* Ann Arbor, Mich.: Institute of Labor and Industrial Relations, 1969.

Lewis, Oscar. *The Children of Sanchez: Autobiography of a Mexican Family.* New York: Random House, 1961.

Lipset, Seymour M., and Reinhard Bendix. *Social Mobility in Industrial Society.* Berkeley and Los Angeles: University of California Press, 1964.

Lubove, Roy. *The Progressives and the Slums: Tenement House Reform in New York City, 1890–1917.* New York: University of Pittsburgh Press, 1962.

McDill, Edward L., Mary S. McDill, and J. Timothy Sprehe. *Strategies for Success in Compensatory Education: An Appraisal of Evaluation Research.* Baltimore: Johns Hopkins Press, 1969.

McPartland, James, and J. Timothy Sprehe. *Some Hypothetical Experiments on Variations in School Components and Selected Educational Outcomes.* Baltimore: Johns Hopkins University, Center for the Study of Social Organization of Schools, 1968.

March, Paul E., and Ross A. Gortner. *Federal Aid to Science Education: Two Programs.* Syracuse: Syracuse University Press, 1963.

Marris, Peter, and Martin Rein. *Dilemmas of Social Reform: Poverty and Community Action in the United States.* New York: Atherton Press, 1969.

Martin, Ruby, and Phyllis McClure. *Title I of ESEA: Is It Helping Poor Children?* Washington, D.C.: Washington Research Project and the NAACP Legal Defense and Educational Fund, 1969.

Meranto, Philip. *The Politics of Federal Aid to Education in 1965: A Study in Political Innovation.* Syracuse: Syracuse University Press, 1967.

Miller, Harry L., ed. *Education for the Disadvantaged: Current Issues and Research,* New York: Free Press, 1967.

Miller, S. M., and Pamela A. Roby. *The Future of Inequality.* New York: Basic Books, 1970.

Mosteller, Frederick, and Daniel P. Moynihan, eds. *On Equality of Educational Opportunity: Papers Deriving from the Harvard Faculty Seminar on the Coleman Report.* New York: Random House, 1972.

Moynihan, Daniel P. *Maximum Feasible Misunderstanding: Community Action in the War on Poverty.* New York: Free Press, 1969.

———, ed. *On Understanding Poverty: Perspectives from the Social Sciences.* New York: Basic Books, 1968.

Munger, Frank J., and Richard F. Fenno, Jr. *National Politics and Federal Aid to Education.* Syracuse: Syracuse University Press, 1962.

Muse, Benjamin. *The American Negro Revolution: From Nonviolence to Black Power, 1963–1967.* Bloomington: Indiana University Press, 1968.

Nathan, Richard P. *The Plot That Failed: Nixon and the Administrative Presidency.* New York: John Wiley & Sons, 1975.

Novick, David. *Program Budgeting: Program Analysis and the Federal Budget*. New York: Holt, Rinehart & Winston, 2d ed., 1969.

O'Hara, William T., ed. *John F. Kennedy on Education*. New York: Teachers College Press, 1966.

Orfield, Gary. *The Reconstruction of Southern Education: The Schools and the 1964 Civil Rights Act*. New York: John Wiley & Sons, 1969.

Ornstein, Allan C. *Race and Politics in School/Community Organizations*. Pacific Palisades: Goodyear Publishing Co., 1974.

Ornati, Oscar. *Poverty amid Affluence: A Report on a Research Project Carried Out at the New School for Social Research*. New York: Twentieth Century Fund, 1966.

Owen, John D. *School Inequality and the Welfare State*. Baltimore: Johns Hopkins Press, 1974.

Panetta, Leon E. and Peter Gall. *Bring Us Together: The Nixon Team and the Civil Rights Retreat*. Philadelphia: J. B. Lippincott Co., 1971.

Parsons, Talcott, and Kenneth B. Clark, eds. *The American Negro*. Boston: Houghton Mifflin Co., 1966.

Passow, A. Harry, ed. *Education in Depressed Areas*. New York: Teachers College, Columbia University, 1963.

Pearl, Arthur and Frank Riessman. *New Careers for the Poor: The Nonprofessional in Human Service*. New York: Free Press, 1965.

Perkinson, Henry J. *The Imperfect Panacea: American Faith in Education, 1865–1965*. New York: Random House, 1968.

Porter, Kirk, and Donald Bruce Johnson, comps. *National Party Platforms, 1840–1964*. Urbana: University of Illinois Press, 1966.

Poverty and Deprivation in the United States: The Plight of Two-Fifths of a Nation. Washington, D.C.: Conference on Economic Progress, 1962.

Rainwater, Lee, ed. *Soul*. Chicago: Aldine Publishing Co., 1970.

Revolution in Civil Rights. Washington, D.C.: Congressional Quarterly Service, 4th ed., 1968.

Ribich, Thomas I. *Education and Poverty*. Washington, D.C.: Brookings Institution, 1968.

Rickover, H. G. *Education and Freedom*. New York: E. P. Dutton & Co., 1959.

Riessman, Frank. *Strategies against Poverty*. New York: Random House, 1969.

Riis, Jacob A. *How the Other Half Lives: Studies among the Tenements of New York*. New York: Hill & Wang, 1957.

Riles, Wilson C. (Chairman). *The Urban Education Task Force Report: Final Report of the Task Force on Urban Education to the Department of Health, Education, and Welfare*. New York: Praeger Publishers, 1970.

Rivlin, Alice M. *Systematic Thinking for Social Action*. Washington, D.C.: Brookings Institution, 1971.

Roach, Jack L., Llewellyn Gross, and Orville R. Gursslin, eds. *Social Stratification in the United States*. Englewood Cliffs, N.J. Prentice-Hall, Inc., 1969.

Rogers, David. *110 Livingston Street: Politics and Bureaucracy in the New York City Schools*. New York: Random House, 1968.

Rogoff, Natalie. *Recent Trends in Occupational Mobility*. Glencoe, Ill.: Free Press, 1953.

Rose, Stephen M. *The Betrayal of the Poor: The Transformation of Community Action*. Cambridge, Mass: Schenkman Publishing Co., 1972.

Rosenthal, Alan. *Pedagogues and Power: Teacher Groups in School Politics*. Syracuse: Syracuse University Press, 1969.

Rossi, Peter, H., and Zahava D. Blum. *Class, Status, and Poverty*. Baltimore: Johns Hopkins University, Center for the Study of Social Organization of Schools, 1968.

Rourke, Francis E. *Bureaucracy, Politics, and Public Policy*. Boston: Little, Brown & Co., 1969.

Rubinstein, Annette T. *Schools against Children: The Case for Community Control*. New York: Monthly Review Press, 1970.

Rushdoony, Rousas J. *The Messianic Character of American Education*. Nutley, N.J.: Craig Press, 1963.

Scheibla, Shirley. *Poverty Is Where the Money Is*. New Rochelle, N.Y.: Arlington House, 1968.

Schlesinger, Arthur M., Jr. *A Thousand Days: John F. Kennedy in the White House*. Cambridge, Mass.: Houghton Mifflin Co., 1965.

Schneier, Edward V., ed. *Policy-Making in American Government*. New York: Basic Books, 1969.

Schreiber, Daniel, ed. *Profile of the School Dropout*. New York: Random House, Vintage Books, 1968.

Schultze, Charles, Edward K. Hamilton, and Allen Schick. *Setting National Priorities: The 1971 Budget*. Washington, D.C.: Brookings Institution, 1970.

Schultze, Charles, Edward R. Fried, Alice M. Rivlin, and Nancy H. Teeters. *Setting National Priorities: The 1972 Budget*. Washington, D.C.: Brookings Institution, 1971.

———— *Setting National Priorities: The 1973 Budget*. Washington, D.C.: Brookings Institution, 1972.

Schwebel, Milton. *Who Can Be Educated?* New York: Grove Press, 1968.

Scott, C. Winfield, Clyde M. Hill, and Hobert W. Burns, eds. *The Great Debate: Our Schools in Crisis*. Englewood Cliffs, N.J.: Prentice-Hall, 1959.

Seidman, Harold. *Politics, Position, and Power: The Dynamics of Federal Organization*. New York: Oxford University Press, 1970.

Seligman, Ben B., ed. *Permanent Poverty: An American Syndrome*. Chicago: Quadrangle Books, 1968.

Sexton, Patricia Cayo. *Education and Income: Inequalities of Opportunity in our Public Schools*. New York: Viking Press, 1961.

————. *The American School: A Sociological Analysis*. Englewood Cliffs, N.J.: Prentice Hall, 1967.

Sheppard, Harold L., ed. *Poverty and Wealth in America*. Chicago: Quadrangle Books, 1970.

Shostak, Arthur B., and William Gomberg, eds. *Blue-Collar World: Studies of the American Worker*. Englewood Cliffs, N.J.: Prentice-Hall, 1964.

Sidey, Hugh. *A Very Personal Presidency: Lyndon Johnson in the White House*. New York: Atheneum, 1968.

Silberman, Charles E. *Crisis in Black and White*. New York: Random House, 1964.

————. *Crisis in the Classroom: The Remaking of American Education*. New York: Random House, 1970.

Sindler, Allan P., ed. *American Political Institutions and Public Policy: Five Contemporary Studies*. Boston: Little, Brown & Co., 1969.

Stanley, David T. *Changing Administrations: The 1961 and 1964 Transitions in Six Departments*. Washington, D.C.: Brookings Institution, 1965.

Stanley, Julian C. *Preschool Programs for the Disadvantaged: Five Governmental Approaches to Early Childhood Education*. Baltimore: Johns Hopkins Press, 1971.

The Status of School Desegregation in the South, 1970. American Friends Service Committee et al., n. d.

Sufrin, Sidney C. *Administering the National Defense Education Act.* Syracuse: Syracuse University Press, 1963.

Summerfield, Harry L. *Power and Process: The Formulation and Limits of Federal Educational Policy.* Berkeley, Calif.: McCutchan Publishing Corp., 1974.

Sundquist, James L. *Politics and Policy: The Eisenhower, Kennedy, and Johnson Years.* Washington, D.C.: Brookings Institution, 1968.

————, ed. *On Fighting Poverty: Perspectives from Experience.* New York: Basic Books, 1969.

Sundquist, James L., and David W. Davis. *Making Federalism Work: A Study of Program Coordination at the Community Level.* Washington, D.C.: Brookings Institution, 1969.

Thernstrom, Stephan. *The Other Bostonians: Poverty and Progress in the American Metropolis, 1880–1970.* Cambridge, Mass.: Harvard University Press, 1973.

————. *Poverty, Planning, and Politics in the New Boston: The Origins of ABCD.* New York: Basic Books, 1969.

Thernstrom, Stephan, and Richard Sennett, eds. *Nineteenth-Century Cities: Essays in the New Urban History.* New Haven, Conn.: Yale University Press, 1969.

Thurow, Lester C. *Poverty and Discrimination.* Washington, D.C.: Brookings Institution, 1969.

Tyack, David B., ed. *Turning Points in American Educational History.* Waltham, Mass.: Blaisdell Publishing Co., 1967.

Valentine, Charles A. *Culture and Poverty: Critique and Counter-Proposals.* Chicago: University of Chicago Press, 1968.

Venn, Grant. *Man, Education, and Work: Postsecondary Vocational and Technical Education.* Washington, D.C.: American Council on Education, 1964.

Waxman, Chaim Isaac, ed. *Poverty: Power and Politics.* New York: Grosset & Dunlap, 1968.

Weaver, Thomas, and Alvin Magid, eds. *Poverty: New Interdisciplinary Perspectives.* San Francisco: Chandler Publishing Co., 1969.

Weeks, Christopher. *Job Corps: Dollars and Dropouts.* Boston: Little, Brown & Co., 1967.

Weinberg, Meyer. *Desegregation Research: An Appraisal.* Bloomington, Ind.: Phi Delta Kappan, 1968.

————. *Research on School Desegregation: Review and Prospect.* Chicago: Integrated Education Associates, 1965.

Weisbrod, Barton A., ed. *The Economics of Poverty: An American Paradox.* Englewood Cliffs: Prentice-Hall, 1965.

Welter, Rush. *Popular Education and Democratic Thought in America.* New York: Columbia University Press, 1962.

Westin, Alan F. *The Uses of Power: Seven Cases in American Politics.* New York: Harcourt, Brace & World, 1962.

White, Sheldon H., Mary Carol Day, Phyllis K. Freeman, Stephen A. Hantman, and Katherine P. Messenger. *Federal Programs for Young Children: Review and Recommendations.* 4 vols. Washington, D.C.: Government Printing Office, 1973.

White, Theodore. *The Making of the President, 1964.* New York: Atheneum, 1965.

Wholey, Joseph S., John W. Scanlon, Hugh G. Duffy, James S. Fukumoto, and Leona M. Vogt. *Federal Evaluation Policy: Analyzing the Effects of Public Programs.* Washington, D.C.: Urban Institute, 1970.

Wicker, Tom. *JKF and LBJ: The Influence of Personality upon Politics.* New York: William Morrow & Co., 1968.

Wilensky, Harold. *Organizational Intelligence: Knowledge and Policy in Government and Industry.* New York: Basic Books, 1967.

Will, Robert E., and Harold G. Vatter. *Poverty in Affluence: The Social, Political, and Economic Dimensions of Poverty in the United States.* New York: Harcourt, Brace & World, 1965.

Williams, Walter. *Social Policy Research and Analysis: The Experience in the Federal Social Agencies.* New York: American Elsevier Publishing Co., 1971.

Wirt, Frederick M., and Michael W. Kirst. *The Political Web of American Schools.* Boston: Little, Brown & Co., 1972.

Woodring, Paul, and John Scanlon, eds. *American Education Today.* New York: McGraw-Hill, 1960.

Articles

Aaron, Henry. "The Foundations of the 'War on Poverty' Reexamined." *American Economic Review* 57 (December 1967): 1229–40.

Allen, James E., Jr. "An Interview with James Allen." *Harvard Educational Review* 40 (November 1970): 533–46.

Alsop, Joseph. "Alsop Fires a Salvo at Schwartz-Pettigrew-Smith." *Nation's Schools* 81 (April 1968): 41–42.

———. "No More Nonsense about Ghetto Education." *New Republic*, 22 July 1967, pp. 18–23.

———. "Reaction to the Coleman Report." *N.E.A. Journal* 56 (September 1967): 27–28.

Anderson, C. Arnold. "A Skeptical Note on the Relation of Vertical Mobility to Education." *American Journal of Sociology* 66 (May 1961): 560–70.

Anderson, W. H. Locke. "Trickling Down: The Relationship between Economic Growth and the Extent of Poverty among American Families." *Quarterly Journal of Economics* 78 (November 1964): 511–24.

Areen, Judith, and Christopher Jencks. "Education Vouchers: A Proposal for Diversity and Choice." *Teachers College Record* 72 (February 1971): 327–35.

Arons, Stephen. "Equity, Option, and Vouchers." *Teachers College Record* 72 (February 1971): 337–63.

Barber, Bernard. "Social-class Differences in Educational Life-Chances." *Teachers College Record* 63 (November 1961): 102–13.

Barber, Rims. "*Swann* Song From the Delta." *Inequality in Education* 9 (August 1971): 4–5.

Beckler, John. "Administration's Proposals for Education Legislation." *School Management* 15 (January 1971): 4, 6–7.

———. "Congress and the Administration Scrutinize the Results of Title I." *School Management* 14 (September 1970): 6–7, 36.

"Benjamin C. Willis: An Interview, *U. S. News and World Report.*" Reprinted in *Integrated Education* 3 (December 1965-January 1966): 38–41.

Benson, Charles S. "Why the Schools Flunk Out." *Nation*, 10 April 1967, pp. 463–66.

Berube, Maurice R. "Community Control: Key to Educational Achievement." *Social Policy* 1 (July/August 1970): 42–45.

Bickel, Alexander M. "Forcing Desegregation through Title VI." *New Republic*, 9 April 1966, pp. 8–9.

Blank, Marion. "Implicit Assumptions Underlying Preschool Intervention Programs." *Journal of Social Issues* 26 (Spring 1970): 15–33.

Bowles, Samuel. "Unequal Education and the Reproduction of the Social Division of Labor." *Review of Radical Political Economics* 3 (Fall-Winter 1971): 1–30.

Bowles, Samuel, and Henry M. Levin, "The Determinants of Scholastic Achievement—An Appraisal of Some Recent Evidence." *Journal of Human Resources* 3 (Winter 1968): 3–24.

Brinkley, David. "Leading from Strength: LBJ in Action." *Atlantic*, February 1965, pp. 49–54.

Broder, David. "Consensus Politics: End of an Experiment." *Atlantic*, October 1966, pp. 60–65.

Bronfenbrenner, Urie. "Is Early Intervention Effective?" *Teachers College Record* 76 (December 1974): 279–303.

Brown, Cynthia. "Nixon Administration Desegregation." *Inequality in Education* 9 (August 1971): 11–16.

Brummitt, Gary W., and Ed Downey. "Title I ESEA Narrows the Education Gap." *School and Community* 55 (April 1969): 17, 45.

Cahn, Edgar, and Jean C. Cahn. "The War on Poverty: A Civilian Perspective." *Yale Law Journal* 73 (July 1964): 1317–52.

Campbell, Donald T. "Reforms as Experiments." *Urban Affairs Quarterly* 7 (December 1971): 133–71.

Carey, William D. "Presidential Staffing in the Sixties and Seventies." *Public Administration Review* 29 (September/October 1969): pp. 450–58.

Carmichael, Stokely, and Charles Hamilton. "Dynamite." *Atlantic*, October 1967, pp. 98–102.

Cass, James. "Do We Really Want Equality?" *Saturday Review*, 17 December 1966, pp. 65–67.

"Chicago Title VI Complaint to H.E.W., The" *Integrated Education* 3 (December 1965-January 1966): 10–34.

Cicirelli, Victor G., John W. Evans, and Jeffrey Schiller. "A Reply to the Report Analysis." *Harvard Educational Review* 40 (February 1970): 105–29.

Clark, Kenneth B. "Alternative Public School Systems." *Harvard Educational Review* 38 (Winter 1968): 100–113.

———. "Eighteen Years after Brown," *Integrated Education* 10 (November-December 1972): 7–15.

Cohen, Bob. "Title I Clothing Grants Found to Improve Student Self-Image and School Attendance." *Inequality in Education* 9 (August 1971): 35.

Cohen, David K. "Compensation and Integration." *Harvard Educational Review* 38 (Winter 1968): 114–37.

———. "Defining Racial Equality in Education." *UCLA Law Review* 16 (1969): 255–80.

———. "Education and Race." *History of Education Quarterly* 9 (Fall 1969): 281–86.

———. "Immigrants and the Schools." *Review of Educational Research* 40 (February 1970): 13–27.

———. "Politics and Research: Evaluation of Social Action Programs in Education." *Review of Educational Research* 40 (April 1970): 213–38.

———. "The Price of Community Control." *Commentary*, July 1969, pp. 23–32.

———. "Public Schools: The Next Decade." *Dissent*, April 1971, pp. 161–70.

Cohen, David K., and Michael S. Garet. "Reforming Educational Policy with Applied Social Research." *Harvard Educational Review* 45 (February 1975): 17–43.

Cohen, David K., and Marvin Lazeron. "Education and the Corporate Order." *Socialist Revolution* 2 (March-April 1972): 47–72.

Cohen Sol. "Urban School Reform." *History of Education Quarterly* 9 (Fall 1969): 298–304.

Coleman, James S. "Equal Schools or Equal Students?" *Public Interest*, Summer 1966, pp. 70–75.

———. "Equality of Educational Opportunity." *Integrated Education* 6 (September-October 1968): 19–28.

———. "Equality of Educational Opportunity: Reply to Bowles and Levin." *Journal of Human Resources* 8 (Spring 1966): 237–46.

———. "Responsibility of Schools in the Provision of Equal Educational Opportunity." *Bulletin of the National Association of Secondary School Principals* 52 (May 1968): 179–90.

———. "Toward Open Schools." *Public Interest*, Fall 1967, pp. 20–27.

"Court Orders Parental Participation in San Jose's Title I Programs." *Inequality in Education* 6 (November 1970): 27–28.

Coser, Lewis. "What Do the Poor Need? (Money)." *Dissent*, October 1971, pp. 485–91.

Crain, Robert L., and David Street. "School Desegregation and School Decision-Making." *Urban Affairs Quarte ly* 2 (September 1966): 64–82.

"Crisis in Education." *Life* reprint, 1958.

Cronbach, Lee J. "Heredity, Environment, and Educational Policy." *Harvard Educational Review* 39 (Spring 1969): 338–47.

Cronin, Thomas E. "The Presidency and Education." *Phi Delta Kappan* 49 (February 1968): 295–99.

Culbertson, Jack. "Introduction." *Public Administration Review* 30 (July/August 1970): 331–33.

Cutright, Phillips. "Occupational Inheritance: A Cross-National Analysis." *American Journal of Sociology* 73 (January 1968): 400–416.

Davie, James S. "Social Class Factors and School Attendance." *Harvard Educational Review* 23 (Summer 1953): 175–85.

Dentler, Robert. "Equality of Educational Opportunity: A Special Review." *Urban Review* 1 (December 1966): 27–29.

———. "Urban Eyewash: A Review of 'Title I/Year II,' " *Urban Review* 3 (February 1969): 32–33.

Deutsch, Martin. "Happenings on the Way Back to the Forum: Social Science, I.Q., and Race Differences Revisited." *Harvard Education Review* 39 (Summer 1969): 523–57.

Drew, Elizabeth Brenner. "Education's Billion-Dollar Baby." *Atlantic*, July 1966, pp. 37–43.

———. "HEW Grapples with PPBS." *Public Interest*, Summer 1967, pp. 9–29.

Effrat, Andrew, Roy E. Feldman, and Harvey M. Sapolsky. "Inducing Poor Children to Learn." *Public Interest*, Spring 1969, pp. 106–12.

Elsbery, James W. "Change the Premise." *Urban Review* 3 (April 1969): 4, 6–11.

Etzioni, Amitai. "On *Crisis in the Classroom*." *Harvard Educational Review* 41 (February 1971): 87–98.

Exton, Elaine. "Federal Program Budgeting is a Step toward Centralized Education Planning." *American School Board Journal* 153 (November 1966): 39, 42–43.

———. "State Legislators Urged to Install Planning-Programming-Budgeting System." *American School Board Journal* 154 (February 1967): 13–16.

————. "USOE Uses Computor-Based Models to Evaluate Education." *American School Board Journal* 154 (January 1967): 15–16, 43–44.

Fairlie, Henry. "Johnson and the Intellectuals." *Commentary*, October 1965, pp. 49–55.

Featherstone, Joseph. "Community Control of Our Schools: Will Children and Teachers Be Better Off?" *New Republic*, 13 January 1968, pp. 16–19.

Folger, John K., and Charles B. Nam. "Trends in Education in Relation to the Occupational Structure." *Sociology of Education* 38 (Fall 1964): pp. 19–33.

Friedenberg, Edgar Z. "The Function of the School in Social Homeostasis." *Rev. Canad. Soc. & Anth./Canad. Rev. Soc. &Anth.* 7 (1, 1970): pp. 5–16.

————. "Requiem for the Urban School." *Saturday Review*, 18 November 1967, pp. 77–79, 92–94.

Galbraith, John Kenneth. "Let Us Begin: An Invitation to Action on Poverty." *Harper's*, March 1964, pp. 16–26.

Gallaway, Lowell E. "The Foundations of the 'War on Poverty.'" *American Economic Review* 55 (March 1965): 122—31.

Gallup, George H. "Fifth Annual Gallup Poll of Public Attitudes toward Education." *Phi Delta Kappan* 55 (September 1973): 38–50.

Gersman, Elinor Mondale. "Progressive Reform of the St. Louis School Board, 1897." *History of Education Quarterly* 10 (Spring 1970): 3–21.

Ginzberg, Eli. "The Economics of the Voucher System." *Teachers College Record* 72 (February 1971): 373–82.

Gittell, Marilyn. "Urban School Politics: Professionalism vs. Reform." *Journal of Social Issues* 26 (Summer 1970): 69–84.

Glazer, Nathan. "Ethnic Groups and Education: Towards the Tolerance of Difference." *Journal of Negro Education* 38 (Summer 1969): 187–95.

————. "The Great Society Was Never a Casualty of the War." *Saturday Review*, December 1972, pp. 49–52.

Glickstein, Howard A. "Federal Educational Programs and Minority Groups." *Journal of Negro Education* 38 (Summer 1969): 303–14.

Goodlad, John I. "The Schools vs. Education." *Saturday Review*, 19 April 1969, pp. 59–61, 80–82.

Gordon, Edmund W. "Information Retrieval Center on the Disadvantaged." *Urban Education* 3 (July 1967): 71–84.

————. "Introduction." *Review of Education Research* 40 (February 1970): 1–12.

Gordon, Edmund W., and Adelaide Jablonsky. "Compensatory Education in the Equalization of Educational Opportunity, I." *Journal of Negro Education* 37 (Summer 1968): 268–79.

Gordon, Margaret S. "U.S. Manpower and Employment Policy." *Monthly Labor Review* 87 (November 1964): 1314–21.

Grant, Gerald. "Developing Power in the Ghetto." *Saturday Review*, 17 December 1966, pp. 75–76, 88.

————. "Essay Reviews: *On Equality of Educational Opportunity: Papers Deriving from the Harvard University Faculty Seminar on the Coleman Report.*" *Harvard Educational Review* 42 (February 1972): 109–25.

Gray, Susan W., and Rupert A. Klaus. "The Early Training Project: A Seventh-Year Report." *Child Development* 41 (December 1971): 900–924.

Greenberg, Jack. "The Tortoise Can Beat the Hare." *Saturday Review*, 17 February 1968, p. 57–59, 68.

Greenfield, Meg. "What Is Racial Balance in the Schools?" *Reporter* 36 (23 March 1967): 20–26.

Greer, Colin. "Public Schools: The Myth of the Melting Pot." *Saturday Review*, 15 November 1969, pp. 84–86, 102.

Guthrie, James W. "City Schools in a Federal Vise: The Political Dynamics of Federal Aid to Urban Schools." *Education and Urban Society* 11 (February 1970): 199–218.

———. "A Political Case History: Passage of the ESEA." *Phi Delta Kappan* 49 (February 1968): 302–6.

Haddad, William F. "Mr. Shriver and the Savage Politics of Poverty." *Harper's*, December 1965, pp. 43–50.

Halloran, Daniel F. "Progress against Poverty: The Governmental Approach." *Public Administration Review* 28 (May/June 1968): 205–13.

Havighurst, Robert J. "Change the Child." *Urban Review* 3 (April 1969): 5, 11–12.

———. "These Integration Approaches Work—Sometimes." *Nation's Schools* 80 (September 1967): 73–75.

Heller, Walter W. "Comment of a Policy Maker." *New Republic*, 20 October 1962, pp. 39–42.

———. "The Economic Outlook of Education." *N.E.A. Journal* 48 (December 1959): 48–50.

Herzog, Elizabeth. "Some Assumptions about the Poor." *Social Science Review* 37 (December 1963): 389–402.

Hess, Robert D., Virginia Shipman, and David Jackson. "Some New Dimensions in Providing Equal Educational Opportunity." *Journal of Negro Education* 34 (Summer 1965): 220–31.

Hunt, J. Mcv. "Has Compensatory Education Failed? Has It Been Attempted?" *Harvard Educational Review* 39 (Spring 1969): 278–300.

Jackson, Elton F., and Harry J. Crockett, Jr. "Occupational Mobility in the United States: A Point Estimate and Trend Comparison." *American Sociological Review* 29 (February 1964): 5–15.

Jencks, Christopher. "Education: The Racial Gap." *New Republic*, 1 October 1966, pp. 21–26.

———. "Johnson vs. Poverty." *New Republic*, 28 March 1964, pp. 15–18.

———. "LBJ's School Program: A Revolution in American Education?" *New Republic*, 6 February 1965, pp. 17–20.

———. "Private Schools for Black Children." *New York Times Magazine*, 3 November 1968, pp. 30, 132–35, 137–39.

———. "A Reappraisal of the Most Controversial Educational Document of Our Time," *New York Times Magazine*, 10 August 1969, pp. 12–13, 34–38, 42–44.

Jencks, Christopher, Judith Areen, et al. "Vouchers and Public Education: An Exchange of Views." *New Leader*, 6 September 1971, pp. 7–16.

Jencks, Christopher, and David Reisman. "On Class in America." *Public Interest*, Winter 1968, pp. 72–85.

Jensen, Arthur R. "How Much Can We Boost I.Q. and Scholastic Achievement?" *Harvard Educational Review* 39 (Winter 1969): 1–123.

———. "Reducing the Heredity-Environment Uncertainty: A Reply." *Harvard Educational Review* 39 (Summer 1969): 449–83.

Kagan, Jerome S. "Inadequate Evidence and Illogical Conclusions." *Harvard Educational Review* 39 (Spring 1969): 274–77.

Karier, Clarence J. "Liberalism and the Quest for Orderly Change." *History of Education Quarterly* 12 (Spring 1972): 57–80.

Karnes, Merle B., James A. Teska, Audrey S. Hodgins, and Earladeen D. Badger.

"Educational Intervention at Home by Mothers of Disadvantaged Infants." *Child Development* 41 (December 1971): 925–35.

Katz, Irwin. "Desegregation or Integration in Public Schools? The Policy Implications · of Research." *Integrated Education* 5 (December 1967-January 1968): 15–28.

Katz, Michael B. "The Present Moment in Educational Reform." *Harvard Educational Review* 41 (August 1971): 342–59.

Keller, Eugene. "Social Priorities, Economic Policy, and the State." *Dissent*, December 1971, pp. 613–32.

Kent, James K. "The Coleman Report: Opening Pandora's Box." *Phi Delta Kappan* 49 (January 1968): 242–45.

Keppel, Francis. "The Emerging Partnership of Education and Civil Rights." *Journal of Negro Education* 34 (Summer 1965): 204–8.

"The Keppel-Page Letter." *Integrated Education* 3 (December 1965-January 1966): 35.

Kirp, David L. "Race, Class, and the Limits of Schooling." *Urban Review* 4 (May 1970): 10–13.

Kolko, Gabriel. "On Blaming the Poor for Poverty." *New Politics*, 3 (Spring 1964), pp. 30–33.

Komatsu, David. "Mr. Johnson's Little War on Poverty." *New Politics* 3 (Spring 1964): 5–29.

Kraft, Ivor. "Integration, Not 'Compensation.' " *Educational Forum* 31 (January 1967): 211–14.

Kraft, Joseph. "Presidential Politics in LBJ Style." *Harper's*, March 1964, pp. 113–16.

Lampman, Robert J. "Approaches to the Reduction of Poverty." *American Economic Review* 55 (May 1965): 521–29.

Land, William G. "Tactics and Strategy of Federal Education Efforts." *Phi Delta Kappan* 46 (January 1965): 211–12.

LaNoue, George R. "The Title II Trap." *Phi Delta Kappan* 47 (June 1966): 558–63.

Lauer, Robert H. "The Middle Class Looks at Poverty." *Urban and Social Change Review* 5 (Fall 1971): pp. 8–10.

Lauter, Paul, and Florence Howe. "How the School System Is Rigged for Failure," *New York Review of Books*, 18 June 1970, pp. 14–21.

Lazeron, Marvin. "Social Reform and Early Education: Some Historical Perspectives." *Urban Education* 5 (April 1970): 84–101.

———. "Urban Reform and the Schools: Kindergartens in Massachusetts, 1870–1915." *History of Education Quarterly* 11 (Summer 1971): 115–42.

Leacock, Eleanor. "Distortions of Working-Class Reality in American Social Science." *Science and Society* 31 (Winter 1967): 1–21.

Leeson, Jim. "Equality of Educational Opportunity: Some Basic Beliefs Challenged." *Southern Education Report* 2 (May 1967): 3–5.

Leifermann, Henry. "Southern Desegregation." *Atlantic*, February 1969, pp. 12, 14, 16, 19–20.

Lekachman, Robert. "The Cost in National Treasure, $400,000,000 Plus." *Saturday Review*, December 1972, pp. 44–49.

———. "Death of a Slogan: The Great Society 1967." *Commentary*, January 1967, pp. 56–61.

———. "Education Report: Vouchers and Public Education." *New Leader* 54 (12 July 1971): 9–14.

Leuchtenberg, William E. "The Genesis of the Great Society." *Reporter* 34 (21 April 1966): 36–39.

Levin, Henry M., James W. Guthrie, George B. Kleindorfer, and Robert T. Sout. "School Achievement and Post-School Success: A Review." *Review of Educational Research* 41 (February 1971): 1–16.

Levine, Abraham S. "Evaluating Program Effectiveness and Efficiency: Rationale and Description of Research in Progress." *Welfare in Review* 5 (February 1967): 1–11.

Lewis, Oscar. "The Culture of Poverty." *Scientific American*, October 1966, pp. 19–25.

Lipset, Seymour Martin. "Social Mobility and Equal Opportunity." *Public Interest*, Fall 1972; pp. 90–108.

McCracken, Samuel. "Quackery in the Classroom." *Commentary*, June 1970, pp. 45–58.

McDill, Mary Sexton, Arthur L. Stinchcombe, and Dollie Walker. "Segregation and Educational Disadvantage: Estimates of the Influence of Different Segregating Factors." *Sociology of Education* 41 (Summer 1968): 239–46.

McDill, Edward, Mary S. McDill, and J. Timothy Sprehe. "Evaluation in Practice: Compensatory Education," in Peter H. Rossi and Walter Williams, eds., *Evaluating Social Programs: Theory, Practice and Politics*. New York: Seminar Press, 1972.

McKissick, Floyd. "A Communication: Is Integration Necessary?" *New Republic*, 3 December 1966, pp. 33–36.

McPartland, James. "The Relative Influence of School and Classroom Desegregation on the Academic Achievement of Ninth Grade Negro Students." *Journal of Social Issues* 25 (Summer 1969); 93–102.

Mahan, Thomas W. "The Busing of Students for Equal Opportunities." *Journal of Negro Education* 37 (Summer 1968): pp. 291–300.

Messerli, Jonathan C. "Controversy and Consensus in Common School Reform." *Teachers College Record* 66 (May 1965): 749–58.

Miller, S. M. "Poverty Research in the Seventies." *Journal of Social Issues* 26 (Spring 1970): 169–73.

Miller, S. M., and Martin Rein. "Participation, Poverty, and Administration." *Public Administration Review* 29 (January/February 1969): 15–25.

Miller, S. M., and Frank Riessman. "The Working Class Subculture: A New View." *Social Problems* 9 (Summer 1961): 86–97.

Miller, S. M., and Pamela A. Roby. "Social Mobility, Equality, and Education." *Social Policy* 1 (May/June 1970): 38–40.

"Modeling in Front of 3-Way Mirror: USOE Tries on Clothing Guide Lines." *Inequality in Education* 6 (November 1970): 32.

Moynihan, Daniel P. "Education of the Urban Poor." *Harvard Graduate School of Education Association Bulletin* 12 (Fall 1967): 2–13.

———. "The President and the Negro: The Moment Lost." *Commentary*, February 1967, pp. 31–45.

———. "Sources of Resistance to the Coleman Report." *Harvard Educational Review* 38 (Winter 1968): 23–36.

"Moynihan Believes Class Is the Issue." *Southern Education Report* 2 (May 1967): 7–10.

Munger, Frank J. "Changing Politics of Aid to Education." *Trans-Action*, June 1967, p. 11–16.

Murphy, Jerome T. "Bureaucratic Politics and Poverty Politics." *Inequality in Education* 6 (November 1970): 9–15.

———. "Title I of ESEA: The Politics of Implementing Federal Education Reform." *Harvard Educational Review* 41 (February 1971): pp. 35–63.

Neelsen, John P. "Education and Social Mobility." *Comparative Education Review* 19 (February 1975): 129–43.

Neufville, Richard de, and Caryl Conner. "How Good Are Our Schools?" *American Education* 2 (October 1966): 2–7.

Nichols, Robert C. "Schools and the Disadvantaged." *Science,* 9 December 1966, pp. 1312–14.

———. "On U.S. Commission on Civil Rights, *Racial Isolation in the Public Schools.*" *American Educational Research Journal* 5 (November 1968): 700–707.

Olneck, Michael R., and Marvin Lazeron. "The School Achievement of Immigrant Children: 1900–1930." *History of Education Quarterly* 14 (Winter 1974): 453–82.

Parenti, Michael, and Dale Marshall. "Review Symposium on Daniel Patrick Moynihan's *Maximum Feasible Misunderstanding.*" *Urban Affairs Quarterly* 5 (March 1970): 329–41.

"Parents of Educationally Deprived May Sue on Title I, Court Rules." *Inequality in Education* 6 (November 1970): 27.

Parmenter, Tom. "Power to the People through Title I? *Maybe.*" *Inequality in Education* 6 (November 1970): 1–8.

"Perspectives on *Inequality.*" *Harvard Educational Review* 43 (February 1973): 37–50.

Pettigrew, Thomas F. "Race and Equal Educational Opportunity." *Harvard Educational Review* 38 (Winter 1968): 66–75.

———. "Racial Implications of Title III, ESEA." *Integrated Education* 5 (October–November 1967): 37–47.

———. "Racially Separate or Together?" *Integrated Education* 7 (January-February 1969): 36–56.

Piven, Frances Fox. "Whom Does the Advocate Planner Serve?" *Social Policy* 1 (May/June 1970): 32–35.

Pressman, Harvey. "The Failure of the Public Schools." *Urban Education* 2 (July 1966): 61–81.

"Providence Suit Alleges Typical Range of Urban Title I Violations." *Inequality in Education* 6 (November 1970): 30–31.

Raab, Earl. "What War and Which Poverty?" *Public Interest,* Spring 1966, pp. 45–56.

"Race and Schools." *New Republic,* 12 October 1968, pp. 7–9.

"Racial Studies: Academy States Position on Call for New Research." *Science,* 17 November 1967, pp. 892–93.

Ravitch, Diane. "Programs, Placebos, Panaceas." *Urban Review* 2 (April 1968): 8–11.

"Recent Trends and Impact of Unemployment." *Monthly Labor Review* 86 (March 1963): 249–54.

Rein, Martin. "Social Science and the Elimination of Poverty." *AIP Journal,* May 1967, pp. 146–63.

———. "Values, Knowledge, and Social Policy," in Sheldon H. White et al., *Federal Programs for Young Children: Review and Recommendations.* (Washington, D.C.: Government Printing Office, 1973. Vol. 3, app. D.

Rein, Martin, and S. M. Miller. "Poverty Programs and Policy Priorities." *Trans-Action,* September 1967, pp. 60–71.

Rice, Roger. "Maine Parents Win Broad Control of Title I Program Funds." *Inequality in Education* 10 (December 1971): 35–36.

Rivlin, Alice M. "Forensic Social Science." *Harvard Educational Review* 43 (February 1973): 61–75.

Roach, Jack L., and Orville R. Gursslin. "An Evaluation of the Concept 'Culture of Poverty.' " *Social Forces* 45 (March 1967): 383–92.

Rudwick, Elliot, and August Meier. "Organizational Structure and Goal Succession: A Comparative Analysis of the NAACP and CORE, 1964–1968," in James A. Geschwender, ed., *The Black Revolt: The Civil Rights Movement, Ghetto Uprisings, and Separation.* Englewood Cliffs, N.J.: Prentice-Hall, 1971.

St. John, Nancy H. "Desegregation and Minority Group Performance." *Review of Educational Research* (February 1970): 111–33.

Sanders, Jacquin. "Gardner Hews Out the Great Society." *Newsweek*, 28 February 1966, pp. 22–30.

Schick, Allen. "From Analysis to Evaluation." *Annals* of the American Academy of Political and Social Science 394 (March 1971): 57–71.

Schrag, Peter. "The New Black Myths." *Harper's*, May 1969, pp. 37–42.

Schultz, Theodore W. "Investing in Poor People: An Economist's View." *American Economic Review* 55 (May 1965): 510–20.

Schwartz, Robert, Thomas Pettigrew, and Marshall Smith. "Collapse of Consensus: Desegregation: Assessing the Alternatives." *Nation's Schools* 81 (March 1968): 61–66, 117.

———. "Fake Panaceas for Ghetto Education: A Reply to Joseph Alsop." *New Republic*, 23 September 1967, pp. 16–19.

Scott, Donald M. "The Social History of Education: Three Alternatives." *History of Education Quarterly* 10 (Summer 1970): pp. 242–54.

Scribner, Jay D., and R. J. Snow. "Comments on Federalism and the Plight of City Schools: An Introduction to Papers by Guthrie and Kirst." *Education and Urban Society*, February 1970, pp. 193–98.

Seely, David. "Southern Desegregation: A Look at the Bright Side." *Nation's Schools* 79 (June 1967): 27–28.

Selden, David. "Vouchers—Solution or Sop?" *Teachers College Record* 72 (February 1971): 365–71.

Seligman, Ben B. "American Poverty: Rural and Urban." *Current History* 55 (October 1968): 193–98, 239–40.

Sewell, William H., Archie O. Haller, and Murray A. Straus. "Social Status and Educational and Occupational Aspiration." *American Sociological Review* 22 (February 1957): 67–73.

Sewell, William H., Leonard A. Marasculo, and Harold W. Pfautz. "Review Symposium: James S. Coleman and Ernest Q. Campbell, Carol J. Hobson, James McPartland, Alexander M. Mood, Frederick D. Weinfeld, Robert L. York. *Equality of Educational Opportunity.*" *American Sociological Review* 32 (June 1967): 475–83.

Shalala, Donna E., and James A. Kelly. "Politics, the Courts, and Educational Policy." *Teachers College Record* 75 (December 1973): 223–37.

Sherwood, Clarence C. "Issues in Measuring Results of Action Programs." *Welfare in Review* 5 (August-September 1967): 13–18.

Sizer, Theodore R. "The Case for a Free Market." *Saturday Review*, 11 January 1969, pp. 34, 36, 38, 42, 93.

———. "Low-Income Families and the Schools for Their Children." *Public Administration Review* 30 (July/August 1970): 340–46.

Smith, Marshall S., and Joan S. Bissell. "Report Analysis: The Impact of Headstart." *Harvard Educational Review* 40 (February 1970): 51–104.

Smith, Timothy L. "Immigrant Social Aspirations and American Education, 1880–1930." *American Quarterly* 21 (Fall 1969): 523–43.

―――. "Progressivism in American Education, 1880–1900." *Harvard Educational Review* 31 (Spring 1961): 168–93.

Smolensky, Eugene. "Investment in the Education of the Poor: A Pessimistic Report." *American Economic Review* 56 (May 1966): 370–78.

Spady, William G. "Educational Mobility and Access: Growth and Paradoxes." *American Journal of Sociology* 73 (November 1967): 273–86.

Spivak, Jonathan. "Education's Muddled Bureaucracy." *Reporter* 32 (8 April 1965): 33–36.

Spring, Joel H. "Education and the Rise of Corporate State." *Socialist Revolution* 2 (March-April 1972): 73–101.

Stambler, Moses. "The Effect of Compulsory Education and Child Labor Laws on High School Attendance in New York City, 1898–1917." *History of Education Quarterly* 8 (Summer 1968): 189–214.

Stevens, Edward W. "School Personnel and Political Socialization: Rochester, New York, 1900–1917." *Urban Education* 6 (July/October 1971): 197–212.

Stringfellow, William. "The Representation of the Poor in American Society: A Subjective Estimate of the Prospects of Democracy." *Law and Contemporary Problems* 31 (Winter 1966): 142–51.

Strom, Robert D. "Education: Key to Economic Equality for the Negro." *Journal of Negro Education* 34 (Fall 1965): 463–66.

Tabb, William K. "The Political Economy and Education." *Urban Review* 5 (January 1972): 29–32.

Thernstrom, Stephan. "The New Poor and the Old." *Social Sciences Forum*, Fall-Winter 1966-67, pp. 5–9.

―――. "Is There Really a New Poor?" *Dissent*, January-February 1968, pp. 59–64.

Thomas, J. Alan. "Institutional Character of Education: Economic and Fiscal Aspects." *Review of Educational Research* 34 (October 1964): 424–34.

Thomas, Norman C., and Harold L. Wolman. "The Presidency and Policy Formulation: The Task Force Device." *Public Administration Review* 29 (September/October 1969): 459–71.

Timpane, P. Michael. "Educational Experimentation in National Social Policy." *Harvard Educational Review* 40 (November 1970): 547–66.

Tyack, David B. "Bureaucracy and the Common School: The Example of Portland, Oregon, 1851–1913." *American Quarterly* 19 (Fall 1967): 475–98.

―――. "Education and Social Unrest, 1873–1878." *Harvard Educational Review* 31 (Spring 1961): 194–212.

Wayson, W. W. "The Political Revolution in Education, 1965." *Phi Delta Kappan* 47 (March 1966): 333–39.

Weiss, Carol. "The Politicization of Evaluation Research." *Journal of Social Issues* 26 (Fall 1970): 57–68.

"Whatever Happened to Comparability?" *Inequality in Education* 5 (June 1970): 22–23.

"Whiston-Cohen Agreement, The" *Integrated Education* 3 (December 1965-January 1966): 35–36.

Wiebe, Robert H. "The Social Functions of Public Education." *American Quarterly* 21 (Summer 1969): 147–64.

Wilkerson, Doxey A. "School Integration, Compensatory Education, and the Civil Rights Movement in the North." *Journal of Negro Education* 34 (Summer 1965): 300–309.

"With Education in Washington." *Education Digest*, 35 (September 1969), pp. 56–58.

Woffard, John. "Community Action: The Original Purposes." *Social Sciences Forum*, Fall/Winter 1966-67, pp. 15–18.

Wolf, Eleanor P. "Community Control of Schools as an Ideology and Social Mechanism." *Social Science Quarterly* 50 (December 1969): 713.

Woock, Roger R. "Community Operated Schools—A Way Out?" *Urban Education* 3 (October 1968): pp. 132–42.

Wrightstone, J. Wayne, et al. "Evaluating Educational Programs: A Symposium," *Urban Review* 3 (February 1969): 4–22.

Yarmolinsky, Adam. "The Origin of 'Maximum Feasible Participation.'" *Social Sciences Forum*, Fall/Winter 1966-67, pp. 19–20.

———. "Shadow and Substance in Politics (2): Ideas Into Programs." *Public Interest*, Winter 1966, pp. 70–79.

Young, Whitney M., Jr. "Order or Chaos in Our Schools." *The National Elementary Principal*, 9 (January 1970), pp. 24–33.

Yudof, Mark G. "The New Deluder Act: A Title I Primer." *Inequality in Education* 2 (December 1969): 1–2, 5–8.

———. "Title and Empowerment: A Litigation Strategy." *Inequality in Education* 5 (June 1970): 11–12, 16–17.

Zigler, Edward. "Social Class and the Socialization Process." *Review of Educational Research* 40 (February 1970): 87–110.

Government Publications

Coleman, James S., et al. *Equality of Educational Opportunity.* Washington, D.C.: Government Printing Office, 1966.

———. *Equality of Educational Opportunity: Summary Report.* Washington, D.C.: Government Printing Office, 1966.

Comptroller General of the U.S. *Report to the Congress: Improved Administration Needed in New Jersey for the Federal Program of Aid to Educationally Deprived Children.* Washington, D.C.: Government Printing Office, 1971.

———. *Report to the Congress: Improvement Needed in Administration of the Federal Program of Aid to Educationally Deprived Children in Ohio.* Washington, D.C.: Government Printing Office, 1970.

———. *Report to the Congress: Opportunities for Improving Administration of the Federal Program of Aid to Educationally Deprived Children in West Virginia.* Washington, D.C.: Government Printing Office, 1970.

84th Congress, 2d Session, Joint Committee, Subcommittee on Research and Development. *Hearings on the Shortage of Scientific and Engineering Manpower.*

85th Congress, 2d Session, Senate, Committee on Labor and Public Welfare. *Hearings on Science and Education for the National Defense.*

88th Congress, 2d Session, House, Subcommittee on the War on Poverty Program. *Hearings on the War on Poverty.*

88th Congress, 2d Session, Senate, Select Subcommittee on Poverty. *Hearings on the Economic Opportunity Act of 1964.*

88th Congress, 2d Session, Senate, Subcommittee on Education. *Hearings on Expansion of Public Laws 815 and 874.*

89th Congress, 1st Session, House, General Subcommittee on Education. *Hearings on Aid to Elementary and Secondary Education.*

89th Congress, 1st Session, House, *Report No. 143: Report of the Committee on Education and Labor, on the Elementary and Secondary Education Act of 1965.*

89th Congress, 1st Session, Senate, *Report No. 146: Report of the Committee on Labor and Public Welfare, on the Elementary and Secondary Education Act of 1965.*

89th Congress, 2d Session, House, General Subcommittee on Education. *Hearings on the Elementary and Secondary Education Amendments of 1966.*

89th Congress, 2d Session, Senate, Subcommittee on Education. *Hearings on the Elementary and Secondary Education Act of 1966.*

90th Congress, 1st Session, House, Committee on Education and Labor. *Hearings on the Elementary and Secondary Education Act Amendments of 1967.*

90th Congress, 1st Session, House, Subcommittee on Research and Technical Programs. *The Use of Social Research in Federal Domestic Programs.*

90th Congress, 1st Session, Senate, Subcommittee on Education. *Hearings on Education Legislation, 1967.*

91st Congress, 1st Session, House, Committee on Education and Labor. *Hearings on the Extension of Elementary and Secondary Education Programs.*

91st Congress, 1st Session, House, General Subcommittee on Education. *Hearings on the Needs of Elementary and Secondary Education for the 70's.*

91st Congress, 1st Session, Senate, Subcommittee on Education. *Hearings on the Elementary and Secondary Education Amendments of 1969.*

91st Congress, 2d Session, House, General Subcommittee on Education. *Hearings on the Needs of Elementary and Secondary Education for the 70's.*

91st Congress, 2d Session, House, General Subcommittee on Education. *Hearings on Emergency School Aid.*

91st Congress, 2d Session, Senate, Subcommittee on Education. *Hearings on Emergency School Aid.*

91st Congress, 2d Session, Senate, Select Committee on Equal Educational Opportunity. *Hearings on Equal Educational Opportunity.*

92d Congress, 1st Session, Senate, Select Committee on Equal Educational Opportunity. *Hearings on Equal Educational Opportunity.*

92d Congress, 1st Session, House, Select Subcommittee on Education. *Hearings to Establish a National Institute of Education.*

92d Congress, 2d Session, Senate, Subcommittee on Education. *Hearings on the Equal Educational Opportunities Act of 1972.*

89th Congress, 1st Session. *Congressional Record.*

91st Congress, 2d Session. *Congressional Record.*

Economic Report of the President Together with the Annual Report of the Council of Economic Advisors. Washington, D.C.: Government Printing Office, 1964.

Howe, Harold, II. *The Human Frontier: Remarks on Equality in Education.* Washington, D.C.: Government Printing Office, 1966.

Mackintosh, Helen K., Lillian Gore, and Gertrude M. Lewis. *Educating Disadvantaged Children in the Middle Grades.* Washington, D.C.: Government Printing Office, 1965.

National Advisory Council on the Education of Disadvantaged Children. *Title I— ESEA: A Review and a Forward Look—1969.* Washington, D.C.: Government Printing Office, 1969.

National Advisory Council on the Education of Disadvantaged Children. *Title I,*

ESEA—The Weakest Link: The Children of the Poor. Washington, D.C.: Government Printing Office, 1971.

National Advisory Council on the Education of Disadvantaged Children. *Educating the Disadvantaged Child: Where We Stand.* Washington, D.C.: Government Printing Office, 1972.

Public Papers of the Presidents of the United States: Harry S. Truman, 1948. Washington, D.C.: Government Printing Office, 1964.

Public Papers of the Presidents of the United States: Harry S. Truman, 1949. Washington, D.C.: Government Printing Office, 1964.

Public Papers of the Presidents of the United States: Harry S. Truman, 1951. Washington, D.C.: Government Printing Office, 1965.

Public Papers of the Presidents of the United States: Lyndon B. Johnson, 1963–1964. 2 vols. Washington, D.C.: Government Printing Office, 1965.

Public Papers of the Presidents of the United States: Lyndon B. Johnson, 1965. 2 vols. Washington, D.C.: Government Printing Office, 1966.

Public Papers of the Presidents of the United States: Richard Nixon, 1969. Washington, D.C.: Government Printing Office, 1971.

U.S. Bureau of Labor Statistics. *Employment and Earnings*, 9 (November 1962).

U.S. Commission on Civil Rights. *Federal Enforcement of School Desegregation.* Washington, D.C.: Government Printing Office, 1969.

U.S. Commission on Civil Rights. *Racial Isolation in the Public Schools.* 2 vols. Washington, D.C.: Government Printing Office, 1967.

U.S. Commission on Civil Rights. *HEW and TITLE VI; A Report on the Organization, Policies, and Compliance Procedures of the Department of Health, Education, and Welfare under Title VI of the Civil Rights Act of 1964.* Washington, D.C.: Government Printing Office, 1970.

U.S. Department of Health, Education, and Welfare, Office of Education. *A Chance for A Change: New School Programs for the Disadvantaged.* Washington, D.C.: Government Printing Office, 1966.

U.S. Department of Health, Education, and Welfare, Office of Education. *Education of the Disadvantaged: An Evaluation Report on Title I Elementary and Secondary Education Act of 1965, Fiscal Year 1968.* Washington, D.C.: Government Printing Office, 1970.

U.S. Department of Health, Education, and Welfare, Office of Education. *Elementary Programs in Compensatory Education.* Washington, D.C.: Government Printing Office, 1969, 1970.

U.S. Department of Health, Education, and Welfare, Office of Education. *Guidelines: Special Programs for Educationally Deprived Children: Elementary and Secondary Education Act of 1965/Title I.* Washington, D.C.: Government Printing Office, 1966.

U.S. Department of Health, Education, and Welfare, Office of Education. *History of Title I, ESEA.* Washington, D.C.: Government Printing Office, 1969.

U.S. Department of Health, Education, and Welfare, Office of Education. *Preschool Programs in Compensatory Education.* Washington, D.C.: Government Printing Office.

U.S. Department of Health, Education, and Welfare, Office of Education. *Report of Meeting of 16 Representatives of Poor People with U. S. Commissioner of Education and Members of His Staff: October 22–23, 1968.* Washington, D.C.: Government Printing Office, 1968.

U.S. Department of Health, Education, and Welfare, Office of Education. *Secondary Programs in Compensatory Education.* Washington, D.C.: Government Printing Office, 1969, 1970.

U.S. Department of Health, Education, and Welfare, Office of Education. *Statistical Report: Fiscal Year 1968: A Report on the Third Year of Title I Elementary and Secondary Education Act of 1965*. Washington, D.C.: Government Printing Office, 1969.

U.S. Department of Health, Education, and Welfare, Office of Education. *Title I Elementary and Secondary Education Act of 1965 (PL 89-10) School Year 1965-1966: Highlights*. Washington, D.C.: Government Printing Office, n.d.

Miscellaneous

Bernstein, Basil. "A Critique of the Concept of 'Compensatory Education.' " Files, Harvard Graduate School of Education. Mimeographed, n.d.

Blumenthal, Richard. "Community Action: The Origins of a Government Program." B.A. thesis, Harvard College, 1967.

Bucher, Richard Henry. "The Elementary and Secondary Education Act of 1965: A Study in Policy Change." Ph.D. dissertation, Duke University, 1971.

Cohen, David K. "The Schools and Social Reform: The Case of Compensatory Education." Unpublished paper, Center for Educational Policy Research, Harvard Graduate School of Education, 1970.

Cohen, David K., Walter J. McCann, Jerome T. Murphy, and Tyell R. van Geel. "The Effects of Revenue Sharing and Block Grants on Education." Unpublished paper, Harvard Graduate School of Education, October 1970.

Davis, Allison. "The Education of Culturally Deprived Children." Address before the Southern California Conference on Human Relations, Los Angeles, May 1962.

DeSilva, John A. "The First Year of the Elementary and Secondary Education Act: An Analysis of Its Implementation in a Suburban School System." Special Qualifying Paper, Harvard Graduate School of Education, 1968.

Dodson, Dan W. "A Hard Look at Cities and Urban Studies." Paper read at the American Sociological Association Convention, 2 September 1965.

Duncan, Beverly, and Otis Dudley Duncan. "Minorities and the Process of Stratification." Files, Harvard Graduate School of Education. Mimeographed, n.d.

Ellison, Keith. "John Kennedy and the 1961 Federal Aid to Education Bill." Unpublished paper, Harvard College, 1972.

Fantini, Mario, and Gerald Weinstein. "Toward a Prescriptive Theory for Teaching the Disadvantaged." Files, Harvard Graduate School of Education. Mimeographed, n.d.

Fitzgibbon, John Gerald. "Implications of Title I of the Elementary and Secondary Education Act of 1965 for Education under Title IIA of the Economic Opportunity Act of 1965." Special Qualifying Report, Harvard Graduate School of Education, 1966.

George Rosemary. "History and Development of the Regulations for Federal Administration of Title I of the Elementary and Secondary Education Act of 1965." Special Qualifying Paper, Harvard Graduate School of Education, 1965.

Gintis, Herb and Sam Bowles. "The Ideology of Educational Reform." Unpublished paper, Harvard Graduate School of Education, n.d.

Grant, Gerald Paul. "The Coleman Report: A Case Study of the Interaction of Social Science and Public Policy." Special Qualifying Paper, Harvard Graduate School of Education, 1970.

Green, Robert L. "Intellectual Development Among Economically and Educationally

Disadvantaged Youth." Paper read at the Detroit School Administrators Workshop, Michigan State University, East Lansing, 16 August 1966.

Greenberg, George Douglas. "Governing HEW: Problems of Management and Control at the Department of Health, Education, and Welfare." Ph.D. dissertation, Harvard University, 1972.

Hansen, W. Lee, Burton Weisbrod, and William J. Scanlon. "Determinants of Earnings: Does Schooling Really Count?" Unpublished working paper no. 5, Harvard University, 1967.

Hanushek, Eric Alan. "The Education of Negroes and Whites." Ph.D. dissertation, M.I.T., 1968.

Hilton, Thomas L. "Cultural Deprivation or Whatever it is." Paper read at American Psychological Association, Los Angeles, September 1964.

Hirsch, Jay G. "Little Squirts in the Great Society: The Search for the Big Squeak." Paper read at the annual meeting of the American Orthopsychiatric Association, 22 March 1967.

Johnson, Lyndon Baines. Papers and Collections. Lyndon Baines Johnson Presidential Library, Austin, Texas.

Kaagan, Stephen S. "Executive Initiative Yields to Congressional Dictate: A Study of Educational Renewal, 1971-72." Ph.D. dissertation, Harvard Graduate School of Education, 1973.

Kearney, Charles Philip. "The 1964 Presidential Task Force on Education and the Elementary and Secondary Education Act of 1965." Ph.D. dissertation, University of Chicago, 1967.

Kennedy, John F. Papers and Collections. John F. Kennedy Presidential Library, Waltham, Massachusetts.

Kent, James K. "The Community School Concept: Panacea or Anachronism for America's Urban Society?" Special Qualifying Paper, Harvard Graduate School of Education, 1968.

Keppel, Francis. "Basic Issues in Education." Address before the Adult Education Council of the Chattanooga Area. Chattanooga, 22 May 1958.

———. "What We Don't Know Can Hurt Us." Address before the Council of Chief State School Officers, Honolulu, 10 November 1965.

Keppel, Francis, Calvin E. Gross, and Samuel Shephard, Jr. "How Should We Educate the Deprived Child?" Three addresses before the Council for Basic Education, Washington, D.C., 23 October 1964.

Landers, Jacob. "An Investigation of the Implementation of Title I of the Elementary and Secondary Education Act of 1965 in New York City during the Fiscal Year 1966." Ed.D. dissertation, New York University, 1971.

Lazeron, Marvin. "Educational Testing and Social Policy." Unpublished paper, Center for Educational Policy Research, Harvard Graduate School of Education, n.d.

Lewis, Ralph Gabor. "Academic Achievement and the Effects of School Racial Composition: A Critical Appraisal of the Literature." Special Qualifying Paper, Harvard Graduate School of Education, 1968.

Mack, Raymond W. "School Integration and Social Change." Paper read at the American Sociological Association, Miami Beach, 31 August 1966.

Merrow, John. "The Use and Abuse of Discretionary Authority in the U.S. Office of Education." Ph.D. dissertation, Harvard Graduate School of Education, 1973.

Mosher, Edith K. "The Origins, Enactment, and Implementation of the Elementary and Secondary Education Act of 1965: A Study of Emergent National Educational Policy." Ph.D. dissertation, University of California, Berkeley, 1967.

Murphy, Jerome T. "Title I of ESEA: The Politics of Implementing Federal Educational Reform." Special Qualifying Paper, Harvard Graduate School of Education, 1970.

National Advisory Council on the Education of Disadvantaged Children. "Summer Education for Children of Poverty." Files, Harvard Graduate School of Education, 1966.

Passow, A. Harry. "Instructional Content for Depressed Urban Centers: Problems and Approaches." Paper read at the Post-Doctoral Seminar of the College of Education, Ohio State University, 23 October 1964.

Pettigrew, Thomas F., and Patricia J. Pajonas. "Social Psychological Considerations of Racially-Balanced Schools." Paper read at the New York State Education Department Conference, New York, 31 March 1964.

Radin, Beryl A., and Richardson White, Jr. "Youth and Opportunity: The Federal Anti-Delinquency Program." Unpublished study for the Institute for Justice and Law Enforcement, University Research Corporation, 1969.

Ratchick, Irving. "Identification of the Educationally Disadvantaged." State Education Department, University of the State of New York, Albany. Mimeographed, 1965.

"Report of the President's Task Force on Education." Mimeographed, 1964.

Saltzman, Henry. "Unequal Education and Family Functioning." Paper read at the National Conference on Social Welfare, New York, 28 May 1962.

Taylor, Ann Boyd, "Revenue-Sharing: An Alternative Model for State Aid to Local Governments." Special Qualifying Paper, Harvard Graduate School of Education, 1974.

Tyack, David. "City Schools at the Turn of the Century: Centralization and Social Control." Unpublished paper, Harvard Graduate School of Education, n.d.

U.S. Bureau of the Budget. Files.

U.S. Department of Health, Education, and Welfare. General Counsel Files.

U.S. Department of Health, Education, and Welfare, Office of Education. "History of the Office of Education," with Appendix. Lyndon Baines Johnson Library, Austin, Texas.

Personal Interviews

Armor, David. Cambridge, Mass., 9 December 1970.

Halperin, Samuel. Washington, D.C., 3 March 1971.

Keppel, Francis. New York, 22 June 1971.

Murphy, Jerome T. Cambridge, Mass., 25 February 1971.

Ratcliff, Shannon. Houston, 18 November 1971.

Yarmolinski, Adam. New York, 21 June 1971.

Index

Achievement test scores: and compensatory education, 144, 158, 189; effect of racial composition on, 146–47, 149, 150–58, 192, 194, 218; effect of teachers on, 157, 228; gap in, between nonwhite and white, 8, 145–46, 151–52, 155, 161, 163, 169, 172, 189, 191, 211; as measure of opportunities, 145; as measure of success, 160, 161, 169, 170, 172; and socioeconomic status, 15, 17, 146–47, 149, 151, 170; and student motivation, 157–58; and successful programs, 130, 167, 168, 229; variations in, due to family, 231–32; variations in, due to genetic factors, 86, 191, 192, 193; variations in measurement of, 160–62

Alexander vs. Holmes County, 212

Allen, James: on Nixon's approach to social policy, 202–3, 208; on need for reform, 210–11; resignation of, 211, 214

Alternative schools, 181–83

Banneker project, 14, 44, 157

Black Power, 116–17, 186. *See also* Carmichael, Stokley

Black movement: division in, 116–17, 227; involvement of, in education, 112, 115–16, 131–35, 157, 165, 183–86; militancy of, 132; rejection of integration by, 117, 186–87

Brademas, John: on feasibility of breaking poverty cycle, 82, 83; on funding, 104

Brown decision, 216; Nixon's views on, 213–15

Bureau of the Budget: and antipoverty legislation, 28, 144; on education and economic growth, 64–65, 70; emphasis of, on economic goals, 203; shift of activity to, 36; on weakness in impacted areas formula, 73

Carmichael, Stokley, 116–17, 186

Catholic church: and allocation of federal funds, 69, 70; compromise by, over aid to parochial schools, 73, 74; on Educational Task Force report, 60; Francis Keppel and, 67, 73; and implementation of ESEA, 105, 106, 107; and National Catholic Welfare Conference, 61, 73; opposition of, to legislation, 61. *See also* Parochial education

4/79

MY 2'79